P9-BIM-807

DREAMLAND AND OTHER POEMS

TECUMSEH: A DRAMA

Literature of Canada

Poetry and Prose in Reprint

Douglas Lochhead, General Editor

Dreamland and Other Poems

Tecumseh: A Drama

Charles Mair

Introduction by Norman Shrive

UNIVERSITY OF TORONTO PRESS

Toronto and Buffalo
Printed in Canada
ISBN (casebound) 0-8020-2073-0
ISBN (paperback) 0-8020-6203-2
LC 73-82586

Literature of Canada 11

This book has been published with the assistance of a grant from the Ontario Arts Council.

Dreamland and Other Poems was originally published in 1868 by Dawson Brothers, Montreal, and Sampson, Low, Son & Marston, London. *Tecumseh: A Drama and Canadian Poems*, 2nd edition, was published in 1901 by William Briggs, Toronto.

Preface

Yes, there is a Canadian literature. It does exist. Part of the evidence to support these statements is presented in the form of reprints of the poetry and prose of the authors included in this series. Much of this literature has been long out of print. If the country's culture and traditions are to be sampled and measured, both in terms of past and present-day conditions, then the major works of both our well-known and our lesser-known writers should be available for all to buy and read. The Literature of Canada series aims to meet this need. It shares with its companion series, The Social History of Canada, the purpose of making the documents of the country's heritage accessible to an increasingly large national and international public, a public which is anxious to acquaint itself with Canadian literature – the writing itself – and also to become intimate with the times in which it grew.

DL

Charles Mair, 1838-1927

Norman Shrive

Introduction

'There is so great a fever on goodness,' remarks the enigmatic Duke of *Measure for Measure*, 'that the dissolution of it must cure it.' This collection of Charles Mair's verse and the introduction to it are both presented on the assumption that a peculiarly Canadian 'goodness,' literary nationalism – or more precisely perhaps, the 'fever' on it – has been dissolved and that its cure is apparent in the healthy objectivity with which we now view our literary achievements, particularly those of the past. And there is really no other way of looking at Charles Mair. If sane, critical evaluation has given Mair's near-contemporaries, Roberts, Carman, Lampman, Scott, a respectable place as poets, Canadian or otherwise, it can rank Mair only in a lower position.

Not that Mair did not at times write good verse, at times, indeed, very good verse. That he was capable of excellence and yet so characteristically did not fulfil his promise posits the key questions that make Mair so significant in Canadian literary history. What is Canadian poetry? Does the inclusion of particular place names or of indigenous flora and fauna make it Canadian? Should it instil a feeling of pride, even of patriotism, in its readers? Such questions have been tiresomely asked and conscientiously answered during the past two or three decades. But they have had to be. We have had to have poets like Charles Mair with their few triumphs and frequent failures in order to see where we have been and where we are going.

The significance of Charles Mair in the development of Canada and of her literature is becoming increasingly recognized. Canadian historians, of course, have long known him as a controversial figure in a controversial event: the Riel uprising of 1869-70. But their accounts, both fair and prejudiced, of the part he played in that historical episode are concerned with only a few months of a life that lasted nearly ninety years, and he has been depicted, therefore, in a very limited context. On the other hand Canadian literary scholars for a long time ignored him altogether or dismissed him condescendingly, preferring to name those poets I have referred to above as their 'Confederation poets,' despite the fact that none of these more famous figures was over the age of seven in 1867 or published anything until almost fifteen years after that date. But Charles Mair not only gave Canada what was regarded in 1868 as its first significant collection of verse; he also offers to the Canadian literary historian an ideal illustration of the struggle of post-Confederation letters for survival and recognition.

Mair's life provides a tableau of some of the most significant aspects of Canadian history – of pioneering in the Ottawa Valley, of the Canada First movement in politics, of both Riel rebellions, of the opening up of the west. Most important is that his writings and the influences behind them reveal the cultural climate in which he lived – more particularly, the way in which literary merit may be confused with national sentiment, not only in the nineteenth century but also in a much later period. Because Mair and his work were so closely associated with the political and cultural development of Canada, there is little wonder that the late Lorne Pierce could describe Mair's life as 'a thrilling romance' and his work as part of 'the structure of our national life.' Or – to point up the whole problem of our 'national identity' – that Louis Riel could find him 'a barely civilized' Upper Canadian who found amusement in 'uttering follies to the world.'

Mair was born in 1838 in Lanark, Upper Canada, a little village by then already prospering in the Ottawa Valley square timber trade. The influences of his early life were most obviously British Colonial. Indeed, Mair fits admirably into a pattern well delineated by A.R.M. Lower in his book with the appropriate title, *Canadians in the Making*. He was one who was 'marked by warm emotions, by passionate concern, sentiment descending to sentimentality, by causes, movements, crusades.' By the time of Confederation he had directed this concern to the romanticism of creating a great Canada. In Mair, a dreamland and his own country in the future became as one.

In the spring of 1868 Mair journeyed to Ottawa to see his first volume of poetry through the press, a momentous journey because there he became associated with the other founding members of the Canada First party – George T. Denison, W.A. Foster, R.G. Haliburton, and Henry J. Morgan – and with the Honourable William L. Macdougall, Minister of Public Works, soon to be designated the first lieutenant-governor of the North-West Territories. These friendships were to direct the course of his life and even of Canadian history.

The book itself, *Dreamland and Other Poems*, is a slim work of thirty-three pieces, most of them short lyrics and some of which had already appeared in journals and newspapers. In a modest preface Mair submitted the book 'to the ordeal of English criticism,' confident, however, that 'at the hands of those accustomed to assess the value of literary productions' he would receive candid criticism that would 'either be a guide to him in future or induce him to abandon the field of poetry altogether.'

From its title and from those of such 'other poems' as 'The North Wind's Tale,' 'Innocence,' 'Our Beautiful Land by the Sea,'

'My Love – A Rhapsody,' and 'Stanzas from the Heart,' it may be rightly inferred that the collection is thoroughly romantic. Even the epigraph from Keats – 'O Poesy! for thee I hold my pen' – suggests the derivative quality of most of the selections. W.A. Foster, in fact, in a curious and yet characteristic illustration of the colonialism that tempered many of even the most ardent nationalists, referred to Mair in a review as 'the Canadian Keats.'

Mair believed he was writing Canadian poetry. But *Dreamland* is a curiously significant reflection of the attitudes that determined the way poetry was written in mid-nineteenth-century Canada. The examples set by the English Romantic poets directed it towards the depiction of the native landscape, and although that landscape might be viewed as through an English filter and interpreted by reference to English models, the poetry was nevertheless considered 'Canadian.' And herein lies a basis of confusion. To be dependent on the literary tradition of England surely cannot be a defect; if it is, perhaps all American poets except Whitman are to be dismissed with their Canadian cousins. But in 1868 it was more important that the verse be written by a Canadian than that it be *poetry*; the comparison was more often between the poet and an accepted English master than between poetry and non-poetry. This approach to criticism, I have already noted, perhaps somewhat hopefully, is virtually extinct, although as late as 1946 A.J.M. Smith could write: 'when it is recognized that the claims of nationalism are less important than those of universality and that a cosmopolitan culture is more valuable than an isolated one, our twentieth-century criticism will be prepared to approach the contemporary Canadian poets.' In 1957, indeed,

Smith could still remark, 'the question of national identity still seems to underlie [our] thinking and haunt [our] imagination.'

Mair's confusion of his objectives in 1868 resulted in singularly uneven verse. The literary escapism of 'Dreamland' or 'Our Beautiful Land by the Sea' is redeemed occasionally by an imaginative sensitivity, by a capacity to see and depict microscopically the minute detail of the animals, birds, and insects of the woods. But far too often Mair's verbosity and his attempts to apply a literary gloss trip him up, and he stumbles. This striving to be 'poetic,' indeed, results sometimes in lines that are ludicrous and grotesque, even bathetic. The 'deadly sick' butterflies of 'Prologue to Tecumseh,' the shouting wind and the mourning peasants of 'The North Wind's Tale,' the 'tapes' and 'coffin worms' of 'To My Photograph,' and the mammary detail of 'Innocence' reflect a highly dubious poetic craft and perhaps, to be charitable, the more unsophisticated aspects of Mair's early life in Lanark.

One selection in *Dreamland* requires special comment – an ode, 'In Memory of Thomas D'Arcy McGee.' This is the only avowedly patriotic work in the volume and its position in the last few pages suggests that Mair was able to have it included only at the last moment. McGee had been assassinated a month before Mair had come to Ottawa, and the poem was quite possibly part of his original manuscript. But in its elegiac treatment of a fervent nationalist it stands so completely apart from the other verse in the book – from the little wrens, the fireflies, the pines, and so on – that one feels Mair originally had no intention of including anything even similar to it, and if this is the case, it presents illustration of the manner in which he was influenced by his meeting in Ottawa with the other young men of Canada First. It was undoubtedly highly satisfactory to them that one of their own number was exemplifying the poets and writers who would help to inculcate a national sentiment; it was highly appropriate that he should include a tribute to a man who had inspired them. As we shall see, Mair was to be similarly influenced later on.

The literary reviews accorded *Dreamland* in the fall and winter of 1868 offer interesting testimony of the kind of criticism a Canadian writer could expect at the time. Canadian comment was almost entirely complimentary, but the English critics were unimpressed. One London paper, for example, while admitting that Mair had proved himself 'to be the possessor of some at least of the characteristics of a poet,' could not say that 'these first fruits of a young Canadian poet's reveries' form an exception to the received rule that 'the New World has been strangely barren in original poets.'

Most important, however, both intrinsically and in respect to its possible future influence upon Mair, were friend R.G. Haliburton's critical judgements. Haliburton wanted to see *Canadian* writing, but unlike Mair at this point he was not concerned with equalling or competing with English models. 'We must bid goodbye,' he wrote, 'to the literary grave-cloths of former years, and strive to create a new school that will interpret the fresh new life of a young nation.' Did he have to suggest, he asked, 'that "Comus and his jolly crew," as emigrants to our woods, are as much out of place as a medieval tournament or Colonial peers would be at Ottawa'? Canada had a fresh, untrodden field for poetry, especially in the west. The boundless prairies, the buffalo, the 'savage and semi-civilized hunters,' the trappers, the half-breeds, were all better worth study 'than Swinburne's Atalanta or Milton's Comus.' More pointedly, concerning *Dreamland*

Haliburton insisted that 'these archaic words set me damning,' and 'for God's sake drop the old style. You're living in a new world and you must write in the language of the living to living men...'

Such criticism, whether influential or not, Mair took quite sturdily. Years later he was to say: 'None of the critics of *Dreamland* hesitated to point out its defects, and I greatly benefited by their strictures.' Certainly, immediately after the work appeared, Mair steps into the pages of Canadian political history, where, for better or for worse, he has been best known.

It would be inappropriate here, although tempting, to detail the fascinating events of the next two years of Mair's life with all their tragi-comic elements of bravado and bloodshed. At least an abstract, however, is necessary. All available evidence indicates that Mair had every intention of returning to medical studies at Queen's in the fall of 1868. During his visit to Ottawa, however, he was asked by William Macdougall to be paymaster of a Government road party to Fort Garry – although actually he was to be a confidential correspondent to the minister about the increasingly tense situation at the Red River Settlement. The vast territories of the Hudson's Bay Company were about to be transferred to the new Dominion but there was much uneasiness about a number of matters – property rights, an immigration policy, American expansionism, to name a few – and it was particularly important to Ontarians that the whole matter should be resolved in a manner satisfactory to them. 'At once we saw the opportunity,' said Denison, 'of doing some good work towards helping on the acquisition of the territory.'

In a very brief time Mair antagonized the settlers of Red River – French Canadians, the Métis, Hudson's Bay Company officials alike – first of all by the letters he wrote to the Toronto *Globe* or to friends and subsequently printed in eastern newspapers, and secondly by his association with John Schultz, already a powerful and, to many, a highly unpopular personality at Red River.

Mair's reports to the newspapers certainly contain some of the most vivid descriptive prose ever written in Canada. Word pictures of the river steamers, the mule-trains, the Red River carts, of the Indians, the half-breeds, the white settlers, are all made more vivid by interpolated accounts of incidents and events that may befall the frontier traveller or immigrant. It is when Mair's depictions seem exaggerated, a little too lush, even though always maintaining a tone of sincerity, that the reader is reminded that the letters were written not for their own sake but to convince Canadians of the desirability of settlement in the northwest. For it is there, he writes, that the Canadian 'for the first time clearly recognizes the significance and inevitable grandeur of his country's future.' Far behind him is 'his glorious old native province' (the singular is significant); before him 'stretches through immeasurable distance the larger and lovelier Canada – the path of empire and the garden of the world.' Commented the Toronto *Globe*: 'We hope to see a new Upper Canada in the North-West Territory – a new Upper Canada in its well-regulated society and government – in its education, morality and religion.'

But to a Red River Settlement already tense over the implications of the approaching transfer the published letters were little short of sensational. In addition to giving an impression of a lazy, self-indulgent Métis and of himself as a rather superior being viewing the lower orders with disdain, some passages were personally offensive to other inhabitants. The result of such journalistic efforts was that Mair was physically attacked on the streets of Red River by some of the settlement's outraged ladies, one of them even resorting to a horsewhip to humiliate Mair publicly. The events which followed and which have become known as the first Riel Rebellion involved Mair even more drastically, even to his being captured by Riel's forces, being sentenced, along with Schultz and other 'loyal Canadians,' to death, and escaping across frozen prairies to St Paul, Minnesota, and thence to Toronto, where he pulled all the stops of rhetoric – particularly in public addresses – to help ensure that an armed expedition would be despatched to Red River.

But perhaps it is the ironies that fascinate us most. In only a few months after he had journeyed to Ottawa with his manuscript of *Dreamland*, a work intended to sound a key-note of a new, unified nation, Mair had by his pen helped to create a situation of potential danger to Confederation itself. As an Upper-Canadian he had brought to the west the attitudes and prejudices that had been formed over a period of thirty years and then sharpened by his alliance with a particularly aggressive group of other Upper-Canadians. In Ontario such pro-British, Protestant attitudes and prejudices could flourish with little or no opposition. In the melting pot of the new west they were almost bound to provoke conflict.

Mair was to live another fifty-seven years and although many of them were to be eventful, none was to be as exciting, as controversial, as fraught with implication both personally and professionally, as that of 1869-70. Within a few years, in fact, he was already settled down as a storekeeper with a wife and growing family in Portage la Prairie. In 1877 he moved even farther west, this time to the tiny settlement of Prince Albert, which he envisioned as becoming, because of the transcontinental railway and expected opening up of the ports of Hudson Bay, a crossroads not only for the commerce of Canada but indeed for the whole world. His friend Schultz was becoming a millionaire in Winnipeg; why should not he in Prince Albert? Within five years Mair had become one of the most important and most prosperous inhabitants of the hopeful little town on the North Saskatchewan River. But again the dreams began to dissolve. The CPR was built far to the south, the Hudson Bay route gave no signs of opening, and the bountiful crops that had been coincident with the land boom suddenly dwindled in two seasons of drought and frost. In addition, Louis Riel's return from Montana presaged new trouble in the west. By 1884, therefore, a somewhat alarmed Mair moved his family to Windsor, Ontario, and here he returned, one eye always on the situation in the west, to the writing he had had to place in the background since the Red River days. Here he wrote *Tecumseh.*

Perhaps the main reason that Charles Mair has been regarded separately as literary figure on the one hand and historical figure on the other is that he himself, despite his ardent literary nationalism, never seemed to envisage the two roles acting together. Here was a Canadian who by word and action fanned the flame of Riel's 1869 uprising, who was a leading participant in the event itself, who avoided Thomas Scott's fate before a Métis firing squad only by a last-minute escape leading ultimately to an almost unbelievable trek across North Dakota, who continued for many years to live a life of some tension and variety – yet who evidently never considered any of this experience as the subject matter for literature. The only direct connection, for example, that he made between his literary endeavours and Riel was that the rebel leader had been indirectly responsible for the loss of poetry manuscripts on the 'Fountain of Bimini' and on 'some incidents in the early life of Zoroaster' – long narrative pieces, evidently of romantic and pseudo-Oriental detail that almost certainly would not have helped Mair's reputation in any way. Not that a writer must write from his own experience. But it seems curious that Mair, so avidly dedicated to what he believed to be the callings of the poetic dramatist and of the nationalist, did not realize that he had unparalleled opportunity to reflect both at once. If he had written such a play, of course, his arch-enemy Riel would have appeared as villain, and John Schultz, or a figure that Mair might have based on his own conception of himself, as hero. Today the work would be a curio. But not so much so, perhaps, as the drama that Mair actually did write.

The great Shawnee chief Tecumseh had for Mair a special fascination. Not only had he been an unusual personality, a brilliant leader of his people, but he had also played a very significant role in defending Canada against armed invasion and indeed saving her from annexation by the hated Yankee. In the story of the final month of Tecumseh's career Mair could reflect some of his own knowledge and experience of the Indian race; but most important, he could urge by means of literature – that touchstone or gauge, as he expressed it, of a nation's desire for greatness – a recognition of Canada's heroic past and of her potentiality for a magnificent future. But he had not composed a line of drama before this time, and either because of this inexperience or because of his simply following the example of a host of nineteenth-century writers from Shelley to Browning, he decided upon the 'literary' or 'closet' drama to tell Tecumseh's story. His feelings of inadequacy led him to depend considerably upon the opinions and advice of others. No sooner had he finished a scene, or even less, than he sent it to Principal George Grant of Queen's or to friend Denison in Toronto, either of whom might then forward it to someone else before it was returned to Mair in Windsor. By the time *Tecumseh* was finished, much of it had been read and criticized by not only Mair's close friends but also by Sir Daniel Wilson, Goldwin Smith, Charles G.D. Roberts – even by Matthew Arnold, who visited Smith in Toronto in 1884. And it is entirely in keeping with Mair's career that the work should be interrupted while Mair joined Denison's militia regiment in the last fight against Riel in the spring of 1885. But the Métis leader finally went to the gallows in November of that year and *Tecumseh* was published a month later.

Mair's almost complete subordination of artistic principles to those of ardent nationalism and of sentimental melodrama makes *Tecumseh* a curious work. With its five acts and twenty-eight scenes, which, if acted, would require at least four hours of presentation, the 'play' is a pageant of stylized and highly rhetorical history – although various patriot groups in Ontario and British Columbia were to bring at least parts of it to the stage in later years. During the depicted period, three heroes, Tecumseh, Brock, and Lefroy (a wandering young Englishman), vie for supremacy with not only invading Americans (including low 'Yankee roughians') but also traitors in their own camps – Tecumseh's villainous brother the Prophet, and Brock's faint-hearted subordinate, Colonel Procter. And since the play is a tragedy, the final 'curtain' falls on a scene of desolation: Tecumseh is dead, Procter has ignominiously retreated, the Americans have won the battle of Moraviantown, and Iena (an Indian maiden) is carried away lifeless in the arms of the distraught

Lefroy. Brock, however, has died gloriously in victory at Queenston Heights, Tecumseh has achieved immortality even in failure, and the Canadian reader is obviously expected to realize that the ultimate outcome of the war was an American defeat.

Tecumseh himself is a superb if wooden figure, a romantic noble savage who acts with consistent gallantry and integrity. As a dramatic creation he is at times Shakespearean, at others Miltonic, and at others Restoration Heroic, but certainly always lofty. Brock is the idealized British soldier. Bold, energetic, decisive, but sensitive to his great responsibility, he is aware of the odds against him, as he occasionally reveals in Shakespearean soliloquy:

> Now might the head of gray Experience
> Shake o'er the problems that surround us here;
> ...
> Could England stretch its full, assisting hand
> Then might I smile though velvet-footed time
> Struck all his claws at once into our flesh.

But the most interesting character is Lefroy; 'a poet-artist, enamoured of Indian life, and in love with Iena.' For this young English expatriate who wanders in and out of the woods searching for love and serenity has a psychological complexity quite lacking in his fellow *dramatis personae.* Fictional though he is, Lefroy is derivative both as a type and as a person, reflecting clearly the literary and historical influences to which Mair was indebted for his creation. His name suggests Chateaubriand's romantic depictions of the wanderings of Atala and René, but more probable is his literary descent from the English Romantics. Lefroy is a Byronic figure, the melancholy poet on a quest, but in

Tecumseh transplanted from a corrupt Europe to an about-to-be-corrupted Canadian wilderness. Like Tecumseh, he deplores the depredations of civilization upon nature, 'the sordid town that here may rise,' the greed and ruthlessness of the white man. But unlike Tecumseh he sees no solution in clearly defined boundaries for different races. Lefroy, as a critic of the time was quick to note, was depicted 'with a dash of socialism of a very modern type, not unlike that of which Mr William Morris is perhaps the most interesting contemporary professor.'

Into Tecumseh, Brock, and Lefroy, Mair obviously projected many of his own attitudes and ideals – humanitarian, patriotic, military, national, romantic, and poetic. By means of three such figures, indeed, he probably managed to resolve satisfactorily, for himself at least, several conflicting points of view, to express through his characters the somewhat confused arguments he may have had with himself. Thus Tecumseh is noble, natural man living in pristine simplicity; but since what he represents has to go in the name of progress, it behooves the enlightened white man such as Brock or militia volunteer Robinson or the United Empire Loyalist to respect him and his prehistoric tradition, to care for him and not to exploit him out of existence as the Americans were doing. Mair declines, however, even to ask how this integrated Utopia can be concretely achieved, for when Lefroy's republican fervour is answered by Brock's authoritarian (and Shakespearean) conviction, they are eventually compelled to 'drop this bootless argument.' One can infer, perhaps, that the romantic poet of *Dreamland* had been confronted by the Prince Albert land speculator.

Two other aspects of *Tecumseh* are particularly noteworthy. By both soliloquy and long passages of descriptive dialogue Mair provides the reader with a vivid picture of the flora and fauna of not only the Upper Canada of Brock's time but of also the still undiscovered west. Usually the setting is pastoral rather than savage, closer to the Forest of Arden than to the wilderness of the contemporaneous Deerslayer. For example, Lefroy's speech in 'Another Part of the Forest' and beginning:

> This region is as lavish of its flowers
> As Heaven of its primrose blooms by night

praises the bounty of nature in terms reminiscent of Friar Laurence's in *Romeo and Juliet.* But when he describes to Brock the 'unrivaled wastes' visited by Tecumseh and himself in order to enroll the western tribes, Lefroy becomes expansive in his vision of 'ocean's paraphrase.' In these passages there is to be noted again the characteristically Mair combination of derivativeness and originality. Reference to only a few lines from Bryant's 'The Prairies' will reveal to the reader the striking similarity of Lefroy's vista of the west and the American poet's in 1832. And yet as he proves in parts of Lefroy's descriptive passages and as he had proved in the best lines of *Dreamland*, when Mair looked at nature directly and allowed his own experience and inspiration to guide him, he wrote verse that rises at times to real poetic achievement. A.J.M. Smith has justifiably praised Mair's 'impressionistic picture of the wilderness, vast and unplumbed, teeming with life, but empty of man,' the intensity and power that resulted when his 'imagination caught fire' and that 'anticipates the more fervid spirit of the later poets.' In such verse

> Mair makes a genuine contribution to the development of Canadian literature. ... It cannot be denied that in a few

> passages where he attains his fullest power there is a firmness and clarity, a hint of Virgilian rectitude, that represents a more universal and truly classical way of looking at things than is exhibited by any Canadian poet except Archibald Lampman.

And thus, as in *Dreamland*, there are reflected in *Tecumseh* strengths and weaknesses, lapses in taste, the unevenness and inconsistency that Mair was never able to overcome, even, in fact, to recognize more than superficially.

His provision of comic relief in *Tecumseh* is an additional example of lack of literary proportion. Just as Shakespeare had his Dogberry and Verges, Snug and Bottom, Bardolph and Pistol, Mair has his Twang and Slaugh, Gerkin and Bloat, low buffoons in the form of 'Yankee roughians' who speak in prose. Such interludes were incorporated, of course, for more than comic effect. The characters are not just white boors; they are American boors, and are intended to express character contrast as well as dramatic contrast to the citizens of York, the brave volunteers who march in a disciplined column and sing a patriotic song.

And to such nationalistic aspects of his drama Mair devoted his most painstaking attention and the larger share of his creative talents. Nowhere in his writings and correspondence does he give evidence of believing his work might live for other than patriotic reasons. The merit of *Tecumseh*, he was always to insist, arose from its being 'a labour of love and patriotism,' from the 'Canadian feeling that is in my bones.' Even the inclusion of parts of it in school texts was to be determined almost entirely, it would appear, by its contribution to the inculcation of national sentiment.

But the reception of *Tecumseh* in 1886 by press and public alike, far more enthusiastic than even that accorded *Dreamland* eighteen years before, suggests that Mair had caught the national pulse. There were, of course, particular factors that attracted notice. The growing awareness of the plight of the Indian, the part he had played in the recent Rebellion, Mair's own exciting involvement with the notorious Riel in 1869 and his subsequent participation in the campaign of 1885, undoubtedly evoked a special response. *Tecumseh* was widely acclaimed as the country's outstanding literary achievement and Mair as its greatest national poet. When his publisher suggested that a second printing be run off as quickly as possible, he declined only when told there was a possibility of financial loss; he estimated that the years of writing had cost him ten thousand dollars and his return but five hundred – 'so I have bled for my country with a vengeance.' But such thoughts were probably farthest from his mind on Victoria Day 1886, as Mrs John Beverley Robinson, the wife of the lieutenant-governor, pinned on his Rebellion Medal and dubbed him 'our warrior bard.' To Mair, at forty-seven and with almost as many years ahead of him, the future seemed redolent with promise. There did remain the problem of resurrecting financial eminence in a post-Rebellion Prince Albert, although, as the Toronto *Truth* remarked, Mair possessed 'much valuable property' and would soon be known as a wealthy as well as a talented Canadian. It may have been yet another irony that a paper called *Truth* should make such a happy prophecy.

And indeed for some time Mair's future looked bright. Having returned to Prince Albert, he began to revive his financial and social position in the community, so promisingly in fact that he endeavoured to keep up his poetry writing. *Tecumseh* had proved his point; given indepedence from financial worry, a Canadian writer might make a worthwhile contribution to national literature. Within a few months of his return to the west, Mair began thinking ahead to the time when he could once again 'retire' from business and compose another drama. Already he had been delving into background, had even chosen a title – *The Conquest* – for a drama based on the beginnings of lasting British influence upon Canada. Meanwhile he found time to write the verse that he contributed during the years 1885-90 to various periodicals and magazines and that was to appear in the collected edition of his works in 1901. In 1889 he was elected to the Royal Society of Canada and the following year contributed a paper to the Society on the American bison – a work that has a rather curious relevance to modern Canada, certainly to modern zoology. As literature it reflects the clarity, the richness of metaphor, the detailed knowledge that had characterized the best of Mair's *Globe* letters of 1869. But as a treatise on Canadian natural history it is a plea for the preservation of a vanishing species, of an animal 'which has been of great service on our continent, which is intimately associated with its history, and whose extinction would be a disgrace to civilized man.' The result of the paper was a renewed interest in the buffalo, and within a short time the Canadian government brought the only available herd from Montana to a sanctuary recommended by Mair, Wainwright Park, Alberta. As the contemporary Canadian knows, this herd has expanded to such an extent that once again the buffalo hunt – now regulated – is an annual event in the Canadian northwest.

But at length, after a succession of rising and falling hopes, after fluctuations of prosperity and minor depressions, both Mair and the little town on the North Saskatchewan that he had helped to build were vanquished. And the degree to which they had depended upon markets and settlers is indicated by the suddenness with which distress struck the community. By midsummer, 1891, long-established families were moving out, going south to the United States, or following the CPR to the west coast. Some of them sold businesses for what they could get; others closed shops to await better times; others left their share of the eighty thousand bushels of wheat no one would buy.

Mair, now over fifty years old, was stricken with a fear he had not known before, the fear of poverty. He went to St Paul, Minnesota, and then to the Chicago World's Fair of 1893 in an attempt to attract settlers to the Canadian prairies. From there he travelled to Kelowna in the Okanagan Valley of British Columbia, where he established a general store. But all was in vain, and by 1894 Mair was pleading with his old friend Schultz, now lieutenant-governor of Manitoba and about to be knighted, and with Denison to do anything they could to save him and his family from absolute ruin. And then, just in time, it would appear, he was appointed to the Immigration Service of Clifford Sifton's Ministry of the Interior. This was in 1898 and Charles Mair was then sixty.

For almost twenty-five years Mair served his department well. He conducted settlers to their new homes in Manitoba, Saskatchewan, Alberta, and British Columbia; he escorted deputations of officials from the United States, Great Britain, and Europe who had been sent to investigate immigration possibilities in a great new country. When not travelling he prepared descriptive pamphlets, wrote articles for newspapers and magazines, and handled the foreign correspondence for the several branch offices to which he was attached over the years. After being stationed in Winnipeg for some time he was placed in charge of the office at

Lethbridge. Shortly afterwards he was moved west, as an inspector, to Fort Steele, British Columbia. In this latter post he retired in 1921, an old man of eighty-three.

One potentially exciting adventure did take place in these later years. In 1899 Mair was appointed English secretary of the Scrip Commission that was sent to the Athabaska and Peace River districts to negotiate with the Indians and half-breeds there for the transfer of their territorial rights to the Dominion. This country of the Mackenzie basin constituted to Mair another frontier of the northwest, another opportunity, surely the last, to be a pioneer before civilization made its inevitable inroad. But this time there were no horse-whippings, no threats of death. Once again Mair wrote of his experiences to the *Globe*, but this time obviously because of the restraints of his official position, his reports were much more subdued than his correspondence of 1868-9. Eventually the narrative of the journey appeared in 1908 as *Through the Mackenzie Basin.*

His poetic reputation Mair tried to keep alive by the volume of collected works that he published in 1901, *Tecumseh, A Drama, and Canadian Poems*, but its reception was less than lukewarm. And the reasons are significant. The 'Canadian Poems,' originally published in periodicals from 1885 to 1892, are romantic to the point of sentimentalism; they are derivative and stylized; they reveal incongruous lapses in technique and taste. But they also reflect, as is to be expected perhaps, the main influences upon Mair in these later years – his western environment, the Indian legends, and above all, the necessity of a Canadian national sentiment. 'A Ballad for Brave Women' begins thus:

A story worth telling our annals afford
'Tis the wonderful journey of Laura Secord!

and continues in this jog-trot metre of " 'Twas the Night before Christmas' to recount the now famous incident of the War of 1812. A eulogy, 'In Memory of William A. Foster,' is poetically insignificant in its urging to

> First feel throughout the throbbing land
> A nation's pulse, a nation's pride –
> The independent life – then stand
> Erect, unbound, at Britain's side!

'The Legend of Chileeli' and 'The Iroquois at the Stake' reflect Mair's detailed knowledge of the Indian but are again derivative from Longfellow, even from Browning, with dramatic monologue and parenthetical 'stage directions.' More interesting is 'Kanata,' which treats the theme of the white man's intrusion upon the Indian, but expresses in addition a note of Mair's personal bitterness for the corruption of true freedom that he feels the European has inflicted upon Canada's previously unspoiled land. The most fantastic selection of all is 'The Last Bison,' in which a 'burdash,' or hermaphrodite bison of tremendous size, bursts into song. The song, lasting for nine Spenserian stanzas, combines praise for the Indian with lament for the departed millions of buffalo, and culminates in a prophetic vision of the passing of the white man himself from the scene.

In this particular group of poems, however, the most significant is undoubtedly 'Open the Bay!' in which Mair versifies, for the most part clumsily, the theme he had so ardently expressed in prose elsewhere. The particular irony of this ringing exhortation is that it reflects a Mair who sees himself as the enlightened patriot pitting the opening of Hudson Bay to navigation (and the consequent prosperous development of Canada) against narrow eastern Canadian interests, and yet who is himself a western land speculator who once wished to impose Upper-Canadian social, political, and economic values upon the west.

The 1901 revision of *Dreamland* provides us, however, with the most fascinating and yet disheartening example of how a poet deliberately set out to 'Canadianize' his work. It must be realized that Mair had met his Canada First friends in Ottawa *after* he had submitted his 1868 *Dreamland* manuscript to the press, and it has already been noted that the D'Arcy McGee eulogy appears to be a *post facto* addition. From that time Mair became a committed, active Canadian nationalist and, as the poet of his group, deliberately set out to inculcate a patriotic sentiment. Haliburton's admonishing comment of 1870 serves mainly to make the whole process concrete, for Mair would undoubtedly have written and revised as he subsequently did without its stimulation. If particular personal influences were significant, the advice of Denison must be considered too. Mair followed most of Denison's critical suggestions faithfully, and thereby excluded the best lines of *Dreamland* – and once again reflected his impressionability and unsure poetic taste.

Now, in 1974, I consider it best to reprint the original *Dreamland* poems from the 1868 work because I believe it to be the superior collection both qualitatively and quantitatively. By reference to the appendix (p xxxiii), however, the reader can note the many quite drastic revisions that Mair made in 1901. In some cases the revisions indicate that Mair, as he confessed, had benefited by the strictures of critics: much of the early crudeness in both matter and technique has been removed or considerably polished, and an attempt has obviously been made to rid the work of what Mair termed 'a young poet's imperfections' – the forced archaisms, the trite epithets, and the evidences of almost snobbish affectation. But the arbitrary substitution in 'Summer,' for example, of Indians, Evangeline, Laura Secord and the War of 1812, for mediaeval knights 'in bout and joust and tournament' is a sadly ironic commentary on Mair's inability to realize that in such verse he was being blatantly 'Canadian' and that in 'August,' for example, as in some of the quite remarkable nature passages of *Tecumseh*, he was really part of an emergent, distinctive poetic tradition.

Mair's last years provide a relevant if poignant note. A much-loved wife whom he had met during the Red River troubles in 1868 had died in 1906. Of his seven children, three, including an indulged son who became a parasitical n'er-do-well, caused him much personal anguish. In the 1920s, now retired from the Civil Service, an aged Charles Mair saw his reputation as a figure prominent in Canadian history and letters become increasingly dim. Then he encountered John W. Garvin, Toronto stockbroker and literary dilettante, and surely one of the more fascinating, if provoking, personalities in Canadian literary history.

I have dealt in detail elsewhere with Mair's relationship with Garvin and can merely note here that for almost the last six years of Mair's life Garvin appeared to the old man as a promise of rescue from the brink of literary and national oblivion; he was, perhaps, if tantalizing hope can keep a man alive, even to prolong his life. Garvin had several plans for republishing Mair's works but they all culminated in his *Master-Works of Canadian Authors* volume of 1925. Originally the energetic Toronto editor proposed to include both versions of *Dreamland*, the 1868 and the 1901, but Mair insisted that only the early poems appear. Professor John Matthews, whose excellent essay on Mair appeared a few years ago in the *Our Living Tradition* series, maintains that Mair's recorded reasons – that the revised edition omitted 'August' and 'Prologue to Tecumseh' and contained abbreviated versions of the earlier poems, and therefore should not be considered – was not the real one. Actually, writes Matthews, Mair 'looked back to the 1901 revisions as a débâcle best forgotten' – a débâcle because of his deliberate attempts to 'Canadianize' by means of historical reference to people and place. This theory is plausible enough (indeed, one would like to believe it represented the truth) but no more so, probably, than that Mair was simply combining sentimentality with his stated reasons. During the last few years of his life, he increasingly looked back to the days of 'dear old Lanark' and of his trip to Ottawa in 1868, and he more than once indicates in his late correspondence that his request to Garvin to publish the original *Dreamland* is based on nostalgic as much as critical reasons. In addition, Mair never once suggested to Garvin that he should omit the later, overtly 'Canadian' poems that had also appeared in the 1901 edition.

Whatever the reason, Mair won his point and it was the 1868 version of *Dreamland* that appeared in Garvin's *Master-Works.* Ironically, however, the collection might better have been left undone. As a piece of bookmaking *Charles Mair's Tecumseh, Etc., Etc.*, from the informality of its title on the spine to the affectation of its deckle-edged Byronic leaves, is almost ludicrous. In any of its three maroon bindings ('buckram, $4.00; half-leather, $5.00; full leather, $8.00') it is over-lavishly decorated with gold tooling and the pretentious escutcheon of the 'Radisson Society'; Garvin's name instead of Mair's boldly graces the title page; many of the photographs, printed on uncoated paper, are poorly reproduced. It is, however, the flamboyant introduction by Robert

Norwood, minister and littérateur, that precludes any serious appreciation of the book. After a highly rhetorical essay on the nature of poetry, replete with references to 'Life Unlimited,' 'the pipes of Pan,' 'the good, brown Mother Earth,' and to the ignorance of contemporary critics, Norwood breathes deeply and states unequivocally that Mair 'is not only the dean of Canadian letters; he is our most authentic poet.' For, he concludes, 'as we look over Canada's host of song, we discover one who, like Saul among the children of Benjamin, towers like a goodly oak above its companion cedars. Charles Mair is our greatest Canadian poet by every count.'

The book appeared in April 1927 and therefore Mair did not live long enough to learn of its failure both critically and financially. He died in Victoria, BC, on 7 July 1927, having been able a week before to send a telegram to the Canadian Authors Association in which he rejoiced for having lived to see the Diamond Jubilee of Canada 'so fittingly celebrated ... and the pride that all Canadians took in it.'

Lanark and Prince Albert, in a way, tell the story of Charles Mair's life. 'Dear old Lanark, embosomed among its hills and vales' and about which Mair felt 'there is a poetry ... which is imperishable,' illuminates the man and his later reputation just as does the town that was to be 'the metropolis of the West.' The influences by which Charles Mair was moulded in his first thirty years directed his aspirations, both literary and material, in Prince Albert. *Dreamland* reflected, as its author noted, 'a young poet's imperfections'; but in the young Mair's case these imperfections were particularly relevant to an environment of backwoods Upper Canada, the indulgences of a proud mother, and a conception of the writer's craft gained from a reading of the more romantic, the more 'manly' of the recognized British authors. By the time he had embarked upon *Tecumseh* Mair had become a practising patriot, and had been involved in one of the most stirring events in Canada's political history. His nationalism, therefore, not only permeates the drama; it provides its very raison d'être. And like *Dreamland* before it, *Tecumseh* was received by Canadians who were searching – almost desperately, one feels at times – for some proof of a literary culture of their own. The work had critical acclaim stimulated more by its purpose and the fervent reflection of that purpose than by any intrinsic artistic merit.

Both Canada and Charles Mair tried to fulfil a vision, and both found their progress marked by long years of discouraging failure. For the man, however, the consequences of both his own and his country's failures were insurmountable. When Canadians were at last able to 'feel the throbbing land / A nation's pulse, a nation's pride,' Charles Mair was old, and had long since seen his personal vision of success fade away. But in Canadian letters of his time there is no better example than Mair of the confusion between literary merit and national sentiment. Nor, perhaps, of the validity in the Canada of his time of an aphorism from Scott that in confident youth Mair himself had quoted so often but never really believed until bitter experience confirmed it – that literature was a good stick, but a very bad crutch.

Appendix

DREAMLAND AND OTHER POEMS

Mair revised most of the early *Dreamland* poems for publication in the 1901 edition of *Tecumseh: A Drama and Canadian Poems.* Many of the changes are quite insignificant – details of capitalization and punctuation – and are not considered important enough to note in this edition. Where, however, they are indicative of a conscious intention to 'benefit by the critics' strictures,' as Mair termed it, and to 'Canadianize,' they provide an instructive commentary upon a Canadian poet attempting to improve his early work and upon a nationalistic writer fervently dedicated to inculcating patriotic sentiment.

The most obvious difference between the 1868 and the 1901 editions is the omission in the latter of a number of poems – an omission explained by Mair himself as one required by cost of publication. The choice of titles for omission, however, seems to have been as much George T. Denison's as his own. In some cases, also, individual titles of poems were changed. Listed below are the significant changes made by Mair in the 1901 edition. The marginal number refers to the page in the 1868 edition on which the poem appears.

1 'Dreamland'

Many changes in capitalization, punctuation, and even phraseology, none of which, however, really improves the poem.

11 'The Pines'

Last four lines, in each case, of stanzas 3 and 4 of the chorus omitted and the eight lines left combined into a single stanza. Stanza 6 omitted completely.

19 'The North Wind's Tale'
This poem, Mair's version of Coleridge's 'The Ancient Mariner,' is reduced to half its length. Its weakest lines and stanzas are preserved but some of the best omitted.

41 'Innocence'
Notable mainly for the attempts to make much of the diction less grotesque. For example, stanza 5 becomes:

Beneath her sloping neck
Her bosom-gourds swelled chastely, white as spray
Wind-tost – without a fleck –
The air which heaved them was less pure than they.

48 'Our Beautiful Land by the Sea'
Retitled 'Ponemah'

51 'The Little Wren'
Omitted.

55 'To a Morning Cloud'
Number of stanzas reduced to nine. Undergoes considerable revision but little improvement. For example, revised stanza 5 becomes:

And yonder there is he, perchance, who tells
Of cloudlands lying westward from the sun,
Within whose vales the mystic rivers run,

By whose banks grow the fadeless asphodels.
  Where every wind is faint with odours won
From Summer boughs, the bees forever feast,
  The rodent dreams not of his wonted store –
For there the snow doth never come to yeast
  The dulcet wave and whiten hill-sides o'er,
Nor bitter frost to seal the forest's pride,
And wretched make the vales and meadows wide.

61 'Lines to Mount St Patrick'
Title revised to 'To Mount St Patrick,' final stanza omitted, and minor revisions made to diction and punctuation.

65 'Address to a Maid'
Omission of fourteen lines and revisions of diction improve this poem but only slightly.

71 'Winter'
Number of revisions increases as poem progresses until the whole last stanza is altered as follows:

But when the solstice chills my friend,
  And steals the sunshine from his heart;
When death's conveyancers descend,
  And he must seal, and we must part;
All gainless grows the Christmas cheer,
  And gloomy seems the New Year's light;
For joys but live when friends are near,
  And vanish when they quit the sight –
    Then, Winter, from thy glamours freed,
    I cry thee false in heart and deed!

75 'Summer'

Drastically revised to become a poem deliberately 'Canadian.' The abstract reminiscences and musings of the 1868 version become much more specific by the references to the War of 1812, the local landscape, the Canadian home – all 'more suited to our land' – and by omission of the original classical imagery. The revision warrants quotation in full.

Hie me now, and give me rest
  In great fields by Summer drest;
Where the moist pea-bloom is seen
Smiling on the tender bean;
Where the maize unfolds its silk,
And unhoards earth's balmy milk;
Or where stand the oaten leaves
Dreaming of the Autumn sheaves;
Or where lovingly entwine
The vetchling and the sweet woodbine.
Or let me entrancèd go
Where the heavy hautboys grow,
And receive the first impress
Of fond Summer's fruitfulness.

Thrilled by brook and forest-tune
He has donned his flowery shoon,
And where Spring was wont to be
Sports in all his gaiety!

Now the lazy lagging Hours
Drowse within his fretted bowers,
And his leafy henchmen keep

Linkèd arms in poppied sleep.
Silently in musky dell
All the listless Zephyrs dwell;
Silently in dewy mead
Birds and painted insects feed,
Whilst the overhanging sky
Feeds his scattered flocks, that lie
Basking neath with sunny smiles
Ere they rally to their toils,
And, in music of the rain,
Dance to mother-earth again.

O Day! give me all your gleams,
All your sun-warm, throbbing beams,
Such as pant in meadow-still,
By the brook or upland hill!
O Fields! give me all your flowers
Which beguile the wanton Hours,
All the windrowed meadow's math,
Every note each small bird hath,
Every breeze by woods delayed,
Each cool place those woods have made!
So may I your treasures prove
Richer still at each remove,
Till bright Vesper, shining through
Evening's haze of tender hue,
Brings the gloaming – the repast
On what day had overcast;
Till – too fine for every ear –
Nature's lover true may hear,

Faery-sweet, the subtile note
Of the opening primrose; float
In pure fancy on the path
Moonlight on the water hath;
Or, in quest of bygone themes,
Lapse into the realm of dreams, –

Dreams of old-world chivalry,
Bout and joust and revelry;
Or, more suited to our land,
Dreams of forest chief and band:
Braves in paint and plume arrayed,
Sun-burnt youth and dusky maid
Paddling down, in days gone by,
Spirit lake or haunted snie;
Huddling in their barks in fear
When strange voices hit the ear;
Or encamped where, mountain-throned,
Star-lit, monarch pines intoned
Earth's primeval homage, backt
By wild chute and cataract;
Hearing Nature's Spirits then
Talking to the souls of men!

Or, if Fancy still would trace
Forms ideal, forms of grace,
Still would haunt, in dreamy trance,
Kindred regions of Romance,
Let her now recall the sweet
Image of lorn Marguerite,

In the forest-screened château
Of the ribald, foul Bigot;
Or restore the restless mien
Of hope-fed Evangeline,
Robbed of love's pure ends by fate
At the very altar's gate;
Follow, and recall her quest
In the wide-spread, savage West,
Seeking, through love's living flame,
Him who never came – yet came!

Or let roving Fancy delve
In the fields of 'Eighteen-Twelve;'
In her dreams recall the sward
Where the wife of lame Secord,
Knowing Boerstler's subtle plan
To surprise the British van
In the far camp where it lay,
Roused her cows at break of day,
Hoaxed the sentry thus, then passed,
Smiling, to the forest vast.
Call up now that sultry morn –
Call up her who sped forlorn
Through the swales and trackless woods,
Wolfish wilds and solitudes,
Till at night, with heart aflame,
To the British camp she came
With her priceless tidings then
For FitzGibbon and his men.

Or let Fancy cease to roam,
And build up a dream of home;
Wide old porches overgrown
With rosebuds or roses blown,
Red-warm walls and gables fine
Hung with clematis and vine,
Latticed casements, roofings steep,
Dormers quaint, eaves cool and deep,
Shady copses, lawns and bowers
Neighboured by old-fashioned flowers,
Water wandering through the ground,
And a boscage all around
To shut out the evil eye
Of the envious passer-by.

Such the dream of outer things –
What's within the vision brings;
In the vestibule, upstanding,
Grizzlies twain; upon a landing
Of the wide stairs in the hall
A haunted clock, antique and tall;
Forest spoils and trophies fine,
Relics of a manly line,
All around, and, everywhere,
Flowers, rare books, and pictures rare;
Rooms for stately life designed,
Rooms for body, rooms for mind,
Sunlit passages, or dim,
Eerie lofts and garrets grim,
Wherein moves with stealthy tread

Something which the youngsters dread –
A lurking shade which haunts the place,
The Spirit of an ancient race.

In that mansion then descry
Gentle forms – a mother nigh,
Midst her children young and old,
Inmate dearest of the fold.
Hither, too, in maiden-quest,
Youth has come at love's behest,
Whilst the Pleasures without pain,
Tenants true of Home's domain,
Bring in gifts of song and rhyme
To beguile old fleeting Time.
And sweet Fancy, ever-flowing,
Still dreams of those dear ones glowing
With delight, and lovely all,
Whilst the rippling laughter-fall
And the roseal strains they breathe
Part their lips and snowy teeth;
Till Fate waves his magic wand
And the Summer-vision fond
Of a home, by love bedight,
Melts into the morning light.

Ye who faint with city moil,
Come and stay with me awhile!
We will travel, we will roam
To the heart of beauty's home,
To the dim and silent land

Where the jewelled larches stand
In their mosses many-hued –
Haunts where still the wood-nymphs brood,
Thither, from a world of pelf,
Led by banished Pan himself!
Or, enravished, we will go
Where the rarest orchids grow
In their valleys. Come along
Through the lowlands thrid with song,
Rich in pools, in runnels rife,
Haunted by primeval life!
Or let's seek the uplands all
Where the red-ripe berries fall
From their spines in juicy sweetness,
Marking, too, the wood-dove's fleetness,
Or, betimes, the inky yeast
Or scared black-birds caught a feast,
Or, that thriller of the soul,
The fire-flash of the oriole!

Then, our pleasures to enhance,
With a last delight, perchance,
Home won, in a dream retrace
All our paths – nay, hit the place
Where, with laughter soft and song,
Dreamland's apparitions throng
Round a form till now unseen,
The Spirit of this dim demesne –
The Poet's Summer steept in rest –
A Vision! undefiled and blest.

93 'Alice'
Omitted.

96 'To my Photograph'
Revisions in diction, particularly at the beginning and the end, and an entirely new stanza, third from the end, is added:

Whereby thou mightest thrill in life,
  Taste of its temper. of its power,
Replace me, quit me of its strife,
  Its fleeting hour.

101 'Stanzas from the Heart'
Omitted.

103 'Prologue to Tecumseh'
Omitted.

109 'Werter'
Omitted.

111 'The Fire-Flies'
Everything before 'Where is thy home?' – eighty-eight lines – omitted and remainder revised and retitled 'To a Captured Firefly':

Where is thy home? On what strange food dost feed,
  Thou fairy haunter of the moonless night?
From what far nectar'd fount or flowery mead
  Glean'st thou by witching spells thy sluicy light?

Thou mock'st at darkness, and thy footsteps are
Where gloom hangs thickest on the silent earth;
And, like a thought, thou comest from afar–
A world-wide thought which with the world had birth.

We fly to outer potencies to win
The solace of our sense, the means to sec;
But thou dost store thy magic light within,
Pale wizard, and art subtler far than we!

And yet thou art of earth, and so must fear,
And hope, and strive, and suffer in its strife,
Wherein we claim a kinship with thee here,
Thy sharers in the mystery of life:

Life which is but effect, perchance each track
The outburst of Infinity behind;
Its manifests, which all at length fall back,
And blend again with the Eternal Mind.

Surely thou has a heart which trembles now
For thy dear young beneath this pulsing dome;
And fond affections which, I know not how,
Find in thy tiny frame a gentle home.

And so, mayhap, thy little lips could tell
Of tender meetings and of ample bliss
In green pavilions where thy loved ones dwell –
Go seek them now, and give them kiss for kiss!

It flits, and disappears; perchance has found
   A grave, and I have marred an innocent life!
Or mingles with its mates, for, all around,
   The air in fitful radiance is rife.

And, musing, I recall them in the past,
   Till chanticleer rewinds his drowsy horn;
And the small pageant vanishes at last
   In the bleached darkness of the drizzly morn.

117 'Frowns and Smiles'
Omitted.

119 'August'
Omitted.

125 'To Memory'
Retitled 'To the Spirit of Memory' and revised as follows:

The forecasts of our lives recall us
   To thoughts and threatenings of decay;
The Present's need and toils inthral us,
   And hold us as their slaves to-day.
O Spirit! bear me on thy pinions bright,
For thunder rends the summer clouds to-night;
And with the morrow comes the sultry light,
   And all the earth's stern traffic vast.

So back my spirit flies, pursuing
   The trail of bygone time again;

Each retrospection still renewing
   The vanished hours – but not their pain;
For savours of the sadness of the years,
Though lingering still, are not the wounds, the tears!
These thou dost heal, and, in thy light, man hears
   Naught but the music of the Past.

O Spirit! gentle, melancholy,
   What benedictions can repay
Thy tenderness to bygone folly,
   Thy hiding of its stains away?
Thou art the Judge, 'tis said, whom God has given
To try our souls from earth, despondent,driven;
And so, perchance, upon the bench of Heaven,
   Thou wilt rule gently at the last.

127 'Wood-Notes'

Considerable revision of diction and omission of several lines, but poem is not improved thereby. Stanzas 3 and 4, however, may reflect an attempt, by removing the classical references to achieve a greater consistency of imagery, also to depict a more 'Canadian' forest:

And here are deep, secluded vales,
   Still by some fond illusion haunted;
The regions dim of fairy tales,
And strains by mystic voices chanted.
   But silent else, no human tread,
   Save ours, is heard the glades among,
   For us the trembling lights are shed,
   For us the forest songs are sung.

Here, by this streamlet's aldered side,
   A Spirit brooded long agone,
And lingers still, tough faith has died,
   And fond affections thereupon.
      The Indian sought it year by year,
      To spend the mellow Autumn hours;
      But he has fled, and we are here,
      And all its rippling now is ours.

133 'The Lament of Andromache'
Omitted.

145 'Midnight'
Retitled 'Germs' and legthened by ten lines, but reflects same theme and mood.

147 'To a Humming-Bird'
Spelling changed to 'Hummingbird' and poem completely reworked, as follows:

'Tis here! This wonder from a distant clime
      Has come again, by procreant love opprest!
   From the South's flaming heart, yet barren nest,
Impelled by Nature's sovran law sublime,
It comes to sweeten and fulfil the time
   Amidst the floriage of the far North-West.
   So, near its thin vangs, thrilled with fine unrest,
Crouched like a boy again I drink their rhyme!
Once more from lips mature my blessing take,
Thou Bird of Faeryland that dost awake
Remembrance of lost song and vanished art!

For, midst the fond illusions of the heart,
Less like a bird thou hast appeared to me
Than some fine image in old poësy!

147 'To – '
Omitted, although an odd phrase used in a new poem, 'Ideals.'

148 'To an Infant'
Considerable revision of final six lines, thus:

But I, who know the shadows yet to come
  Of care and sorrow and of solitude,
Well-springs of deeper tears, here lay my heart
  To hers in silence, passionate though dumb –
Foreseeing thee upon Life's weltering flood
  Drifting who knoweth whither? but apart.

150 'Love's Empery'
Retitled 'Love's Land' and revised, particularly in opening lines.

Select Bibliography

WRITINGS BY MAIR

a/ *Books*

Dreamland and Other Poems Montreal: Dawson Brothers; and London: Sampson Low, Son and Marston 1868 [all but approximately two hundred copies were destroyed by fire at the Ottawa bindery]

Tecumseh, a Drama Toronto: Hunter, Rose; and London: Chapman and Hall 1886 [despite the imprint, not even distributed in England]

Tecumseh, a Drama, and Canadian Poems Toronto: Briggs 1901

Tecumseh, a Drama, and Canadian Poems; Dreamland and Other Poems; The American Bison; Through the Mackenzie Basin; Memoirs and Reminiscences Introduction by Robert Norwood. Vol. XIV of *Master-Works of Canadian Authors* [edited by John W. Garvin]. Toronto: Radisson Society 1926. [did not actually appear until April 1927]

Through the Mackenzie Basin: A Narrative of the Athabasca and Peace River Treaty Expedition of 1899; also Notes on the Mammals and Birds of Northern Canada, by Roderick MacFarlane. Toronto: Briggs 1908. [also published without MacFarlane's 'Notes' and in paper covers, but with the same imprint]

b/ *Articles and Letter-articles Contributed to Newspapers and Periodicals*

'The American Bison: Its Habits, Methods of Capture and Economic Use in the North-West, with reference to Its Threatened Extinction and Possible Preservation,' *Transactions of the Royal Society of Canada*, 1st ser. VIII (1890) Section II, 93-108

Correspondence from the Red River to eastern newspapers, 1868-9: Perth Courier 1, 14 Jan. 1869; Montreal *Gazette* 25 Dec. 1868; 23 Jan., 27 Feb. 1869; Toronto *Globe* 14, 27 Dec. 1868; 4 Jan., 16 Feb., 14, 28 May 1869

'The New Canada,' *Canadian Monthly and National Review* VIII (July and Aug. 1875) 2-8, 156-64

DOCUMENTS AND MANUSCRIPTS

Canada, *Journals of the House of Commons.* Report of the Select Committee on the Causes of the Difficulties in the North-West Territory in 1869-70. Vol. VIII, Appendix No. 6, 1874

Public Archives of Canada. Denison Papers

- Public Works Files, series 98, subject 429, correspondence, the Department of Works and C. Mair

Queen's University Library, Kingston, Ontario. Garvin Papers

- Mair Papers

BOOKS

Begg, Alexander *The Creation of Manitoba; or, a History of the Red River Troubles* Toronto: Hovey 1871

- *'Dot-It-Down,' A Story of Life in the North-West* Toronto: Hunter, Rose 1871 (Toronto Reprint Library of Canadian Prose and Poetry 1973)

Broadus, E.K., ed. *A Book of Canadian Prose and Verse* Toronto: Macmillan 1924

Brown, E.K. *On Canadian Poetry* Toronto: Ryerson 1943

Creighton, Donald G. *Dominion of the North* Boston: Houghton Mifflin 1944

Denison, George T. *Reminiscences of the Red River Rebellion of 1869* Toronto: privately printed 1873

- *Soldiering in Canada* 2nd ed. Toronto: Morang 1901
- *The Struggle for Imperial Unity* Toronto: Macmillan 1909

Haliburton, Robert G. *The Men of the North and Their Place in History* Montreal: John Lovell 1869

Hargrave, Joseph J. *Red River* Montreal: John Lovell 1871

Lower, A.R.M. *Canadians in the Making* Toronto: Longmans, Green 1958

Matthews, John P. *Tradition in Exile: A Comparative Study of Social Influences on the Development of Australian and Canadian Poetry in the Nineteenth Century* Toronto: University of Toronto Press 1962

Morgan, Henry J. *Bibliotheca Canadensis, or a Manual of Canadian Literature* Ottawa: Desbarats 1867

- *Canadian Men and Women of the Time: A Handbook of Canadian Biography* Toronto: Briggs 1898

Morton, William L. *Alexander Begg's Red River Journal* Toronto: The Champlain Society 1956

Pacey, Desmond *Creative Writing in Canada* 2nd ed. Toronto: Ryerson 1961

Pierce, Lorne *An Outline of Canadian Literature* Toronto: Ryerson 1927

Shrive, Norman *Charles Mair: Literary Nationalist* Toronto: University of Toronto Press 1965
Smith, A.J.M., ed. *The Book of Canadian Poetry* 3rd ed. Toronto: Gage 1957

ARTICLES

Bailey, A.G. 'Literature and Nationalism after Confederation' *University of Toronto Quarterly* XXV (July 1965) 409-24
Bissell, C. 'Literary Taste in Central Canada during the Late Nineteenth Century' *Canadian Historical Review* XXXI (Sept. 1950) 237-51
Matthews, John 'Charles Mair' *Canada's Past and Present: Our Living Tradition* Fifth Series. University of Toronto Press 1965, pp 78-101
Pratt, E.J. 'Canadian Poetry, Past and Present' *University of Toronto Quarterly* VIII (Oct. 1938) 1-10
Shrive, Norman 'Poet and Politics: Charles Mair at Red River' *Canadian Literature* 17 (Summer 1963) 6-21
– 'Poets and Patriotism: Charles Mair and Tecumseh' *Canadian Literature* 20 (Spring 1964) 15-26
– 'What Happened to Pauline?' *Canadian Literature* 13 (Summer 1962) 25-38
Smith, A.J.M. 'Colonialism and Nationalism in Canadian Poetry before Confederation' *Report of the Canadian Historical Association* (1944) 74-85
– 'Nationalism and Canadian Poetry' *Northern Review* I (Dec.-Jan. 1945-6) 33-42
– ' "Our Poets": A Sketch of Canadian Poetry in the Nineteenth Century' *University of Toronto Quarterly* XII (Oct. 1942) 75-94

Dreamland and Other Poems

TO

MRS. WILLIAM MACDOUGALL,

OF OTTAWA, CANADA,

THIS VOLUME

IS RESPECTFULLY DEDICATED

AS AN EARNEST OF

THE SINCERE FRIENDSHIP AND ESTEEM OF

THE AUTHOR.

PREFACE.

It is not without much hesitation and many misgivings that the author of the following poems allows them to pass the press. Perhaps no poet, and certainly no young poet, can estimate with precision the value of his work. Familiarity with his subjects, the reproduction of sympathies and emotions peculiar to himself, the very delight attending composition, all conspire to delude him, and to endear to him productions which may find but little place in the esteem of readers competent to judge. Hence it is that the author submits this, his first venture, to the ordeal of English criticism. He feels convinced that at the hands of those accustomed to assess the value of literary productions he will receive that candid criticism which will either be a guide to him in future or induce him to abandon the field of poetry altogether.

Perth, Ontario, August 1st, 1868.

CONTENTS.

DREAMLAND AND OTHER POEMS.

O Poesy! for thee I hold my pen,
That am not yet a glorious denizen
Of thy wide heaven—should I rather kneel
Upon some mountain-top until I feel
A glowing splendour round about me hung,
And echo back the voice of thine own tongue?

Keats.

DREAMLAND

WE are not wholly blest who use the earth,
  Nor wholly wretched who inherit sleep.
Behold, it is a palace of delight
Built beyond fear of storms by day or night;
  And whoso enters doth his station keep,
Unmindful of the stain upon his birth.

Sin hath no hold on it; yea, men may take
  Their loves into their arms tenaciously;
For sleep is as a chamber high and fair,
Wherein warm love makes light of cold despair;
  And wives may deem their faithless lords are nigh,
And maids may kiss false lovers for love's sake.

Thou canst not fetter it, for it is free ;
  No tyrant yokes it to the labouring oar.
It is a solemn height, wind-visited,
And touched by sunlight when the sun is fled—
  Where bondsmen lift their aching brows no more,
And men have peace, and slaves have liberty.

See now it hath a tender bloom, like light
  Viewed at the autumn's latest outgoing.
It is the faithful summer of our sorrow,
A kindly year whose winter is the morrow.
  See now 'tis like the firstlings of the spring,
Which win their fragrance in the snow's despite.

Faint, far-off sounds are blown unto our ears,
  Faint, far-off savours steal unto our lips,
When orient dreams assemble manifold,
And sleep doth throne himself on royal gold.
  Then night is noon-tide, morning the eclipse
Wherein no comfort is but in our tears.

Man may not say unto himself: "Time fills
  Day's even measures with matched bitterness,"
Whilst he hath sleep—a jewel without peer,
Which hath the light as but its bezel here.
  For there are days which curse, and nights which bless,
And unseen forces striving with our ills.

We are not equal with the unseen powers,
  Who eat but bread, and suffer strange decay.
Yet there are pleasant environs which make,
Mid adverse things, a heaven for our sake.
  Beyond the precincts of the open day
There is an easy entrance which is ours.

I entered in thereat, and I had peace;
  By ancient ways I went and I had rest;
And space was far about me, murmurings,
And 'wildering speed of undulary wings:
  My limbs were lissom, and my soul possessed
Of thousand fantasies which would not cease.

Beyond me were wide plains of amber light,
And sunless regions stained with solemn gold.
And there the myriad wild-fowl soared on high,
Scattered and strewn like dust against the sky.
And, in the east, a tender shadow rolled
Forth from the distant antres of the night.

Aërial mountains of their substance gave
To beamless forests where the breezes stirred
Faintly, and faintly shook the leaves. I saw
The rising mists behind the mountains draw
Like phantoms to the hovering clouds, and heard,
Far-off, the sullen thunder of the wave.

Not any space of all the world's desire
Was fairer to mine eyes, and, when my death
Seemed instant on my head, mine eyes grew dim,
And all my life fled out of every limb.
My fears I felt as one who holds his breath,
And fears betwixt the thunder and the fire.

For I was falling, falling from on high
  With the deceitful earth, which sunk away.
Unmeasured depths were sounded as I fell,
And there was peace no more, nor could I tell,
  For dizziness, the darkness from the day,
So numb of sense, so dead with fear was I.

O blessed was the hand that caught my hand,
  Unseen, and swung me thrice throughout all space !
Blessed that sought me at the ocean's brink,
And gave me hope as food and love as drink,
  And fanned with snowy flowers mine anguished face,
And soothed me with her kisses as she fanned.

Lo, she was holy and most strangely fair,
  Sleek-throated like a dove, and solemn-eyed.
Her lips were, as an infant's, small and sweet,
And as an infant's were her naked feet ;
  And scarf-like flowed and shimmered at each side
Her cloven tresses of untrammeled hair.

The melancholy waste of wave was dead,
  And silence haunted the Marmorean hills;
Nor any sound of any breeze or bird
Within the sunshine or the shade was heard
  When as she said, "O love! 'tis life that kills,"
When as she sighed, and touched my lips, and said:

"Small light have they, O love! who love their lives,
  Calling the dead the past, and fearing death.
For these our ways aforetime have been trod
By patient suffering ones who now are God,
  Being immortal, with abiding breath,
And joy that ravishes, and hope that strives.

"'Tis but a terror which entreats control,
  A baseless fear which thwarts us of the dues
Of sacred death—things effable above,
And roomy thrones, and light of endless love.
  Wherefore 'tis meet to seal our fate and use
The trodden path which disenthralls the soul.

"For I am weary of the day which dips,
  And, faint with love, I hunger for thy sighs.
They who have tasted of my limbs, and felt
My veins and the keen life that in them dwelt
  Like fire, and felt as fire my kindling eyes,
And caught my tears upon their trembling lips :

"These shall be hateful to me for thy sake,
  If thou, O love! wilt drink of this with me,"
Whereat a tiny, vase-like amethyst
She pressed from lip to lip, and then I wist
  Our steps were God-like and our souls were free,
For all our flesh fell from us flake by flake.

And all our bones we gathered in a pyre,
  Like faggots, and the flesh thereon we laid :
And all the mystery of baleful years,
And all our mortal sleep, and sin, and tears
  We heaped upon the pile which we had made,
And closed them in and burnt them with swift fire.

And in the smoke thereof we faded thence,
  Away into empyreal regions blest,
Beyond the extreme cloisters of the skies,
And, like a flame, the lightning of her eyes
  Burnt in my path, and endless was our rest.
Endless our love and love's omnipotence.

And in our strength and everlasting youth,
  Arising in clear dawn and light which saves,
We found a realm wherein earth's sorrowings
Were heard no more, where myriad blameless things
  Rose from their venal and lethean graves,
And found a resting-place, and called it Truth.

They rose from island and from continent,
  Pale-featured spirits in apparel bright ;
They rose from ancient rivers and the sea
In human shapes and garbs of chastity ;
  They came from sepulchres of death and night,
Faint with despair and long imprisonment.

And all these shapes found each its own desire,
Whate'er its faith on earth, whate'er its creed.
The Christian saw at last the Son unsoiled;
The Prophet's God upon his creatures smiled.
The Indian found his Manitou indeed,
Lama his life, the Magian his fire.

For all these souls were innocent below,
And loved God well who loved what he had made;
And, loving all things, though they found not truth,
Were yet received of heav'n, and gat them youth,
And pleasant sleep, and shelter in the shade,
And endless mitigation of their woe.

For God, who is our Master and our Lord,
Took pity on their helpless ignorance,
And, from their wives, their children and their pelf,
And all their idols, took them to himself,
And clad them round with glorious circumstance,
And all the joys high heaven doth afford.

O could I sleep for ever in a dream,
Or dream such dreams for ever while I slept!
Onwards they went, and sung their mystic psalms,
Screening their pallid faces with their palms,
Whither the Unimaginable kept
His kingly state as doth Him best beseem.

Onwards they went unto the Paraclete,
With far-heard sound of voice and instrument,
I could not follow them, I could not tread
Where passion burns not, and where lust is dead;
For love had caught me in his arms, and bent
My will to his, and bound my feeble feet.

Yes, love possessed me, and, with keen desire,
I took her eyes' wild light into my soul.
I clasped her spirit-form, and drunk her breath,
And then our lips, more near than life and death,
Clung each to each in silence, and control
Vanished as snow-flakes vanish in the fire.

That moment there was darkness, and the lists
  Of heav'n gave place unto the gloom of day.
Whereat I woke to deadly fears and pain,
To misery of the thunder and the rain,
  And crime, and subterfuge, and fierce affray
Of warring creeds and brawling mammonists.

THE PINES.

O heard ye the pines in their solitude sigh,
When the winds were awakened and night was nigh?
When the elms breathed out a sorrowful tale,
Which was wafted away on the wings of the gale;

When the aspen leaf whispered a legend dread,
And the willows waved darkly over the dead;
And the poplar shone with a silvery gleam,
And trembled like one in a troublesome dream;

And the cypresses murmured of grief and woe,
And the linden waved solemnly to and fro,
And the sumach seemed wrapt in a golden mist,
And the soft maple blushed where the frost had kissed;

And the spectral birch stood alone in the gloom,
Like an unquiet spirit uprist from the tomb;
And the cedar outstretched its lone arms to the earth,
To feed with sweet moisture the place of its birth;

And the hemlock, uplifted above the crowd,
Drunk deeply of mist at the brink of a cloud;
And the balsams, with curtains of shaggy green,
Like tents in the distance were dimly seen.

I heard the pines in their solitude sighing,
When the winds were awakened, and day was dying;
And fiercer the storm grew, and darker its pall,
But the voice of the pines was louder than all:

The Voice of the Pines.

"We fear not the thunder, we fear not the rain,
  For our stems are stout and long;
Or the growling winds, though they blow amain,
  For our roots are great and strong.
Our voice is eternal, our song sublime,
  And its theme is the days of yore—
Back thousands of years of misty time,
  When we first grew old and hoar!

"Deep down in the crevice our roots were hid,
  And our limbs were thick and green
Ere Cheops had builded his pyramid,
  Or the Sphinx's form was seen.
Whole forests have risen within our ken,
  Which withered upon the plain;
And cities, and race after race of men
  Have arisen and sunk again.

"We commune with the stars thro' the paly night,
  For we love to talk with them;
The wind is our harp, and the marvellous light
  Of the moon our diadem.
Like the murmur of ocean our branches stir
  When the night air whispers low;
Like the voices of ocean our voices are,
  When the hurtling tempests blow.

"We nod to the sun ere the glimmering morn
  Prints her sandals on the mere;
We part with the sun when the stars are borne
  By the silv'ry waters clear.
And when lovers are breathing a thousand vows,
  With their hearts and cheeks aglow,
We chant a love strain 'mid our breezy boughs,
  Of a thousand years ago!

" We stand all aloof, for the giant's strength
Craveth naught from lesser powers ;
'Tis the shrub that loveth the fertile ground,
But the sturdy rock is ours !
We tower aloft where the hunters lag
By the weary mountain side,
By the jaggy cliff, by the grimy crag,
And the chasms yawning wide.

" When the great clouds march in a mountain heap,
By the light of the dwindled sun,
We steady our heads 'gainst their misty sweep,
And accost them one by one.
Then our limbs they jostle in thunder-mirth,
And the storm-fires flash again ;
But baffled and weary they sink to earth,
And the monarch-stems remain.

"The passage of years doth not move us much,
  And Time himself grows old
Ere we bow to his flight, or feel his touch
  In our 'limbs of giant mould.'
And the dwarfs of the wood, by decay oppressed,
  With our laughter grim we mock;
For the burden of age doth lightly rest
  On the ancient forest folk.

"Cold winter, who filches the flying leaf,
  And steals the floweret's sheen,
Can injure us not, or work us grief,
  Or make our tops less green.
And spring, who awakens her sleeping train
  By meadow, and hill, and lea,
Brings no new life to our old domain,
  Unfading, stern and free.

"Sublime in our solitude, changeless, vast,
  While men build, work, and save,
We mock—for their years glide away to the past,
  And we grimly look on their grave.
Our voice is eternal, our song sublime,
  For its theme is the days of yore—
Back thousands of years of misty time,
  When we first grew old and hoar."

THE MORNING-LAND.

The light rains grandly from the distant wood,
  For in the wood the hermit sun is hid;
So night draws back her curtains ebon-hued,
  To close them round some eastern pyramid.

The listless dew lies shining on the grass,
And o'er the streams the light darts quick away,
And through the fields the morning sunbeams pass,
Shot from the opening portals of the day.

Still upward mounts the tireless eremite,
(While all the herald birds make loud acclaim)
Till o'er the woods he rounds upon our sight,
And, lo ! the western world is all aflame.

From out the landscape lying 'neath the sun
The last sea-smelling, cloud-like mists arise ;
The smoky woods grow clear, and, one by one,
The meadow blossoms ope their winking eyes.

Now pleasèd fancy starts with eager mien—
A-tiptoe, looking o'er the silent fields,
Where all the land is fresh and calm and green,
And every flow'r its balmy incense yields.

And I, who am upon no business bent,
  A simple stroller through these dewy ways,
Feel that all things are with my future blent,
  Yet see them in the light of by-gone days.

THE NORTH WIND'S TALE.

I am the lord of frost and snow,
  My home is on the northern deep,
Where lofty berg and sunless floe,
  Their cold, eternal vigils keep.

I prowl about the dreary main,
  I roam along the sleepless sea;
The burden of my tale is pain,
  And sighs and tears and agony.

For I am he who lays full low
  The pleasant flow'r in loathsome death;
I churn the rivers while I blow
  Great gusts which sweep away men's breath.

What time I lurk in icy halls
  They say 'tis summer, and the earth
Throbs, buds and glows—the fruitage falls;
  Each cottage rings with peasant-mirth.

But, often, ere the tender blade
  Hath filled its spike with sappy corn,
I hurtle from my piny glade,
  And shout till all the peasants mourn.

The winter cometh, chill and drear,
  A slave—the offspring of my power;
And soon the daisies find a bier,
  A common grave each tender flow'r.

And cold and dull as an old man's blood
  Earth's pulses beat; within the air
No joyous sound, no warbled flood:
  The leaves fall down in mute despair.

The mighty forests pant and heave,
  Like drunken bacchanals they call;
My hand goes forth and, lo! they grieve;
  My fingers touch them and they fall.

I look upon the glimmering stream
  Which woos the stars from heaven's breast,
And quickly vanishes the gleam:
  Each ripple finds an icy rest.

The torrent-music and the hush,
  The lonely whisper of the woods
Grow faint and die; their spirits rush
  To other haunts and solitudes.

The nut-brown cheek, and matron grace
  Of autumned earth, the dewy eye
Which gazeth on her quiet face,
  Alike must shrink, alike must fly.

And over hills and mountains drear
  I sift and heap my whirling snow ;
I sweep away the leaflets sear,
  And hide them in the vales below.

I load the green-armed balsams down,
  And robe them in a kirtle white ;
I front the cedars with a frown,
  And hide their darkness from the light.

About the plains I lash and roar,
  And surge as doth the billowy ocean,
Casting my wreaths behind, before—
  Cloud after cloud in hasty motion.

I heap my flakes upon each roof,
  I huddle them about the eaves;
The mantle hath no warp, no woof,
  Which the chill-fingered winter weaves.

Men shrink aghast when I draw nigh,
  And quake as seized with sudden dread;
Then quickly to their cov'rings fly,
  To mansion, cottage, or to shed.

The parents gather round the fire,
  The youngsters perch upon each knee,
And all are still, while higher, higher
  My tingling tongue shrieks mournfully.

All night I hunt with snow and storm
  The wretched mother, wandering, lost;
And shake with sleet her tender form,
  And bind her tears with links of frost.

And when the infant, mute-mouthed, slips,
  Dead, from the sighing mother's teat,
I freeze the milk which slowly drips
  Adown, and steal her bosom's heat.

And chiller, fiercer in my glee,
  I blow along the paths of night;
Till o'er them sweeps the winter free,
  And buries them from mortal sight.

I track great armies on their path,
  And harass them with sleet and snow;
They shrink, they cower before my wrath—
  In vain their pomp and martial glow.

Down, down they sink, those stern-faced men,
  Down, one by one, all silently,
In sleep which hath no dream of pain,
  So calm, so cunning death can be.

Then I arise in awful might,
  And howl their requiem aloud;
And stealthily at dead of night
  Weave over them a snowy shroud.

And over them I shout and brawl,
  Day after day upon the plain;
Till spring comes forth with breezy call,
  And straight unburies them again.

Long years ago a ship set out
  From a far city in the West:
With brawny hull and timbers stout
  She cleaved the sounding ocean's breast.

And on she sped: her hardy crew
  Feared neither tide nor wave nor wind.
Into the dim expanse they flew—
  The earth-world soon was left behind.

And naught but sea and sky was seen,
  Naught but the sky and murm'ring sea;
And midnight whispers rose between,
  Voices and deep-born harmony.

And hope was there; nor fear nor dread
  Found resting place—swoll'n was each sail;
And northward like a cloud they fled,
  Urged by the wing-stroke of the gale.

Softly the shrouds, tuned to my voice,
  Harped a faint music through the air—
Sweet tones which made each soul rejoice,
  Mazing and threading here and there.

The jest passed round from mouth to mouth,
  The echoing laugh rung clear and bold;
And many a legend of the south,
  And many a pleasant tale was told.

Some told of brave, advent'rous men
  Forsaking home in dauntless bands,
That home they ne'er might see again,
  To roam in quest of other lands.

And how, in wretched, leaky craft,
  They battled with the wind and wave;
How hunger pinched them till they laughed
  Like maniacs in a living grave!

How thirst consumed them until death
  Stared in each haggard cheek and eye:
They gasped for thirst, they gasped for breath,
  When lo! the land dawned suddenly.

And such a land! A land of gold,
  And fruitage mellowing in the sun;
Of myriad joys, of wealth untold,
  And hope, and peace, and pleasure won.

Some told how settlements were made,
 And cities rose in haughty pride,
Where gloomed erstwhile the forest glade,
 Or by the lordly river's side.

And how wealth flowed, an endless stream,
 And days and years went flocking past,
Like the procession in a dream,
 Or heav'nly boons too sweet to last.

And others told of balmy isles,
 Where lovers might their griefs assuage;
Of scenes where nature ever smiles—
 Of youth, and innocence and age.

Of fame, and power, and empires great,
 Of kings—how millions fear their wrath ;
And of the poor, the rich estate
 The poet, painter, sculptor hath.

Ah, well-a-day! what themes were these,
  Ere I arose in vengeful might!
What hopeful morns, what nights of ease,
  What pleasant thoughts, what fancies bright!

But I had tracked them many a mile,
  Remorseless as the yearning grave,
And all unseen had mocked each smile,
  Each laugh one to the other gave.

And cunning as an asp I reared
  The unseen danger of my mouth;
And swept the spoon-drift as I veered,
  And blew from east and west and south.

Till to the desolate ocean's brink
  And dreary waste of wave they came,
Where frosty planets rise and sink
  In sheeny fields of wandering flame.

And now I scowled upon the sea,
And fetched great clouds to hide the sky,
And quench its twinkling, starry glee,
While tempest, storm and fears drew nigh.

And fiercely still I urged them on—
On to the land of frost and snow,
Where night and morn and eve are one,
The sunrise and the sunset glow.

The talking billows rose and gave
Strange stories 'twixt the lightning gleams;
And all dark thoughts that murd'rers have,
Dim visionings and lonely dreams,

And ev'ry wild and dreadful thing,
Fear and despair, remorse and pain,
That hour I o'er the deep did fling
In mist, in thunder and in rain.

The white foam winked upon the deep ;
  The great masts bent before the gale ;
Each blast made th' strong ship surge and leap,
  And bulged and strained each dripping sail.

Each strong blast made her creak and groan,
  As 'twere a soul in misery ;
She swayed, she lurched with many a moan,—
  No rest, no peacefulness had she.

And yet I spared her ; day and night
  She fled before me. While my breath
Grew fiercely cold none marked her flight
  Onward to the abode of death.

And colder, colder still I blew—
  A horrible and intense cold ;
It numbed the fingers of the crew,
  It froze the water in the hold.

They fed the fires, their fuel spent,
With short'ning wine, and oil, and grain,
And chafed in wild bewilderment
Their stony limbs, and wept with pain.

They fed the feeble fires till naught
Was left for fuel or for food;
And still the icy drift I brought,
And chilled the torrent of their blood.

And blist'ring snow fell thick and fast,
On deck it lay in dreary hills;
Thick ice clung round each rope and mast,
And hung in sheeny icicles.

And, sealed with frost as with a seal,
The big blocks stood in icy mails;
The great sheets hung like bars of steel—
So stiff they could not reef the sails.

At length the ocean ceased to flow—
It froze and bound her; far and near
Great crags of ice and peaks of snow
Lifted their foreheads chill and drear.

And through the shrouds I whistled keen,
And drave the luckless vessel fast,
'Twixt icebergs, and the awful sheen
Of crashing floes and hummucks vast.

Then, like a frightful dream which fills
The soul with loathing, in a trice
I wrought a horror in the hills
And whuling caverns of ice.

And round the ship I shrieked and howled;
What mortal crew could bravė my glee?
Their souls fled upward as I scowled,
And left the lifeless clay with me.

The attitude each body had
  When life departed still it kept;
Some clutched the ropes, despairing, mad—
  Some knelt in pray'r, some crouched and wept.

One even smiled—a strange, sweet smile,
  Tinged with regret and musing thought—
As nothing could his soul despoil
  Of the deep joy with which 'twas fraught.

The look-out man upon the mast
  Still seemed as he was wont to be,
On watch—but he was frozen fast:
  He peered into eternity.

The captain sat before his log,
  Holding his pen as if to trace
Some words, and at his feet a dog
  Lay crouched, and looking in his face.

And near him his fond sister leant
  Her weary head upon her hand;
In her fair, lovely face were blent
  Pity and hope and high command.

And all were dead, and stony cold,
  As cold as ever the dead can be;
And the frost of years, and the rime of old
  Still cling to their flesh and garmentry.

For, though all dead, they still are there:
  No more by toil and trouble worn,
Silent as shadows, free from care,
  They wait the dreadful coming morn.

NIGHT AND MORN.

THE sun is stepping upward in his might
To wake the West from sleep;
And, while his shining hair and brows of light
Lift like a giant's o'er the Western deep,
He fills with shadow every Eastern eye
Which saw him sink in bright obscurity—
In cloudy canopy of gold-like cloud.

The Mufti saw him sink, and cried aloud
To Allah and his seer,
Then straightway every Arab knee was bowed.
The Moor in the wide sand-wave struck his spear,
Gazed a mute prayer to Mecca and the shrine
Where sleeps the dust of Mahomet divine,
And slipt into the darkness of a dream.

The patient Hindoo caught his latest gleam,
  In penance for his caste,
Self-tortured by the ancient sacred stream.
  The Parsee viewed the glory fading fast,
And wept his banishment from Khonzar's vale.
The Guebres sighed to see their god-head fail,
  And felt the powers of darkness round them strong.

In distant China there was heard a song;
  The mystery, and the doom
Of viewless ancestry employed it long
  Where maids at shut of eve burnt sweet perfume.
The dreamer watched him fade into the West,
And sorrowed till his opiate wreathings blest
  Wrought sleep in mystic palaces divine.

The Abyssinian saw the light decline,
  And felt his amulet.
All ebon limbs grew cold beneath the line,
  Though not a Libyan leaf with dew was wet.
The driver on his noiseless camel strove
To gain the desert fountain and the grove,
  Ere howling monsters met him on the plain.

He sank from sight beyond the ancient main
  Of Egypt, and the Nile.
The awful tombs of Djizeh gloomed again,
  The Sphinx, unmoved, turned from his setting smile.
Then did the mourning women moot their sighs
In chambers of the East, and aching eyes
  Bewept the dead who never could return.

Far Abyla and Calpe saw him burn
  The ocean in his ire,
And, like a god indignant, from him spurn
  The glorious sea-swell in a mist of fire.
Once more he looked, then plunged into the wave,
And left a myst'ry brooding on his grave,
  And o'er the land a solemn darkness drew.

So Asia's flow'rs sloped to the West anew,
  And closed their leaves in sleep.
So Afric's sons forgot their cursed hue,
  So Europe's outposts lay in darkness deep.
Helvellyn saw the flaming light no more,
And sacred Snowdon hid his summits hoar
  In domes of mist and vaults of sullen gloom.

And now he stands above the wat'ry doom,
  And views our songless shores.
No sea-maid doth her glassy eyes illume
  With fatal light, nor any siren pours
Her treacherous melody at ocean's brink.
No elf doth seek the cloud, no fairies shrink
  Into their primrose tents of shady gold.

But, in the ancient woods the Indian old,
  Unequal to the chase,
Sighs as he thinks of all the paths untold,
  No longer trodden by his fleeting race.
And, Westward, on far-stretching prairies damp,
The savage shout, and mighty bison tramp
  Roll thunder with the lifting mists of morn.

INNOCENCE.

Oft I have met her
In openings of the woods and pleasant ways,
Where flow'rs beset her,
And hanging branches crowned her head with bays.

Oft have I seen her walk
Through flow'r-decked fields unto the oaken pass,
Where lay the slumb'ry flock,
Swoll'n with much eating of the tender grass.

Oft have I seen her stand
By wandering brooks o'er which the willows met;
Or where the meadow-land
Balmed the soft air with dew-mist drapery wet.

Much patting of the wind
Had bloomed her cheek with colour of the rose ;
Rare beauty was entwined
With locks and looks in movement or repose.

Beneath her sloping neck
Her bosom-gourds plumped mellow-white as spray ;
Stainless, without a fleck,
The air which heaved them was less pure than they.

Strolling in evening's eye,
There came unto her airy laughter-chimes,
Nature's night-hymn and cry,
Leaf-stirring madrigals and river-rhymes.

The floriage of spring,
And summer's coronals were hers in trust,
Till came the winter-king
To droop their sweetness into native dust.

His sharp, embracing wind,
And wavering snow, or heaped in rimy hills,
She loved ; ay ! she could bind
On Fancy's brow his charmèd icicles.

The dingle and the glade,
The brown-ribbed mountains and tall, talking trees
Seemed fairer while she stayed,
And drank of their dim meanings and old ease.

Thoughts such as day unfolds
From starry quietude and noiseless sleep ;
Scenes which the fancy holds
In easy thraldom in her joyous keep ;

Visions of high delight,
And storied legends, cool as the dim eve,
Came thronging faintly-bright,
The habit of her inner life to weave.

Nor was she dead to pain—
Another's was her own ; all griefs, all care
Which crush souls down amain,
She ever sought for, always wished to share.

And chiefly she did love
To soothe the widow's ruth, and orphans' tears ;
With counsel from above,
Alleviating woe, allaying fears.

All these, and more, were hers :
What man may speak not of, but think upon ;
What the pure soul avers
In secret solitude before God's throne.

There was a quiet grace
In all her actions, tok'ning gentleness,
Yet firm intent to trace
The paths of duty leading up to bliss.

He who created night,
Earth, and the biding stars, was all her guide ;
She worshipped in his sight,
She sighed, she wept, she flung away her pride.

She thought of One who bore
The awful burden of the world's despair—
What could she give him more
Than blameless thoughts, a simple life and fair ?

She was and is, for still
She lives and moves upon the grass-green earth,
And, as of old, doth fill
Her heart with peace, still mingling tears with mirth.

O ! could we find her out,
And learn of her this wild'ring maze to tread
And, eased of every doubt,
Let deadly passions linger with the dead.

But truth is hard to find,
And simple souls are oft in error's thrall,
And faith too oft is blind:
We know a part and yet we know not all.

THE BEAUTIFUL LAND BY THE SEA.

FAR away in the West there's a beautiful land,
  And it lies by the shore of the sea,
And spirits have flown to that region unknown,
  To welcome and wait you and me.

And all the way there we will travel with care,
  Nor the frost nor the rain shall you see,
For the angels of sleep will come with us and keep
  The fair weather for you and me.

And the region of dreams, which with wondrous forms teems,
  Shall be travelled by you and me,
Ere we see the far light of the waves day and night
  In that beautiful land by the sea.

But when we, unwearied, have reached it at last,
What shall we do there ? Let me see :
We will build us a home of the starlight and foam
In our beautiful land by the sea.

We will build us a home of the starlight and foam,
And the waves' voice our music will be,
And the Zephyrs will play by our doors night and day
In our beautiful land by the sea.

And ev'ry sweet smell that in Summer doth dwell,
And ev'ry fair flow'r of the lea
Shall be wasted no more as in seasons of yore
In our beautiful land by the sea.

For the music which flows from the wide open rose
With the lily's voice blended will be,
And with us will come to inhabit our home
In our beautiful land by the sea.

And ev'ry fair thing, which the ocean can bring,
  Shall be wafted for you and me
By the waves and the winds, till a harbour it finds
  In our beautiful land by the sea.

And up from the shore shall the relics of yore
  Be carried for you and me :
Old songs of the dead whose wild echoes have fled
  From the dim world of memory ;

And the vases which keep the pale nectar of sleep,
  And the weird books of destiny,
And the vans which upraise the spirit to gaze
  O'er the blue hills of reverie ;

And the gems and the gold of the realms of old,
  And the rich embroiderie,
And the sumptuous things of embalmed kings
  From the crypts of the isles of the sea.

And the ocean shall flow, and time come and go,
  And ages on ages shall flee,
And bear to the glooms of their spiritless tombs
  The dust of the slave and the free.

But the footsteps and breath of malevolent death
  Shall be shorn, ere they reach you and me,
Of their ailments unclean and corruptions obscene,
  In our beautiful land by the sea.

THE LITTLE WREN.

A LITTLE wren comes hopping slowly,
  Picking, hopping by the gate;
Picking, hopping, bending lowly:
  "Little wren, where is thy mate?"

"I neither know nor care," said she—
  And little wren here cocked her head—
"For he has used me cruelly,
  I wish, indeed, that he were dead!"

"Ah, little wren, how can you say
  You wish your little husband dead,
When he, perhaps, is far away,
  For you and yours a-gath'ring bread?"

"Why no," said she, "'tis not quite that :
This morning, ere we left the nest,
He billed and cooed and was quite pat,
Yet, afterwards, may I be blest,

"If, when some cherries we had found,
He did not snap up two to one,
And then went piping round and round,
And swore he did it all in fun!

"And that's not all ; for, yesterday,
When we flew down to have a drink—
Down yonder by the little bay—
What did he do to me ? Just think !

"He pitched me from the margin slickly,
And, sure as I am not a marten,
If me he had not picked out quickly,
I should have been, sir, drowned, that's certain.

"And that's not all; for, one night, he,
After that sort of time called 'old,'
Came home and railed and swore at me—
Ay, swore! because the nest was cold.

"And that was true, for, purposely,
I made the nest unpleasant all;
And that was right, for why dared he
To stay away from me at all?

"And all day long with tricks like these
He vexes, angers me," she said;
"And so, because he loves to tease,
I wish indeed that he were dead!"

"Ah, little wren, can you so hate
Your little friend, you spiteful elf?"
"Why there's the rub," said she, "my mate
I love as dearly as myself."

"Yet he so frets me with his ways,
And keeps me in such fear and dread,
That I have thought these last few days
'Twere better far if he were dead."

"You little wren, come, tell me truly:
Before the wretched cherry feud,
Had he not brought the rations duly
For you and for the callow brood?"

"Why, yes, that's true; but, then, I say,
'Tis no more than he ought, I think;
And, then, what earthly right had he
To duck me when I went to drink?"

"Why, little wren, he did reclaim
You from the flood, as you have told";
"Yes! yes! But, yet, why did he blame
His wren because the nest was cold?"

And so this silly wren went on,
And teazed her silly little head,
Still crying out, with many a moan,
"I wish that he or I were dead!"

TO A MORNING CLOUD.

WHY stray'dst thou from the unseen realm of wonder,
To mock my soul, which fain would visit thee,
And roam unwearied, exploring eagerly
Thy furthest vale where sleeps the infant Thunder?
Alas, so fair art thou I fain would be
As one who knew not, and who ne'er could know
Those yearnings deep which sicken in the heart;
Those idle thoughts which have in fancy's flow
Their frenzied utt'rance and unvalued part.
Then the fair form of things would I pass by,
And view thee, glorious cloud, unheedingly.

What tortured rocks are those? What mountains rolling?
What healthy throng of men and maidens sing
By yonder lake, and all unseen? What echoing
And shouts are those? What unheard voices calling?
And, far away, by frequent brook and spring,
And leafy woods, behind yon snowy hills,
What jocund shepherds welcome in the morn
With out-poured beakers ta'en from sparkling rills
Which sing forever through the tasselled corn?
Ah me! what happy, happy swains are there!
What happy maids! what trysts! what joyance fair!

Who built those palaces and lofty towers,
With crownèd battlements and standards drooping?
And, see! what knights pass through the arched ways stooping,
In haste to join fair ladies in their bowers,
Or bevy-laughers in yon gardens grouping?
From what far city do those strange folk bring
Their gleaming sapphires and manorial gold?
And whence the uncouth people following
Their fleecy flocks escaping from the fold—
Those mounting herds whose lives so long have been
In scented meadow-lands and pastures green?

Methinks I hear the rolling murmur deep
Of cascades tumbling o'er the lofty heights,
Where often, often on the starlit nights,
The elves go dancing down each rocky steep,
And never stop until each one alights
On grassy plains low-stretching to the sea.
There late have come, from islands far away,
The long-lost Argonauts with shouts and glee.
Their moorèd craft I see within yon bay—
Large galleons, scathed by many a whistling breeze,
And barks, and amber-freighted argosies.

And yonder there is he perchance who tells
Of cloudlands lying westward from the sun,
Where forest-threading creeks and streamlets run,
By whose banks grow the fadeless asphodels,
Where every wind is faint with odours won
From summer boughs, and bees are feasting ever,
Nor dream at all of laying by their store
Against the hateful snow which cometh never—
No, not one hour,.to whiten hill-sides o'er,
And droop, and quite abash the forest's pride,
And wretched make the vales and meadows wide.

Why comest thou to edge our mortal cares,
Dissembler of the tempest and the storm ?
The glory of thy perishable form
Is as a momentary dream, which bares
Mysterious feet in fields and forests warm.
We know thee, that for our ancestral sin
Thy beauty shall be wasted like our toil.
Ruin shall come upon thee, darkness win
Thy stainless peaks, and poison-fires uncoil
Like asps within thy vales, yet enforced here,
Our minds invite thy fleeting fancies dear !

O golden shape! Fair, full-blown flow'r of heaven !
Gift of the dawn and far-possessing sea !
Thou foster-child of sunshine and the free
Wild air of summer, wherefore art thou given
To mock us with delights which quickly flee
Th' inviting of our souls ? Art thou, O God !
Offended that thy weary children groan,
And wither in their anguish at thy rod,
And think it but small ill to walk alone
On this thine earth, wishing their cares away,
Yet finding them grow deadlier day by day ?

O 'tis enough that the sharp solstice brings
Numb snow and frost to bite us to the heart;
That devilish pain and sickness smite apart
Ease and keen pleasure in the face of things.
Those gifts from heaven could we take athwart
Our little eager paths, and bear the cross
Meekly; yet they are nought to these: hope dies
And leaves us desolate, and love is loss,
And hatred burns our bones, and mercy flies
Our sundering souls, and progress funeral
Towards the love that reigns and rules o'er all.

Our pain hath no dismissal, and our joys
But speed us to our ashes. In life's charm
There lifts a cold, intolerable arm
Which smites the very infant at its ploys.
Our comfort wastes, and fair forms come to harm—
Naught lasts but sorrow, all things else decay,
And time is full of losing and forgetting,
Our pleasure is as iron and rusts away,
Our days are grief, and scarcely worth their setting.
Wherein there is repose and slumber deep,
And therefore are we thankful for our sleep.

We all are thankful for a little sleep,
For therein there is peace and easy death,
And solace for our sad, impatient breath.
Perchance therein we lose ourselves, and keep
Part of an ageless silence ; yet one saith
We are but born to linger and to fear,
To feel harsh fleeting time and aimless woe.
Th' inscrutable decree which brought us here
Makes myriads wretched and shall keep them so
Till death uplifts the bars for those who wait
And yearn along the soundless gulphs of fate.

Still let us wait beneath the glorious sun,
And, be his light or strengthened or subdued,
Let light come to our eyes, for it is good
To see the small flow'rs open one by one,
And see the wild wings fleeting through the wood.
They grow and perish uncomplainingly,
And blameless live and end their blameless years.
And mayhap we are blind, and cannot see
The rainbow shining in a mist of tears ;
And mayhap we are dull, and cannot feel
The touch which strengthens and the lips which heal.

What sudden haste ! Why art so quickly going,
Thou fair beatitude ? Ah, canst not stay
To drowse our aching sense one summer day,
And feed the light within so faintly glowing ?
Alas, it heedeth not, and, far away,
The breezy standards wave o'er happier fields.
But are we fixed ? O soul, is there no dawn,
No rising of some brighter sun which yields
A welcome recompense for pain ? Drift on,
Thou mimic world ! Thou art not all alone—
We, too, are drifting to the dim unknown.

LINES TO MOUNT St. PATRICK.

Oft have I wandered by the pebbly shore,
And in the woods have had mine own delight,
And quiet pleasure.
Far-seen expanses, both by day and night,
Have warmed my sight,
And caused my longing spirit soar
From common sounds up to a lofty measure.

Yet never did I greet the clear sublime,
Until with patient steps I clomb thy steep,
And looked beyond
A thousand forests yielding music deep ;
And saw the thunder leap
In mist from cataracts, nor heard their rhyme
Tired in dim distance though mine ear was fond.

Out o'er the pleasant villagès I looked,
While morning swept the haze from meadows wide.
And, far away,
In op'ning woods I saw where Bonnechère brooked
To swell great Uttwa's tide,
And where large streams grew small, and little rills
Were dimmed from sight afar by distance grey,
Wedged in the heavens stood the dark blue hills.

What antique forms I wot lay undescried
Beyond those hills in lonely valleys deep
Sweet Fancy drew—
Of captive maidens weeping side by side,
Or fairy hermitages lost in sleep.
For there the distance blent with dim romance,
And clasped my thought away in regions old.
I saw the shadows creep
From ancient days, while dream-like forms anew
Bestrode the earth, and, in a waking trance,
Lived o'er again the wondrous age of gold.

O happy, happy mount, which doth extend
  A wild outlying space for roving thought;
        Spurning the plain
Where sorrowing eyes and rankling cares abide;
Where hapless men in weary tangle caught,
      Narrow life's circumstance to purpose base:
Thee would I ever seek to ease my pain!
Nor long, while up thy silent slopes I wend,
  Or loll in idlesse on thy swarthy side,
For Heav'n to take me from the summer days,
  Away from thee to view Creation wide.

ADDRESS TO A MAID.

If those twin gardens of delight,
Thine eyes, were ever in my sight,
I would no pinks or roses seek,
Save those which bloom upon thy cheek.
I would no pleasant perfume breathe
Save that which parts thy snowy teeth,

Or in sweet warblings e'er rejòice,
Save when I listened to thy voice.
Than in the citadel of love
I would no other dwelling have.
For neighbours, then, the jewelled pair,
Who part each night thy long, loose hair,
Or other twain who sit upon
Thy swelling breast as on a throne,
Or those two, wand'rers since their birth,
Who set small seals about the earth.
I would no other seasons find
Than the reversals of thy mind.
Thus, thy delight and joy would be
Enough of summer warmth for me;
And thy displeasure next would hold
A season short of wintry cold.
No other food would I beseech
Than such as thy smooth chin could reach,
Or what I otherwise might sip
About its suburbs, on a lip,
Or cheek, or, higher, where the snow
In stainless white the brow doth show.

No other sickness should I feel
Than what thy queenly touch could heal,
Or any weariness or pain
That thou couldst not remove again.
Thus all delights would meet in thee,
And I should live, and live to be,
(Whilst dwelling in thy many graces)
A scorner of those paltry places
Which cumber pleasant spots of earth,
And wis not of the wondrous birth
Of love, or of the keen degrees
Of love's wan languor and disease.

Why laugh, my love, all love to scorn,
And, like a stalk of fruitless corn,
Nor yield nor fill one golden ear
With promise for the Future's wear?
Why hide those eyes? Enough that night
Finds each, like some starved eremite,
Shut in with coffin-lids of snow,
Which chill the fateful forms below.
Why hide them? They their lustre win
From fairer fields and floods within,

And whatsoever thence is ta'en
Those eyes, my love, must give again.

Why turn, O love, why turn away,
Like sunshine from an April day?
The past is dreary, dumb and cold,
And love and youth are growing old.
The past doth wear no weather-locks,
Bestirs no fields, and feeds no flocks.
The past is like a hidden grot,
For years unseen, and so forgot
Till stumbled on—and then are found
Some relics. When no longer sound,
Or form of thine is heard or seen,
Thou art the past, and then I ween
Thou art forgotten, too, and, lo!
Art buried, though thou think'st not so.

Why look so haughty and so proud,
As Time himself to thee had bowed,
And cringed and craved with humble air
Permission to preserve thee fair?

Time cares no whit for thy delight
In beauty, or in beauty's might.
Thou canst not coax him with thine eyes,
Or bluff him with asperities!
Thou canst not hold him in thy fee,
A vassal to thy sovereignty;
For Time his obligation pays
With silv'ry nights and golden days,
Till all are quit at last, and paid
In full by mattock, trench and spade.

This Time shall come with finger cold
And wrinkle up thy smooth-set mould;
Shall come like hoar-frost in the night,
Shall come like darkness in the light,
And blind thy sombre eyes with tears,
And darken thought with sullen fears,
And, taking thee within his arms,
Shall husk thy body of its charms,
And, for a garment, clothe thee in
A frosty snood and wrinkled skin,
And for the music of thy voice
Shall give thee groans, and for thy choice

A stick, or crutch, to pick thy way
Adown some autumn's golden day.

Then, being mortal, be not proud,
And—love confessed, and love allowed—
I'll shield thee with my soul and give
Thee kiss for kiss, and, as I live,
Use the deep wonder of thine eyes
As daily food. And thy sweet sighs
Shall melt into the warmth of mine,
And my pale breath shall meet with thine,
And my lips cling to thee, and sleep
Shall part us not. Not any deep
Or the wan, waney light of dreams,
Or utter space, or height, or gleams
Of wasteful lightning, or the blore
Of storms, or any misty shore
Of sightless sea, or wealth, or fame,
Or any voice that calls thy name,
Or pestilence, or pois'nous breath
Of calumny—not even death,
Or the cold, far-averted eyes
And angry mouths of deities,

Or the cold unseen feet which press
Earth's sullen graves shall dispossess,
In hell beneath or heaven above,
My soul of thee, O love!

WINTER.

WHEN gadding snow makes hill-sides white,
And icicles form more and more;
When niggard Frost stands all the night,
And taps at snoring Gaffer's door;
When watch-dogs bay the vagrant wind,
And shiv'ring kine herd close in shed;
When kitchens chill, and maids unkind,
Send rustic suitors home to bed—
Then do I say the winter cold,
It seems to me, is much too bold.

When winking sparks run up the stalk,
  And faggots blaze within the grate,
And, by the ingle-cheek, I talk
  With shadows from the realm of fate;
When authors old, yet ever young,
  Look down upon me from the walls,
And songs by spirit-lips are sung
  To pleasant tunes and madrigals,—
    Then do I say the winter cold
    Brings back to me the joys of old.

When morn is bleak, and sunshine cool,
  And trav'llers' beards with rime are grey;
When frost-nipt urchins weep in school,
  And sleighs creak o'er the drifted way;
When smoke goes quick from chimney-top,
  And mist flies through the open hatch;
When snow-flecks to the window hop,
  And childrens' tongues cling to the latch,—
    Then do I sigh for summer wind,
    And wish the winter less unkind.

When merry bells a-jingling go,
  And prancing horses beat the ground;
When youthful hearts are all aglow,
  And youthful gladness rings around;
When gallants praise, and maidens blush
  To hear their charms so loudly told,
Whilst echoing vale and echoing bush
  Halloo their laughter, fold on fold,—
    Then do I think the winter meet,
    For gallants free and maidens sweet.

When great pines crack with mighty sound,
  And ice doth rift with doleful moan;
When luckless wanderers are found
  Quite stiff in wooded valleys lone;
When ragged mothers have no sheet
  To shield their babes from winter's flaw;
When milk is frozen in the teat,
  And beggars shiver in their straw,—
    Then do I hate the winter's cheer,
    And weep for springtime of the year.

When ancient hosts their guests do meet,
And fetch old jorums from the bin;
When viols loud and dancers' feet
In lofty halls make mickle din;
When jokes pass round, and nappy ale
Sends pleasure mounting to the brain;
When hours are filched from night so pale,
And youngsters sigh and maids are fain,—
Then do I hail the wintry breeze
Which brings such ripened joys as these.

But, when the winter chills my friend,
And steals the heart-fire from his breast;
Or woos the ruffian wind to send
One pang to rob him of his rest—
All gainless grows the Christmas cheer,
And gloomy seems the new year's light,
For joy but lives when friends are near,
And dies when they do quit the sight.—
Then, winter, do I cry, "thy greed
Is great, ay, thou art cold indeed!"

SUMMER.

HIE me now, and give me rest
In great fields by Summer drest;
Where the moist pea-bloom is seen
Smiling on the tender bean;
Where the corn unfolds its silk,
And unhoards earth's balmy milk;
Or where stand the oaten leaves,
Dreaming of the autumn sheaves;
Or where lovingly entwine
The vetchling and the sweet woodbine.
Or let me entrancèd go
Where the heavy hautboys grow,
And receive the first impress
Of the summer's fruitfulness.

Urged by silver-footed June,
Summer dons her flowery shoon,

And, where Spring was wont to be,
On the green, herd-haunted lea,
Sports in youthful gaiety.
Now she lays her cheek full low,
Bosoming all flow'rs which grow,
Till the blinkards ope their eyes,
And from prison-dreams arise,
Wond'ring at the fond caress
Which sets free their loveliness.
Now she roams the valleys through,
Licking up the clammy dew
Which bows down the tender grass,
Sick-sore with the wealth it has.
This she takes where roses pine,
And drops it softly from her eyne,
Till they quick forget again
Irksome days and faintish pain.

Now the lazy, lagging hours
Drowse within her sun-built bowers,
And her leafy henchmen keep
Linkèd arms in poppied sleep.

Silently in musky dell
All dew-dropping zephyrs dwell,
While the smooth, eloinèd sky
Feeds her flocks of clouds which lie
Basking 'neath with sunny smiles
Ere they hasten to their toils,
And from ocean bring again
Thunder-gloom and panting rain.

O Day ! give me all thy beams,
All thy warm, embodied dreams,
Such as pant in meadow still,
By streamlet brink, or upland hill.
O Fields ! give me all your flow'rs
Which beguile the wanton Hours,
All sweet dews which night distils,
All your shallow, whisp'ring rills,
All your deeply perfumed breath,
Ev'ry note each small bird hath,
Ev'ry breeze by woods delayed,
Each cool place those woods have made—

So may I thy riches prove
Till Sleep bring me dreáms of love,

Dreams of by-gone chivalry,
Wassailing and revelry,
And lordly seasons long since spent
In bout, and joust, and tournament.
And, mid visioned feats of arms,
Fierce attacks and rude alarms,
Let my dreams run back to thee,
Chastely fair Eurydice !
To the lover and the lute,
Which made the mighty torrents mute,
And rumbling hell itself grow meek,
While iron tears from Pluto's cheek
Rolled down. Then let processions pass—
Bacchanals, each with his lass,
Waving mighty clusters round,
Tipsily, until the ground
Purples with the clammy juice,
Spoilt for quaffing, spoilt for use.
And let nymph-attended Pan
Come in habit of a man,
Singing songs of reeds and rushes,
Elder brakes and hazel bushes.

See him swing and jig about,
Whilst the merry, rabble rout
Chases round with joinèd hands,
Twitching slily, when he stands,
At his back, his garments tearing,
All his swart, brute-buttocks baring.
And let Comus and his crew
Shout until the welkin blue
Claps its hands in quick refrain,
And echoes o'er and o'er again.
Flushed and jolly is his face,
With something of Olymp'an grace
Still ling'ring on his beamy brow :
Now lolls he on the ground, and now
His youthful revellers recline,
Draining beakers full of wine,
Or, upstarting from the green,
With a wild, unsteady mien,
Tread a measure on the sod,
In honor of the mirthful god.

Then let my spirits sink or swim,
And now grow bright, or now grow dim ;

For Hermes waves his mystic wand,
And all is hushed—the rivers stand;
The rain sleeps midway from the earth,
And lab'ring mothers long for birth;
The birds hang motionless in air,
And, Silence, aching everywhere,
A dumb and heavy darkness brings
Upon all manner of sweet things.
Lo! creepeth in my hearing then
The windy tread of lifeless men—
Grim skeletons in rattling hosts,
Wan spectres, and unhouseled ghosts!
They draw anear, they lean upon me,
They lay their clammy fingers on me!
Hell-doomed, of floating gloom I drink,
And none to save, I sink! I sink!
Dear Mother! hear a mortal's call,
And help me, save me ere I fall.

Awake! Awake! The woods are bright
With mirror-leaves and slumb'ry light.
The streams are singing madrigals,
And bird to bird in gladness calls.

Buzzing whispers float about,
And, from afar, the ploughman's shout
And dinner-hollas are upborne
From trumpet-wood and valley-horn.

Ye who faint with city moil,
Come and stay with me awhile.
We will find a mossy bed,
With awning branches overhead,
And juicy coolness of large leaves,
Much longed for by the swelt'ring beeves,
And, enravished, we will go
Where the honeysuckles grow—
We will pluck them. Come with me,
To the vales and forest free,
Where the runnels, as of yore,
Keep for us a varied store
Of gleams and glooms and pebbled edges,
Mallows, pipy reeds and sedges.
We will haunt the meadows all,
And barren leas where berries fall
From spiny twigs in juicy sweetness,
And mark betimes the nimble fleetness

Of startled wild-deer breaking cover,
Or lazy flight of fat-winged plover,
And, our pleasures to enhance
With a new delight, perchance
Waylay some Driad as she broods
In silence mid leaves-dropping woods.

Now the big, full-breasted sun
All his downward course hath run,
And silent vesper shineth through
Her heavenly shroud of purple hue.
The hour has come for greetings sweet,
The quiet hour for blessings meet,
And sober souls may now repast
On what the day had overcast;
For Summer quiteth not the sight,
But dwelleth, mingleth with the night,
And crowns her hulky crags and trees
With light from starry palaces.
Now weird Imagination finds
A cave where lodge night-whisp'ring winds,
Sees Hecate gleaning baleful dew
By lonely tarn or rustling yew,

Or hears the night-hag muttering
O'er bubbling brook or haunted spring.
Aghast she flies the hated scene,
With wild affright and startled mien,
Then stops, and broods, and starts again
At thievish shadows on the plain

But purer fancies will be ours!
We will haunt the moon-lit bow'rs,
Where matchless odours faint in flight
From primrose fountains of the night.
And, amid our varied joys,
We will muse on Summer's ploys:—
How no partial gifts are hers,
But now the palms and now the firs
Are dozed with kisses balmy-sweet
From lips which breathe a pulsing heat.
How she is the blessed wafter
Of forest tunes and streamy laughter,
When Spring hath lifted in a trice
The Winter's heavy lid of ice,
And travels east, and travels west,
Till the nations all are blest.

Then will we mingle sad with sweet,
And think how wonderfully fleet
Are brightest things, how quick o'ercast
With the shadow, with the past;
And how to blackened embers turn
The hearts of those poor ones that mourn
Excess of joy; ay, how they waste
Their fateful lives who ever haste
From shine to shine, till in the shade
Of darkling years, where truth has made
A bitter tomb for king and clown,
They lay their loathèd pleasures down.
Then will we think upon, and bless
The wise whose heart ne'er beats amiss;
Whose charity is large, whose hand
Is full of counsels featly planned
To trick despair of ev'ry spoil,
And quicken hope, and brighten toil;
Who knows the pleasures without pain,
Fast-followers in Virtue's train,
And, 'neath their softly-dropping balm,
Lightly layeth palm to palm,
Till his hands are incense-full.

Sleep, now, and dream of fruitage cool
Mellowing on the heavy boughs.
Sleep and dream of upturned brows
Ever gazing where afar
The heav'ns' own tender blossoms are
Ev'ry moment fainter growing.
Sleep and dream of dear ones glowing
With delight, and lovely all,
While the rosy music-fall
Leaps 'twixt their snowy-tinted teeth.
Sleep and dream of ev'ry heath
Where blooms resort for peacefulness,
And unseen fingers love to dress
Fair, healthy bow'rs and leafy ways
Through the long Summer's shining days.

MY LOVE—A RHAPSODY.

Who hath not seen my love? Her violet eyes
  Like morning blooms awake, and, all aglow,
The heav'nly fruitage yet untasted lies
  On the full lip which swells and smiles below.
The movements of her noiseless feet keep time
  To tremulous music of a world-old song
Which all the Hours do breathe into her ear;
  And many, many languish in their prime,
For hopeless love of her who hath been long
  My chiefest joy through the full-seasoned year.

Be not too boist'rous, or to free to take
Those curls into thy lap, O Summer wind!
But, ever gently, let the faint breeze make
Cool places for her midst the leaves, or find
Some dome-like cloud to hide her from the sun.
And, Winter Solstice, when you draw anear,
Breathe not too rudely on her tender form—
Ah, make not chill my love! for she hath won
My very soul from me, and I do fear
The rash snow-wreathing, and the heedless storm!

Who hath not seen my love? Ye twining flow'rs,
I know she hath been with you, for you droop,
And pine for her fond presence, and the hours
Seem dull and dark when she no more doth stoop
To kiss away the dew-drops from each lip;
And, O sad streamlets, tell me why ye mourn!
Mayhap it is for lack of those twin feet
Which she all carelessly is wont to dip,
And lave within your flood at eve's return,
When love's hours run to moments swift and sweet.

Mayhap ye grieve for her divided care—
(O fondest care which e'er did grace the earth !)
Yet still ye seem not unto her less fair,
Though love hath come to quiet down her mirth.
And, though sweet fancy flees your wanderings,
And lurks in love's own world within, and fears
And hopes new-born within her bosom swell,
Yet ev'ry lucent, dew-clad morning brings
Its cool delight, and, list'ning, still she hears
The vestal Nature hymning in her cell.

Here let me linger by my love's own stream,
And gaze into the water where it frets
In endless monotone, till, in a dream,
It slips away with me, and quite forgets
Its ancient haunts amid the peaceful woods.
Then, in another land, my love with me
Will sit and sing old summer-songs of youth
By its green banks, and take the amber floods
Of sunset, or the silence of the sea
To witness our firm oaths and plighted truth.

Yea, though she loved me not, still would I bring
A vision of her beauty to the mead,
Midst hummings soft, and music on the wing,
And daisies huddling with the tangled weed.
Still would I place pale blossoms in her hair,
And, in her lap, moist lillies, white and wan,
And meadow-sweet which rarest scent distils.
And all the wilds would know that she was there,
For I would call her name till Echo ran
From vale to vale, far-questioning the hills.

I ask not how this pleasing fondness came
Into my heart, and yet, for many a time,
I have been mirthfúl at love's very name,
Who now, alas! am vanquished ere my prime.
I ask not. 'Tis enough for me to feel
The quick pulse throbbing and the hastened breath,
When all the soul-fed brightness of her eyes
Doth gleam upon me: then my senses steal
Away from me, as from some saint who saith
Deep pray'rs, or maketh holy sacrifice.

O that the twinkling eve were come again,
  To feed with dew the soft melodious leaves,
And wake the nodding primrose which hath lain
  For hours and hours unseen, like one who weaves
Forever his day-dreams and sits apart.
  So to my love's own bower might I repair,
Where she, in slumber and sweet fancies wreathing,
  Doth steal all beauty from the night—and there
Be mute, and still the beatings of my heart,
  And kneel and listen to her quiet breathing.

Ay, I will listen while the wan stars wheel
  Along the dusk, and watch each cloudy lid
Of thine, my love, until thou dost reveal
  Those clearer planets which beneath lie hid.
Then wilt thou place thy paly cheek to mine,
  And feel the sadness of love's ecstacy,
And I will kiss away thy painless tears.
  Ah, closer, closer, may our thoughts entwine
This night, sweet love, this night while you and I
  Make patient promise for the future years.

ALICE.

"OH, where is the Spring, mother dear,
  And when will it come back again?
For this sad snow fills me with fear,
  And I long for the soft-falling rain.
And I long for the glad, green leaves,
  And the sweet little birds on the wing,
And the swallows which chirp round the eaves—
  Oh, Mother, let's go seek the Spring."

And then the fond mother did chide,
  Leaning over her sick one's brow,
Nor her sad, swift tears could she hide,
  Nor her sighs could she stifle I trow.
For the drooping child still cried, "Come!
  To the sweet spring mead let us pass,
For I long for the wild bee's hum,
  And the grasshopper's chirp in the grass."

"No! The rough winds are blowing, my child,
  And the sad snow falls far and wide,
And the bleak woods are leafless and wild,
  And sigh on the gloomy hill-side.
And all the eave-cabins are still,
  And the linnets in other lands sing,
And the thrush and the lone whippoorwill—
  Let us wait yet awhile for the Spring.

" Oh no, let us seek it, I pray,
  While yet I have strength, mother dear,
To roam o'er the hills far away,
  And find the sweet bud of the year.
For I dream of the rivulet's brink,
  And I sigh at the sad thoughts they bring,
When of all the sweet blossoms I think
  Which gleam far away in the Spring."

But the death-flakes began to fall,
  And the soft cheeks grew white as snow,
And the eye-lids closed down like a pall
  On the little round orbs below.
'Twas winter within and without,
  For the fond little spirit took wing,
Nor could the bereaved mother doubt
  That her soul was away to the spring !

TO MY PHOTOGRAPH.

GHOST of Myself! Go seek my fair,
  And tell her of the days we've seen,
In pleasant palaces of air
  Where we have been.

And tell my love how you and I
  Have seen strange suns on dream-lakes glow,
And seen the night-mare-moon on high,
  Ay, long ago.

How, often from the world unseen
  We've slipt into the realm of things,
Where chance hath led through fields of green
  Our wanderings.

How, often in the warm old woods,
Drowsed with the forest-fumes we've lain;
Or studied all their changing moods
In shine or rain.

Or traced the small streams to their source
High up amidst the meadow lands,
And parted branches in our course
With patient hands.

And studied out the storied hill,
The lake, the legendary vale,
Or read, midst leaves and shadows still,
Some breezy tale.

And drank where the wild Indians drank,
And walked together where they walked;
Ay, met their shades by many a bank,
And with them talked.

Or on the mountain summit stood,
High-gazing o'er the forests wide,
And stayed against the solitude
With silent pride.

Or caught the muse where myriads kept
Their hideous strife and needless wars,
Or where the silent city slept
Beneath the stars.

Or waked, amidst the hum of men,
From dreams of temples by the sea,
Of stolèd priests, and old world ken,
And harmony.

Yes ! waked to find some men unkind,
And others vain, and others false—
Cold, sordid reptiles who would bind
One's very pulse.

And women, too, with paltry shapes
  Teazed out of nature's flowing forms—
The early devotees to tapes
  And coffin-worms.

With here and there a pleasant soul
  To cheer our travel to the grave,
And calm us ere we reach the goal
  Where willows wave.

And art thou then my very sprite,
  And not some crafty, cunning elf,
Deceiving me—my own glad light?
  My second self?

Come, then, and toast with me my love
  In one ripe draught—'tis meet, I think
That thou and I our joy should prove—
  What! canst not drink?

Drear, voiceless shape, thou know'st not, then,
The cheerful usage of the vine;
Its keen delights, beyond your ken,
Alone are mine.

Alack, poor shade! I pity thee,
And, if the mode I could but know,
I quickly here would set you free
From your Limbo.

Yet this revenge there is in store,
This vantage hast thou over me,
That, though it seems not, I am more
A ghost than thee.

For, though thou canst not weep, or groan,
Or take life's pleasant things on trust,
Thou shalt, perchance, be looked upon
When I am dust.

STANZAS FROM THE HEART.

THE morning dew, and eke the gentle rain
    Are grateful to the earth;
    They usher in the birth
Of flow'rs and fruitfulness. The scorchèd plain
Drinks deep the draught and all things bloom again.

The sweet winds fan the leaves until they lisp
    Soft music in our ears,
    And drop the pearly tears
Aurora wept on them ere morning broke,
And am'rous Day from fev'rish dreams awoke.

They kiss the water till the wavelet swells,
    And lifts its glassy face
    To an unseen embrace.
Then sigh away where some fond maiden trips
And steal the nectar from her coral lips.

Like wanton thieves they wander mongst the flow'rs,
Kissing the violet
With od'rous moisture wet,
And waft those sweets where suff'rers moan with pain,
Making them long for primrose meads again.

All these do move me much, fair girl, but thou
Dost wield a mightier power,
For one dim fleeting hour
Of bliss with thee creates what ne'er can cloy—
A world, an exaltation and a joy.

Give me those kisses—they are mine! In truth,
Desire and love of thee
Are as a boundless sea
Which ebbeth, floweth, swelleth in my heart,
Bearing deep thoughts from which I may not part.

Garland thy milky arms around my neck,
And let thine orbèd eyes
Their orient merchandize
Discover in the wasting of the light
Like stars which shed their glory in the night.

Or let me sleep, as doth a wearied child,
    Clasped to thy beating breast,
    In dreamy mansion blest,
And wake to find thine ageless smiles indeed
The fragrant dew on which young love doth feed.

PROLOGUE TO TECUMSEH.

Call in the last few leaves, yes, call them in,
For ev'ry bird hath ceased its shrilly din,
And all the butterflies are deadly sick.
Beneath the sallow walks the dew-worms sleek
Lie many-coiled, and all the toiling bees
Grow tired of bootless journeys to the leas.
Sheep that do wend far distances afoot,
Nipping crisp herbage close unto the root,
Now leave much fleecy wealth in thorny passes,
Seeking in vain the tangled summer grasses.

And he who loves wood-violets now must part
Wan leaves thick strewn in coverts close and start
More than one centipede or crooked worm
Before he hath delight. The pleasant form
Of many a tiny flow'r in blue and white
And crimson-spotted meets no more the sight.
Belike those flow'rs of which none knows the name,
Yet, if you ask, some youth with eye aflame,
And reddened cheek will tell you that they come
With screaming blue-jays and the early hum
Of yellow bees, and through whole months bestreak
Damp places where the mad-weed and false leek
Allure the rav'nous kine which largely feed,
Then quick return with nostrils all ableed'
And milk that curdles sudden in the pail.
He now that listens hears the tamping flail
Quick-plied, or, if the yellow fields have been
Profuse of pipy straw, now may be seen
Their rustling gold heaped high above the eaves,
And horses panting while the brainèd sheaves
With stour and din drift from the barn-ways wide.
The balsam thickets by the meadow side

Are green and still. Should one here fall asleep
In pastoral dreaminess, small flies will keep
A little mid-day uproar overhead.
Nor will one wake until the sun hath sped
And lowings loud one's drowsy sense affright.
The glossy milk plant's scarfs of snowy white
Have blown away into the neighb'ring fields,
And little pleasure now the meadow yields
Save 'tis the permeant joy of odours strange
From reed and flag outborne, and the wide range
Of sallow rushes and the sunburnt fern.
Ah ! now the loneliest very loneliest tarn,
With prickly ash engirt, seems lonelier far
Than when with flushing eve the summer star
Tapered her beams aslant the smooth-topt wood.
And lonelier now seems each wan solitude,
With little lake low-couched among the hills,
And noisy murmurings of hidden rills
Swoll'n with the steady fall of autumn rain.
Once more the oak is humbled, and again,
With ragged stems and spray quite tempest-shorn,
The aged elms and hoary birches mourn.

He that doth listen now will something hear—
'Tis Winter's hounds a-baying up the year.
Therefore the timid hare with all his kin
Grows winter-white, and squirrels have gathered in
Their forest spoils. Therefore the wild fowl takes
Its seaward flight and leaves its peaceful lakes
Lost in the mighty bosom of the wood.
The faintest winds which blow there are imbued
With old traditions, but the brave of yore,
Who gave them meaning, tread the paths no more.

Their mem'ries haunt adown the wid'ning years,
Still teazing us from quiet into tears;
And restless longings, amid all our ploys
And fev'rish ventures, with unwonted noise
Of leaves and stony brooks are ever coming
Troubling our minds as doth a wild bee's humming
The dungeoned captive. Straightway then we seek
O'erbranchèd forest-ways and haunt each creek
Till teeming Fancy, profuse of her powers,
Peoples the woods. Once more th' heroic hours
Flare up within the overcultured brain.
We see the camp-fires gleaming, and again

We see the wigwams by the river-side
Outpour their crafty breed, and swart forms glide
From thickets noiselessly. Amidst the thrông
Powhattan comes, Tomocomo the strong,
Bold Wingina and lofty Ensenore.
What Wampanoag strideth quick before
With haughty port? 'Tis great Massassoit!
The cunning Uncas hastes, his dark eye lit
With fury, and from Pokanoket's glade
Canonchet, too, the last, the lost has strayed
With hapless Weetamore.
Again we hear
The wild, mad war-whoop ringing loud and clear—
'Tis Pontiac! 'Tis Pontiac the fierce!
I saw his vengeful, horrid weapon pierce
The pale-face enenee. I saw him lift
His sun-burnt arm, and straight out flew a gift
Of warriors from the woods, and after them
A melancholy madman sighing came—
'Twas Logan, sad old Logan, who hath sent
A thrilling plaint for nations' wonderment
Through the wide world. But whence that sudden stir—
Those voices reaching through the woods? The fir

Gives solemn utt'rance, and the steady oak
Prospers against full many a laboured stroke
Of rough and bullying wind. Yet 'tis not these;
For now they shout, and all the forest trees
Shake to their roots; and now they shout, and all
The last encrimsoned autumn leaves down fall.
I hear them shout 'tis great Tecumseh hastes
O'er creek and moor, and wild outlying wastes.
They shout again, and then, with lofty stride,
Tecumseh comes to weld the nations wide.

WERTER.

FAREWELL! the night hath closed at last
O'er my day dream of happiness.
Hope, joy and peace—all these are past,
The loving look, the kind caress.

The dear delight which warmed my heart—
The body and the mystery
Of love, divinest, purest part
Of the soul's wealth—has fled from me.

Throb, tender heart! It throbs in vain—
In vain ye tender passions burn!
The generous bliss, the pleasing pain—
Ah, these can never more return.

Back, back, ye thronging thoughts, no more
Me mock with your delusive light!
The fancies which your glad beams bore
Have faded in eternal night.

Frown solemnly, ye dizzy clouds,
And cast dull shadows o'er the earth—
Drink up the moon! my griefs, as shrouds,
Have muffled up the heart's quick mirth.

Wave high, ye overhanging woods,
And whisper sadly of the tomb.
Lonely I trace your solitudes,
And haunt your melancholy gloom.

The hour of darkness, storm and fears
Broods o'er the dim, benighted plain.
There let me go, and mingle tears
With passionate weeping of the rain.

THE FIRE-FLIES.

LIKE an ill-favoured thief, the murk hath crept
Into the air, and greedily devoured
Eve's last, wan smiles. One shaggy cloud which wept
Great puddling drops upon the ground, and show'red
Its tepid moisture, till the mists arose,
Earthborn, and, like a cloud, all reeking went
From out the meadows, where the saffron grows,
Up to the summer height—one shaggy cloud,
Which the tressed Morning from the east had sent,
Against her coming, to o'erspread and shroud
Earth's fruited bosom from the blist'ring sun,
Still hangs above the drowsy hills, quite spent
And wretched-looking; while the black fiend, Night,
In vales and hollow places 'reft of light,
Broods o'er the spoils he from the day hath won.

How dreamy-dark it is!
Men yawn for weariness, and hoard their gains,
While careful housewives drown the kitchen fires,
Then slip to bed to snore away their pains,
And bury for a time all low desires.
The plodding oxen, dragging creaky wains
O'er bosky roads, their ancient horns entwine,
Lick their huge joles, and think of bedded stalls,
And munching of sweet corn. The lick'rous swine
Huddled in routed turf, neglect the calls
And pinches of their young, and hide their dugs,
Swoll'n with a lazy milk; whilst timid sheep,
Far from their winter-folds of knotty fir,
Dream of lean wolves and bleatings in their sleep.

Yet there are those that oft the silence mock,
For life wings through the darkness everywhere,
And night's dull, ugly brood is all astir.
The flapping bat and hungry-snapping hawk
Now glut themselves with innocent, droning flies,
Whisked from the dingy commonwealth of air.
The loathsome toad, which foul infection breeds
And lep'rous sores, hops o'er the dusty walk,

And, in the hollows where the river lies,
The hoarse frogs sprawl among the bedded reeds,
And croak harsh ditties to their uncouth mates.
The moon-eyed owl unto the forest prates,
And greedy cranes and herons wade about,
Draggling the weedy stream in search of food—
While far around the darkling woods àgree
To hide their dancing leaves and gloomy be.

This is the very hour when witches ride
Through barren air unto the elfish rout,
Where trickish spells and sorcery are brewed;
When jack-o'-lanterns o'er the quagmire glide,
Seen by the tipsy hind, who straightway thinks
Of alehouse uproar, and in fancy drinks
Great, cheering goblets of the beaded stout:
And them he follows until quite worn out
With perilous trudging o'er the hummocks damp,
When, all at once, they flicker off, and leave
The lazy lubber in the foggy swamp,
Knee-deep in oozing sludge. This is the hour
When fire-flies flit about each lofty crag,

And down the valleys sail on lucid wing,
Luring their spouses to the love-decked bower.

I see them glimmer where the waters lag
By winding bays, and to the willows sing;
And, far away, where stands the forest dim,
Huge-built of old, their tremulous lights are seen.
High overhead they gleam like trailing stars,
Then sink adown, until their emerald sheen
Dies in the darkness like an evening hymn—
Anon to float again in glorious bars
Of streaming rapture, such as man may hear
When the soul casts its slough of mortal fear.
And now they make rich spangles in the grass,
Gilding the night-dew on the tender blade;
Then hover o'er the meadow-pools to gaze
At their bright forms shrined in the dreamy glass
Which earth, and air, and bounteous rain have made.
One moment, and the thicket is ablaze
With twinkling lamps which swing from bough to bough:
Another, and like sylphids they descend
To cheer the brook-side where the bell-flow'rs grow.

Near and more near they softly come, until
Their little life is busy at my feet;
They glow around me, and my fancies blend
Capriciously with their delight, and fill
My wakeful bosom with unwonted heat.
One lights upon my hand, and there I clutch
With an alarming finger its quick wing:
Erstwhile so free, it pants the tender thing!
And dreads its captor and his handsel touch.

Where is thy home? On what strange food dost feed,
Thou fairy haunter of the moonless night?
From what far nectar'd fount, or flow'ry mead
Glean'st thou, by witching spells, thy sluicy light?

Thou mock'st at darkness, and thy footsteps are
Where gloom hangs thickest on the swart, damp earth;
And, like a thought, thou comest from afar
In fitful glee—say hadst thou e'er a birth?

Mayhap thou hast a heart which trembles now
For thy dear young, beneath this shining dome;
And fond affections which, I know not how,
Find in thy tiny frame a gentle home.

And mayhap, too, thy little lips could tell
Of am'rous meetings, and of ample bliss,
In green pavilions where thy loved ones dwell—
Go seek them now and give them thy fond kiss.

It flits, and disappears, perchance has found
A grave, and I have marred an innocent life;
Perchance 'tis with its mates, for, all around,
The air in fitful radiance is rife.
They gleam and shimmer in a guileless strife,
A heav'n of stars, sprung from the earth's warm breast,
Clad with inservient fire, and sprightly all,
Touched by no sorrow, by no cares oppressed!
The moving hours speed on apace, and fall
Like faded garlands in the lap of time;
Yet still the fire-flies sparkle ev'rywhere,
And seem like wandering Peris as they climb
Up through the gloomy vault of misty air.

At length the sky is flecked with dingy streaks,
And Morn comes striding o'er the eastern hills,
Muffled in angry trappings which foretell
A coming storm; and now each fire-fly seeks

Its distant home, to drink from leafy rills,
And feed on mulse and sweetest hydromel.
Hark to the chirrup and the tinkling bell!
Rude chanticleer now winds his drowsy horn
To the bleached darkness of the drizzly morn.

FROWNS AND SMILES.

I THOUGHT the world was cold and dull,
That clouds on clouds were darkly piled,
All bleak and sombre, anguish-full—
I fancied this till Cathos smiled.

I thought the world was warm and bright,
That mirth and laughter floated round
The heart's bright chambers day and night—
I fancied this till Cathos frowned.

She frowns, she smiles, by turns my heart
Is sad, is glad—its ev'ry tone
Of gay or grave she doth impart
By that strange magic all her own.

But let me only laugh or weep,
I would not have another gain
Those frowns, those smiles which she doth keep
To woo my tears, to ease my pain.

AUGUST.

DULL August! Maiden of the sultry days,
And Summer's latest born! When all the woods
Grow dim with smoke, and smirch their lively green
With haze of long-continued drought begot;
When every field grows yellow, and a plague
Of thirst dries up its herbage to the root,
So that the cattle grow quite ribby-lean
On woody stalks whose juices all are spent;
When every fronded fern in mid-wood hid
Grows sick and yellow with the jaundice heat,
Whilst those on hill-sides glare with patchy red;
When streamlets die upon the lichened rocks,
And leave the bleaching pebbles shining bare,
And every mussel shell agape and parched,
And small snail-craft quite emptied of their crews;
When not one angel-cloud is to be seen
To image coolness and the coming rain,
But all the air with stour and dust is filled,

Through which the sun stares with a pallid face
On which one long may look, and turn, and read
Some prophecy of old with eyes undimmed;
When every morn is fiery as the noon,
And every eve is fiery as the morn,
And every night a prison hot and dark,
Where one doth sleep and dream of pleasant snow,
And winter's icicles and blessed cold,
But, soon awakes, with limbs uneasy cramped,
And garments drenched, and stifled, panting breath;
When life itself grows weary of its use,
And mind is tarnished with the hue of things,
And thoughts are sickened with o'erdarkened food;
When man uneasy strolls, a listless mome
In museless misery, a wretch indeed—
Say, fiery maiden, with the scorching eyes,
What hast thou left to chain us to the earth?

Ah, there are busy forms which, all unsought,
Find yet a relish in thy scanty store.
And, for that blooms are scarce, therefore the bee
Wades knee-deep in the purple thistle tops,

And shares their sweetness with the hungry wasp.
Therefore the butterfly comes sailing down,
And, heedless, lighting on a hummer's back,
Soon tacks aloft in sudden strange alarm,
Whilst bee and wasp quick scurry out of sight,
And leave their treasures to the plodding ant.
The beetle in the tree-top sits and sings
His brassy tune with increase to the end,
And one may peep and peer amongst the leaves,
Yet see him not though still he sits aloft,
And winds his reedy horn into the noon.
Now many a sob is heard in thickets dim,
Where little birds sit, pensive, on the spray,
And muse mayhap on the delights of Spring;
And many a chitmunk whistles out its fear,
And jerks and darts along the panneled rails,
Then stops, and watches with unwinking eyes
Where you do stand, as motionless as death;
But should you wag a finger through the air,
Or move a-tiptoe o'er the crispy sod,
'Twill snudge away beneath the balsam brush,
Quick lost and safe among the reddened spray.

Now one may sit within a little vale,
Close to the umbrage of some wood whose gums
Give heavy odours to the heavy air,
And watch the dusty crackers snap their wings,
Whilst gangs of blue-flies fetch a buzzing teaze
Of mad, uneasy whirlings overhead.
Now one may mark the spider trim his web
From bough to bough, and sorrow at the fate
Of many a sapless fly quite picked and bare,
Still hanging lifeless in the silken mesh,
Or muse upon the maze of insect brede
Which finds a home and feeds upon the leaves
Till naught but fibre-skeletons are hung
From branch to branch up to the highest twig.
And many a curious pleasance may be seen
And strange disport. Of such the wondrous glee
The joinèd gnats have in their headlong flight;
The wild'ring quest of horse-flies humming past
In twos and threes, and the small cloud of wings
Which mix and throng together in the sun.
A num'rous kin dart shining o'er some pool
Spared from the general wreck of water store,

And from the lofty woods crow-blackbird trains
Chuck o'er the barren leas with long-drawn flight.
Far o'er the hills the grouse's feath'ry drum
Beats quick and loud within a beechen copse,
And, sometimes, when the heavy woods are still,
A single tap upon a hemlock spire
Dwells with the lonely glades in echoes deep.

Then with the eve come sounds of varied note.
The boys troop clam'ring to the woods, and curs
Yelp sharply where the groundhog's lair is found.
The horn has called the reapers from the fields,
And, now, from cots half-hid by fruited trees,
The homely strains of fiddle or of fife,
Which distance sweetens with a needed art,
Come dropping on the ear. And sometimes, too,
If sparks are deemed sincere, and rustic love
Run smooth, the merry milkmaids sing
A fallow's length with pails at elbow slung,
Or, while they thrust the draw-well dangler down,
'Gainst which the swains oppose their yielding strength,
Laugh loud and long, or scold with mimicked heat.

These find a pleasure in the waste of days,
And strive against the mis'ry of the time
With am'rous snares and artifice of love.
Not less those faithful ones who look upon
This weather-sorrow with sufficing joy—
The old, who still would linger with their seed,
And snatch a little comfort from the earth.
Still would they gaze upon the simmering sun,
And take the warmth into their aged bones,
Nor cavil with the hindrances which stay.
The lethal hour when death shall come and bend
Their reverend heads into the restful grave.

Hail August! Maiden of the sultry days,
To thee I bring the measured meed of praise.
For, though thou hast besmirched the day and night,
And hid a wealth of glory from our sight,
Thou still dost build in musing, pensive mood,
Thy blissful idyls in the underwood.
Thou still dost yield new beauties, fair and young,
With many a form of grace as yet unsung,
Which ripens o'er thy pathway and repays
The toil and languor of the sultry days.

TO MEMORY.

THE unknown future years appal us
With dreadful threat'nings of decay;
The Present's need and toils enthral us,
And hold us as their slaves to-day.
Ah, Mem'ry! bear me to thy mountain-height,
For thunder rends the summer clouds to-night,
And with to-morrow comes the sultry light,
 And all the earth's stern traffic vast.

We dare not ask when life will leave us—
Instinctively we hold our breath.
Though passing hours like tyrants grieve us,
Still would we shun the pains of death.
But rising from the grave of bygone years,
A spirit comes to pacify our fears;
'Tis Memory, and in her light man hears
 Naught but the music of the Past.

O spirit, gentle and most holy!
What thanks or blessings can repay
Forgetfulness of fruitless folly
Or wiping of our tears away?
Thou art the judge, 'tis said, whom God hath given
To try our souls from dusty temples driven;
O may'st thou smile as tenderly in heaven,
And shrive as gently at the last!

WOOD-NOTES.

THE moss is green upon the tree,
The leaves are green upon the spray,
And I will rest beneath the shade,
And watch their ceaseless revelry.
Know ye the wild anemone ?
'Tis blooming here alone for me,—
The lilies and the blue-bells too,
And violets gemmed with drops of dew.

The leaves half hide and yet reveal
The far-off dimples of the sky,
As a maiden's veil which should conceal
Yet makes more languishing her eye;
And 'twixt the branches overhead
A brightness with their shade is shed—
A trembling, dancing, furtive light,
Appearing oft in dreams by night.

And here are green, inviting bowers,
Such as of old the Dryads haunted,
And perfumes shed by unseen flow'rs,
And strains by mystic voices chanted.
But silent all, no human tread,
Save mine, is heard the glades among:
For me the fragrance all is shed,
For me the mystic lay is sung.

Here is a streamlet by whose side
The Naiads wandered long agone,
Ere old mythology had died,
And mankind's heart was turned to stone.
The Indian sought it year by year,
And listened to its rippling glee;
But he is gone, and I am here,
And all its rippling is for me.

The woodland grass is tall and rank,
And hath a soothing, mead'wy smell
The antlered ranger loveth well,—
In truth 'tis no unwholesome thing;

And here are leaflets grim and lank,
Besmeared with mildew cold and dank,
 The relics of a by-gone spring.
The rocks are all with moss o'ergrown,
 And ivy creepeth up and down;
The owl, in distant woods alone,
 Sleeps soundly in his feathers brown;
But all the birds are carrolling
As Morning's stars were wont to sing.

As the low murmur of a brook,
 (Go listen for the music's sake)
So is the murmur of the trees
 But now a louder voice they take,
Look how they bend before the breeze!
 The distant forest reels at length,
In vain the oak, the elm's strength,
 Their waving tops now cleave the air.
O'er mountain brow, through hidden dell,
Where twilight gloom delights to dwell,
Hark! how their mighty voices swell
 Like giants shouting in despair.

At length the breeze has reached the plain,
And silent are the woods again,
And, at my feet, the crazy light,
Which danced so wildly in my sight,
Lies in that still, calm dreaminess
Which man may feel but ne'er express.

Again there comes a roaring wind,
  And with it drifts a murky cloud
As black and angry as the look
  To Satan by the world assigned.
The pealing thunder rattles loud—
  God ! how yon sturdy hemlocks shook !
Down come the rain-drops in a crowd,
  And whiten o'er the little brook.
Hark, how they dance amongst the leaves
  And patter thence unto the earth,
While fiercer still the tempest heaves
  The forest in its riant mirth !

Like wearied soldiers after fight,
  At length the clouds have ceased to frown ;
The rain comes slower, slower down,
  And to the west a streak of light,

By wid'ning eastward glads the sight.
  The foam has vanished from the rill,
The woods are marvellously bright,
  The thirsty earth hath drunk its fill,
But all the trees are raining still!

Awake ye woods, unwonted strains!
  They wake indeed afar and near.
The wild blood dances through my veins,
  And glorious breathings meet mine ear.
The sounds, the voices and the throng
  Of joyful birds, the whisper low
Of tree and stream entrance me long,
  And thrill my being as they flow.

True are the friends that nature gives,
  Their voices ever are the same;
The rock, the tree, the streamlet lives—
  Each speaks to him who knows its name.
But Nature's heart is cold indeed
  To sullen souls that cannot see
Some comfort in her face, and read
  The warning and the mystery

THE LAMENT OF ANDROMACHE.

(From the Iliad.)

And thou hast died, O husband young in years,
And thou hast left me widowed and in tears.
The son to whom thy hapless wife gave birth
Shall ne'er touch manhood's prime upon the earth;
For ere that hour this city shall be thrust
From its proud summit prone unto the dust.
Ay! thou art dead, Protector of its wives,
And all its prattling throng of infant lives;
And these shall soon be held in sad array
In hollow barks, and with me borne away.
But thou, my son, wilt either with me go,
Where thou shalt labour for the heartless foe
At basest tasks, or some enragèd Greek
Will grasp thy wrists, and with fierce hurlings wreak
A sad destruction from a turret's height;
To him, thy father, Hector, hath in fight

A brother slain, a parent, or a son;
For many Greeks have faced him, and, undone,
Have bitten the enormous earth.
'Twas he
Who sought the conflict with the fiercest glee;
Wherefore the people mourn him through the streets.
Hector! Ah me, what sorrowful death-beats
Sound at thy parents' hearts of joy bereft;—
While still to me the bitterest griefs are left.
For thou didst not, when dying, stretch thy palms
Forth from the couch to me, nor any calms
Fell from thine ashen lips in prudent speech.
Nor through my future journeyings shall reach
One word to be remembered far away
While fall my silent tears by night and day.

IN MEMORY OF THOMAS D'ARCY McGEE.

Jam fuerit neque post unquam revocare licebit.—LUCRETIUS.

OUR eyes are full of tears,
Of sounds of grief our ears,
   And anger thrills our veins and clenchèd hands;
And vaguely we await,
As from the lips of fate,
   The murmur of the wrath of many lands,
The travel of a fire which brings
The horror of an empire on its wings.

For he who knew to touch
Our ears with language such
   As charmed the infant earth when time was young;
Which brought us from the night
Of darkness to the light
   Wherein a nation into being sprung,
Lies colder than our thoughtful fears,
Born of the madness of these guilty years.

Cold is the agent brow,
And cold the lips ere now,
  Which parted, and strange rapture and delight
Came to men's hearts and minds
Like journeyings of the winds,
  Or stars which shine, or flowers which blow by night,
And Fancy, like a dream, drew by
The curtains of a cloudless destiny.

Yea, we like children stood
When in his lofty mood
  He spoke of manly deeds which we might claim,
And made responses fit
While heavenly genius lit
  His melancholy eyes with lambent flame,
And saw the distant aureoles,
And felt the Future thunder in our souls.

Of more he dreamed than this—
What was not nor yet is,
  But in the far-off Æon is to be—
Of tyrant Wrong dismayed,
And Crime in ruins laid—
  Cast under foot, nor found on earth or sea,
Of every realm, when hate shall cease,
Made glorious with a heritage of peace.

For he had caught a gleam
Beyond the sacred stream
  Which steals betwixt the twin Phædriades,
Or that far mountain scene
Where flows the Hippocrene
  Which struck the wingèd steed between his knees,
Beyond the gloom and awful smoke
Of Pythos' cave or Hella's whispering oak.

A later glory caught
From holier founts, and fraught
  With simpler love of life and sacrifice
Of wayward, wild desire,
Which eats the flesh like fire,
  And binds our souls with iron beneath the skies ;
And thence he rose on flashing wings
Beyond the seeming fate and changeless things.

And in his songs was light,
And in his words was might,
  To lift our hopes unto the wished-for end,
When jealousies of creed
Shall, like a loathsome weed,
  Be cast away, and man with man be friend,
Nor any think the souls unpriced
That linger sadly at the feet of Christ.

And in his visions true
There came high forms anew—
  Dim outlines of a nation yet to stand,
Knit to the Empire's fate,
In power and virtue great,
  The lords and reapers of a virgin land—
A mighty realm where Liberty
Shall roof the northern climes from sea to sea.

And when 'gainst the emprise
Arose those enemies
  Whose house is hell with chambers full of death,
Who knit their hands and weep,
And curse us in their sleep,
  And drink the wine of madness with their breath,
He wrung the secret from their minds,
And cast their schemes unto the shuddering winds.

For as a spirit stood
Before the seer good,
  Bright-eyed, with amber ribs and limbs of fire,
And caught him to the skies,
Whence, with reluctant eyes,
  He viewed the wicked's sin and mad desire,
And saw beneath the waning day
His haunts and chambers of dark imagery.

So, not by feeble chance
Of time or circumstance,
  He scanned their features and their turpitude,
But his unclouded sight
Burned through the blackest night,
  And in our midst unscreened the felon brood,
And warned them from our blameless doors
Back to their hateful fields and alien shores.

For this they slew him! Now
We lift his abusèd brow
  And in our anguish vainly cry to Thee
Who art our God! How long
Shall hellish crime be strong
  And slavish spirits tamper with the free?
Alas, that all our days are bleak
With hate which chills, and crime which pales the cheek.

Yea, these our days are cold
With driftings manifold
  Of keener sorrows deep'ning with the past;
And time, slow-swift in flight,
Still brings its ancient blight,
  And shadows from increasing clouds are cast;
And hearts still ache, and heavy hands
Grow weary with their toil in many lands.

For far and near seem blent
With hollow merriment,
  The groanings of the travail of the earth ;
And grey-haired grace is old,
And coward hearts grow bold,
  And shameless cheeks are creased with soulless mirth ;
And, everywhere, who looks espies
A world's swift tears, or cold, hard-hearted eyes.

Yet as blooms melt in fruits,
Or dead flow'rs live in roots,
  So time may bring the fabled after-age
When Knowledge shall be found,
Emboldened and unbound,
  And Heav'n shall grow more kind as men grow sage,
And earth, no longer tempest-tost,
Shall snatch again the grace she once hath lost.

SONNETS.

MIDNIGHT.

THE silent shadows lay about the land,
  In aching solitude, as if they dreamed;
And a low wind was ever close at hand,
  And, though no rain-drops fell, yet alway seemed
The rustle of the leaves like falling rain.
  I could not tell what life-long ease or pain
Found hoarse expression by the river's brink,
  Where moving things mysterious vigils kept.
These had their joys, perchance, whilst I did link
  Sad thoughts of bygone pleasure till I wept.
Then entered I my house, and sat and heard
  The lonely cricket chirp until I feared
Some ghost had hid me in a wilderness.
  And long I gazed on one who slept. "I guess
'Twas frightful," for away I trembling stole,
  As if some murder-stain lay on my soul.

BARDOLPH REDIVIVUS.

(To a Friend.)

When Plato in his cradle slept, the bees
Swarmed at his lips, for so the legend goes;
But, fickle creatures, coy and hard to please,
They sure mistook, and settled on your nose!
Mayhap it is your wife who loves to teaze,
And on your patient knob incessant blows
Doth strike for her own sweet amusement's sake.
Perchance it cometh of the drams you take,
This subtle, fiery redness—who can tell?
Ay, who can tell, great nasal organ bright!
What vintages and distillations dwell
Pent in those caverns awful in our sight?
Dark with the morn, but, in the darkness, light,
A purple cloud by day, a flame by night!

TO A HUMMING-BIRD.

It comes! This strange bird from a distant clime
  Has fled with arr'wy speed on flutt'ring wing.
From the sweet south, all sick of revelling,
  It wanders hitherward to rest a time,
And taste the hardy flora of the west.
  And now, O joy! the urchins hear the mirth
Of its light wings, and crouch unto the earth
  In watchful eagerness, contented, blest.
Bird of eternal summers! thou dost wake,
  Whene'er thou comest and where'er thou art,
A new-born gladness in my swelling heart.
  Go, gentle flutterer, my blessing take!
Less like a bird thou hast appeared to me
Than some sweet fancy in old poësy.

TO ———

THOU lov'st me not, and seldom have we met,
Nor ever have thy dreams mine image borne.
Some other hand thy loving tasks shall set,
Some other lip shall bless thee night and morn.
Yet have I dreamt such happy fate was won—
To be with thee forever, still to hear,
Adown the pathway of each fading year,
Thy gentle voice like music lead me on.
Ah, generous dream of unsubstantial joy,
Go with me where my star shall rise or set!
For, though thou imagest but to destroy,
And ever mock'st me with delusive art,
I would no charm to teach me to forget
The still and silent worship of the heart.

TO AN INFANT.

SMILE on! thou tiny mystery, nor ope
  Those tear-fed eyes now curtained down by sleep.
Wake not nor start, thou mother's tender hope!
  A mother's fond eye doth a vigil keep.
Now bends she o'er thee, and recalls the kiss
  And throes which gave thee being on a time,
And made thee doubly dear. Be hers the bliss
  Of building summer castles for thy prime.
'Tis left for me to sigh, yea I could weep
  To think how Care and Grief may come and flood
Thy cheeks with tears—rough-visaged pards which creep
  Into men's hearts and steal their vigorous blood.
Then wilt thou pray release from mortal pain,
  And wish thou wert a sleeping child again.

LOVE'S EMPERY.

O LOVE! if those clear faithful eyes of thine
  Were ever turned away there then should be
No heav'nly looks to take the gloom from mine,
  Nor any hills, nor any dales for me,
Nor any honeyed cups of eglantine,
  Nor morning spilth of dew on land or sea.
No sun should rise, and leave his eastern tent
  To wake the music of the rambling wave,
Nor any freshness of the West be sent
  To sweep away night's savours of the grave.
But, when I gaze into those fadeless eyes,
  Methinks I am in some mysterious land,
Where far-off seas take colour from the skies,
  And voiceless on a mountain-top I stand.

TIME.

WHEN but a child thou cam'st in friendly guise,
O Time! and I was happy in thy flight;
For faithful sleep was tender to mine eyes,
And morning filled them with increasing light.
At length came knowledge, and the slow surprise
Of common death, and sin's inhuman blight.
And now I take thee, Time, for what thou art—
Death's porter. The immeasurable sea,
And the green continents it smites apart
Are borne to their sublime decay by thee.
Stern servitor! though stronger than the earth,
And mightier than the deep, I yet shall know,
In jails eternal, or in haunts of mirth,
Thy bitter end, and mark thine overthrow.

THE END.

TO THE SURVIVORS

OF THE

"Canada First" Association

THIS VOLUME IS

AFFECTIONATELY DEDICATED.

PREFACE.

THE first edition of "Tecumseh," published in Toronto in 1886, had a quick sale, but, not being stereotyped, ran out of print, and a re-issue is now called for. The author has often been asked to republish his youthful venture, entitled "Dreamland, and other Poems," only a limited number of copies of which saw the light. Whilst the edition was passing through the binder's hands in Ottawa, and the author himself in the then wilderness of Prince Rupert's Land, the greater part of it was burnt in the Desbarats fire in 1869. In the following pages (Part II.) the major portion of that unfortunate volume is included, with such revision as seemed desirable.

For the shortcomings of his work, of which the author is but too conscious, his only excuse is that he has done his best. Our romantic Canadian story is a mine of character and incident for the poet and novelist, framed, too, in a matchless environment; and the Canadian author who seeks inspiration there is helping to create for a young people that decisive test of its intellectual faculties, an original and distinctive literature—a literature liberal in its range, but, in its highest forms, springing in a large measure from the soil, and "tasting of the wood." Any work of this kind, therefore, is on the right path, and, though of slender pretensions otherwise, may possess the merits of suggestiveness and sincerity. For his own part, the writer may say, with regard to the book now in hand, that its colouring, at any rate, is due to a lifetime's observation of those primitive inter-racial and formative influences which, together with a time-honoured polity, are the source of the Canadian tradition.

In "Tecumseh" the author attempts to depict dramatically the time and scenes in which the great Indian so nobly played his part—at first independently, and in his own country, and afterwards in alliance and leadership with General Brock in the War of 1812. That war was the turning point of Canada's destiny. It was maintained mainly within her borders—a community of some 70,000 souls in Upper Canada, with about thrice that number in the Lower Province, being pitted against a nation of 8,000,000. Upper Canada was then a wilderness almost unbroken, save by the clearings of the United Empire Loyalists and their sons. There were only 1,500 Imperial troops in the Province, scattered along an immense frontier; and England, when the United States declared war, was in the throes of her deadly struggle with Napoleon. In the face of such emergencies, the courage and vigor of the Canadian people of both races can be truly appreciated. Enrolling during the war over 500,000 men, and repeatedly entering Canada at many points, the invaders were at last everywhere discomfited, and at its close had been driven to a man from Canadian soil. The bitter feelings engendered by the long struggle have died down, and racial sympathies, wantonly alienated on the one hand by despotic statecraft in the previous century, and, on the other, by a criminal and unprovoked attack upon Canada, have revived, and are rightly taking their place. The tradition lives, but the feelings begot of it, like the ancient memories of Flodden and Bannockburn in the mother-land, are now academic. In this altered spirit Americans, in their fiction and histories, restore the body and pressure, even the rancours of the time, without offence; whilst Canadians, in like manner, call to mind the decisive victories which preserved their liberties.

Both preface and notes to the drama are, no doubt, superfluous to many home readers; but, as the book is to be published in the Old Country, and as the persons of the drama move in an atmosphere—a domain of Nature's things—unfamiliar to people there, the notes may be read with advantage perhaps before turning to the text, especially as the study in England of Canadian history subsequent to the Conquest is said to be confined to experts—the general reader being familiar only with the captivating pages of Parkman. Certainly knowledge of such a momentous event to Canada as the War of 1812 must be far from common, since its greatest names seem to be unknown. Lieut.-Colonel G. T. Denison, in his recent book, "Soldiering in Canada," states that "few even of the well-educated people of England have ever heard of Brock, and, if his name is mentioned, the question is generally asked, Who was General Brock?" If such be the case, no doubt Tecumseh is also unknown, yet these are names familiar as household words in the mouths of Canadians. Both were men of transcendent ability, to whose genius and self-sacrifice at the most critical period in her history is due the preservation of Canada to the Empire. At the outbreak of the war numbers of aliens domiciled in the Upper Province had contrived to spread dismay amongst a timid and wavering section of the community. It was at this juncture that the bold stroke of Brock and Tecumseh at Detroit electrified the people. Both heroes subsequently fell, but not until all Canada, inspired by their example, had resolved to fight it out to the end. It seems strange that well-read Englishmen should be ignorant of this vital record, whose stirring chapters exhibit in the clearest light the spirit and the springs of action which have made Canada what she is. If the prophetic soul of a wide empire, "dreaming on things to come," is already prefiguring an imperial adjustment in which the larger, if not the greater, Britain shall be the outworks, and the mother-country the citadel, it is surely important that she should know something of the history and idiosyncrasies of her offspring. The habitudes of each colony are largely the products of distinct environments which can never be transfused, and must be reckoned with hereafter as constant factors in the interaction of imperial politics. Certain it is that, even if the characteristic features and incidents of Canadian history were unrecorded, they would still survive in tradition, and influence for generations, perhaps for ages to come, the feelings and sympathies of both sections of her people. Not that thereby they are less true to their institutions; on the contrary, loyalty has crystallized in Canada. Nowhere has judgment been less warped or a people's insight been more clear and penetrating regarding the great question of a United Empire. Nowhere has public opinion been more instinctively opposed to disintegration. With all her faults, Canada has ever been true to the high ideal. Even when the mother-country seemed ignobly to falter and fall away, she saw in it the indispensable safe-guard of our common interests, and with enlarged confidence in her own future, looks forward to its fulfilment still with abiding faith. For then Canada shall cease to be a dependency, and become a nation. Then shall a whole family of young giants stand

> "Erect, unbound, at Britain's side—"

her imperial offspring oversea, the upholders in the far future of her glorious tradition, or, should exhaustion ever come, the props and support of her declining years.

CONTENTS.

PART I.

"When the white men first set foot on our shores, they were hungry; they had no places on which to spread their blankets or to kindle their fires. They were feeble; they could do nothing for themselves. Our fathers commiserated their distress, and shared freely with them whatever the Great Spirit had given to his red children."

From TECUMSEH'S *speech to the Osages.*

TECUMSEH

A DRAMA

DRAMATIS PERSONÆ.

INDIANS.

TECUMSEH (*Chief of the Shawanoes*).
THE PROPHET (*Brother of Tecumseh*).
TARHAY (*a Chief in love with Iena*).
STAYETA (*Chief of the Wyandots*).
MIAMI, DELAWARE, KICKAPOO and DAHCOTA CHIEFS.
Warriors, Braves, Josakeeds and Runners.
MAMATEE (*Wife of Tecumseh*).
IENA (*Niece of Tecumseh*).
WEETAMORE, WINONA, *and other Indian Maidens.*

AMERICANS.

GENERAL HARRISON (*Governor of Indiana Territory*).
GENERAL HULL.
COLONEL CASS.
BARRON (*an Indian Agent*).
TWANG, SLAUGH, GERKIN and BLOAT (*Rough Citizens of Vincennes*).
Five Councillors of Indiana Territory, Officers, Soldiers, Volunteers, Orderlies and Scouts.

BRITISH AND CANADIANS.

GENERAL BROCK (*Administrator of the Government of Upper Canada*).
COLONEL (*afterwards General*) PROCTOR.
GLEGG, MACDONELL, } (*Aides-de-camp to General Brock*).
NICHOL, BABY, ELLIOTT, } (*Colonels of Canadian Volunteers*).
MCKEE, ROBINSON, } (*Captains of Canadian Volunteers*).
LEFROY (*a poet-artist, enamoured of Indian life, and in love with Iena*).
Two Old Men of York, U. E. Loyalists, and other Citizens, Alien Settlers, Officers, Soldiers, Volunteers, Orderlies and Messengers.

TECUMSEH.

ACT I.

SCENE FIRST.—The Forest near the Prophet's Town on the Tippecanoe.

Enter the PROPHET.

PROPHET. Twelve moons have wasted, and no tidings still!
Tecumseh must have perished! Joy has tears
As well as grief, and mine will freely flow—
Sembling our women's piteous privilege—
Whilst dry ambition ambles to its ends.
My schemes have swelled to greatness, and my name
Has flown so far upon the wings of fear
That nations tremble at its utterance.
Our braves abhor, yet stand in awe of me,
Who ferret witchcraft out, commune with Heaven,
And ope or shut the gloomy doors of death.
All feelings and all seasons suit ambition!
Yet my vindictive nature hath a craft,
In action slow, which matches mother-earth's:
First seed-time—then the harvest of revenge.
Who works for power, and not the good of men,
Would rather win by fear than lose by love.
Not so Tecumseh—rushing to his ends,
And followed by men's love—whose very foes
Trust him the most. Rash fool! Him do I dread,
And his imperious spirit. Twelve infant moons

Have swung in silver cradles o'er these woods,
And still no tidings of his enterprise,
Which—all too deep and wide—has swallowed him,
And left me here unrivalled and alone.

Enter an INDIAN RUNNER.

There is a message in your eyes—what now?
RUNNER. Your brother, great Tecumseh, has returned,
And rests himself a moment ere he comes
To counsel with you here.

[*Exit Runner.*

PROPHET. He has returned!
So then the growing current of my power
Must fall again into the stately stream
Of his great purpose. But a moment past
I stood upon ambition's height, and now
My brother comes to break my greatness up,
And merge it in his own. I know his thoughts—
That I am but a helper to his ends;
And, were there not a whirlpool in my soul
Of hatred which would fain ingulf our foes,
I would engage my cunning and my craft
'Gainst his simplicity, and win the lead.
But, hist, he comes! I must assume the rôle
By which I pander to his purposes.

Enter TECUMSEH.

TECUMSEH. Who is this standing in the darkened robes?
PROPHET. The Prophet! Olliwayshilla, who probes
The spirit-world, and holds within his ken
Life's secrets and the fateful deeds of men.
The "One-Eyed!" Brother to the Shooting Star—
TECUMSEH. With heart of wax, and hands not made for war.
PROPHET. Would that my hands were equal to my hate!
Then would strange vengeance traffic on the earth;
For I should treat our foes to what they crave—

Our fruitful soil—yea, ram it down their throats,
And choke them with the very dirt they love.
'Tis you, Tecumseh! You are here at last,
And welcome as the strong heat-bearing Spring
Which opens up the pathways of revenge.
What tidings from afar?

TECUMSEH. Good tidings thence!
I have not seen the Wyandots, but all
The distant nations will unite with us
To spurn the fraudful treaties of Fort Wayne.
From Talapoosa to the Harricanaw
I have aroused them from their lethargy.
From the hot gulf up to those confines rude,
Where Summer's sides are pierced with icicles,
They stand upon my call. What tidings here?

PROPHET. No brand has struck to bark our enterprise
Which grows on every side. The Prophet's robe,
That I assumed when old Pengasega died—
With full accord and countenance from you—
Fits a strong shoulder ampler far than his;
And all our people follow me in fear.

TECUMSEH. Would that they followed you in love! Proceed!
My ears are open to my brother's tongue.

PROPHET. I have myself, and by swift messengers,
Proclaimed to all the nations far and near,
I am the Open-Door, and have the power
To lead them back to life. The sacred fire
Must burn forever in the red-man's lodge,
Else will that life go out. All earthly goods
By the Great Spirit meant for common use
Must so be held. Red shall not marry white,
To lop our parent stems; and never more
Must vile, habitual cups of deadliness
Distort their noble natures, and unseat
The purpose of their souls. They must return
To ancient customs; live on game and maize;
Clothe them with skins, and love both wife and child,
Nor lift a hand in wrath against their race.

TECUMSEH. These are wise counsels which are noised afar,
And many nations have adopted them
And made them law.
PROPHET. These counsels were your own!
Good in themselves, they are too weak to sway
Our fickle race. I've much improved on them
Since the Great Spirit took me by the hand.
TECUMSEH. Improved! and how? Your mission was to lead
Our erring people back to ancient ways—
Too long o'ergrown—not bloody sacrifice.
They tell me that the prisoners you have ta'en—
Not captives in fair fight, but wanderers
Bewildered in our woods, or such as till
Outlying fields, caught from the peaceful plough—
You cruelly have tortured at the stake.
Nor this the worst! In order to augment
Your gloomy sway you craftily have played
Upon the zeal and frenzy of our tribes,
And, in my absence, hatched a monstrous charge
Of sorcery amongst them, which hath spared
Nor feeble age nor sex. Such horrid deeds
Recoil on us! Old Shataronra's grave
Sends up its ghost, and Tetaboxti's hairs—
White with sad years and counsel—singed by you!
In dreams and nightmares, float on every breeze.
Ambition's madness might stop short of this,
And shall if I have life.
PROPHET. The Spirit Great
Hath urged me, and still urges me to all.
He puts his hand to mine and leads me on.
Do you not hear him whisper even now—
"Thou art the Prophet?" All our followers
Behold in me a greater than yourself,
And worship me, and venture where I lead.
TECUMSEH. Your fancy is the common slip of fools,
Who count the lesser greater being near.

Dupe of your own imposture and designs,
I cannot bind your thoughts! but what you do
Henceforth must be my subject; so take heed,
And stand within my sanction lest you fall.

PROPHET. You are Tecumseh—else you should choke for this!

[*Crosses the stage and pauses.*

Stay! Let me think! I must not break with him—
'Tis premature. I know his tender part,
And I shall touch it. [*Recrosses.*
Brother, let me ask,
Do you remember how our father fell?

TECUMSEH. Who can forget Kanawha's bloody fray?
He died for home in battle with the whites.

PROPHET. And you remember, too, that boyish morn
When all our braves were absent on the chase—
That morn when you and I half-dreaming lay
In summer grass, but woke to deadly pain
Of loud-blown bugles ringing through the air.
They came!—a rush of chargers from the woods,
With tramplings, cursings, shoutings manifold,
And headlong onset, fierce with brandished swords,
Of frontier troopers eager for the fight.
Scarce could a lynx have screened itself from sight,
So sudden the attack—yet, trembling there,
We crouched unseen, and saw our little town
Stormed, with vile slaughter of small babe and crone,
And palsied grandsire—you remember it?

TECUMSEH. Remember it! Alas, the echoing
Of that wild havoc lingers in my brain!
O wretched age, and injured motherhood,
And hapless maiden-wreck!

PROPHET. Yet this has been
Our endless history, and it is this
Which crams my very veins with cruelty.
My pulses bound to see those devils fall
Brained to the temples, and their women cast
As offal to the wolf.

TECUMSEH. Their crimes are great—
Our wrongs unspeakable. But spare our own!
These gloomy sacrifices sap our strength;
And henceforth from your wizard scrutinies
I charge you to forbear. But who's the white
You hold as captive?
PROPHET. He is called LEFROY—
A captive, but too free to come and go.
Our warriors struck his trail by chance, and found
His tent close by the Wabash, where he lay
With sprainèd ankle, foodless and alone.
He had a book of pictures with him there
Of Long-Knife forts, encampments and their chiefs—
Most recognizable; so, reasoning thence,
Our warriors took him for a daring spy,
And brought him here, and tied him to the stake.
Then he declared he was a Saganash—
No Long-Knife he! but one who loved our race,
And would adopt our ways—with honeyed words,
Couched in sweet voice, and such appealing eyes,
That Iena, our niece—who listened near—
Believing, rushed, and cut him from the tree.
I hate his smiles, soft ways, and smooth-paced tread,
And would, ere now, have killed him but for her;
For ever since, unmindful of her race,
She has upheld him, and our women think
That he has won her heart.
TECUMSEH. But not her hand!
This cannot be, and I must see to it:
Red shall not marry white—such is our law.
But graver matters are upon the wing,
Which I must open to you. Know you, then,
The nation that has doomed our Council-Fires—
Splashed with our blood—will on its Father turn,
Once more, whose lion-paws, stretched o'er the sea,
Will sheathe their nails in its unnatural sides,
Till blood will flow, as free as pitch in spring,
To gum the chafed seams of our sinking bark.

This opportunity, well nursed, will give
A respite to our wrongs, and heal our wounds;
And all our nations, knit by me and ranged
In headship with our Saganash allies,
Will turn the mortal issue 'gainst our foes,
And wall our threatened frontiers with their slain.
But till that ripened moment, not a sheaf
Of arrows should be wasted, not a brave
Should perish aimlessly, nor discord reign
Amongst our tribes, nor jealousy distrain
The large effects of valour. We must now
Pack all our energies. Our eyes and ears
No more must idle with the hour, but work
As carriers to the brain, where we shall store,
As in an arsenal, deep schemes of war!

[*A noise and shouting without.*

But who is this?

[*Enter* BARRON *accompanied and half dragged by warriors. The* PROPHET *goes forward to meet him.*

BARRON. I crave protection as a messenger
And agent sent by General Harrison.
Your rude, unruly braves, against my wish,
Have dragged me here as if I were a spy.

PROPHET. What else! Why come you here if not a spy?
Brouillette came, and Dubois, who were spies—
Now you are here. Look on it! There's your grave!

[*Pointing to the ground at* BARRON'S *feet.*

TECUMSEH. (*Joining them.*) Nay, let him be! This man is not a spy.
(*To* BARRON.) Give me your message!

BARRON. The Governor of Indiana sends
This letter to you, in the which he says (*Reading letter*)
"You are an enemy to the Seventeen Fires.
I have been told that you intend to lift

The hatchet 'gainst your father, the great Chief,
Whose goodness, being greater than his fear
Or anger at your folly, still would stretch
His bounty to his children who repent,
And ask of him forgiveness for the past.
Small harm is done which may not be repaired,
And friendship's broken chain may be renewed;
But this is in your doing, and depends
Upon the choice you make. Two roads
Are lying now before you: one is large,
Open and pleasant, leading unto peace,
Your own security and happiness;
The other—narrow, crooked and constrained—
Most surely leads to misery and death.
Be not deceived! All your united force
Is but as chaff before the Seventeen Fires.
Your warriors are brave, but so are ours;
Whilst ours are countless as the forest leaves,
Or grains of sand upon the Wabash shores.
Rely not on the English to protect you!
They are not able to protect themselves.
They will not war with us, for, if they do,
Ere many moons have passed our battle flag
Shall wave o'er all the forts of Canada.
What reason have you to complain of us?
What have we taken? or what treaties maimed?
You tell us we have robbed you of your lands—
Bought them from nameless braves and village chiefs
Who had no right to sell. Prove that to us,
And they will be restored. I have full power
To treat with you. Bring your complaint to me,
And I, in honour, pledge your safe return."

TECUMSEH. Is this it all?

BARRON. Yes, all. I have commands
To bear your answer back without delay.

PROPHET. This is our answer, then, to Harrison:
Go tell that bearded liar we shall go
With forces which will pledge our own return!

TECUMSEH. What shall my answer be?
PROPHET. Why, like my own—
There is no answer save that we shall go.
TECUMSEH. (*To* BARRON.) I fear that our complaint lies all too deep
For your Chief's curing. The Great Spirit gave
The red men this wide continent as theirs,
And in the east another to the white;
But, not content at home, these crossed the sea,
And drove our fathers from their ancient seats.
Their sons in turn are driven to the Lakes,
And cannot farther go unless they drown.
Yet now you take upon yourselves to say ·
This tract is Kickapoo, this Delaware,
And this Miami; but your Chief should know
That all our lands are common to our race!
How can one nation sell the rights of all
Without consent of all? No! For my part
I am a Red Man, not a Shawanoe,
And here I mean to stay. Go to your chief,
And tell him I shall meet him at Vincennes.

[*Exeunt all but* TECUMSEH.

What is there in my nature so supine
That I must ever quarrel with revenge?
From vales and rivers which were once our own
The pale hounds who uproot our ancient graves
Come whining for our lands, with fawning tongues,
And schemes and subterfuge and subtleties.
O for a Pontiac to drive them back
And whoop them to their shuddering villages!
O for an age of valour like to his,
When freedom clothed herself with solitude,
And one in heart the scattered nations stood,
And one in hand. It comes! and mine shall be
The lofty task to teach them to be free—
To knit the nations, bind them into one,
And end the task great Pontiac begun!

SCENE SECOND.—ANOTHER PART OF THE FOREST.

Enter LEFROY, *carrying his rifle, and examining a knot of wild flowers.*

LEFROY. This region is as lavish of its flowers
As Heaven of its primrose blooms by night.
This is the Arum which within its root
Folds life and death; and this the Prince's Pine,
Fadeless as love and truth—the fairest form
That ever sun-shower washed with sudden rain.
This golden cradle is the Moccasin Flower,
Wherein the Indian hunter sees his hound;
And this dark chalice is the Pitcher-Plant,
Stored with the water of forgetfulness.
Whoever drinks of it, whose heart is pure,
Will sleep for aye 'neath foodful asphodel,
And dream of endless love. I need it not!
I am awake, and yet I dream of love.
It is the hour of meeting, when the sun
Takes level glances at these mighty woods,
And Iena has never failed till now
To meet me here! What keeps her? Can it be
The Prophet? Ah, that villain has a thought,
Undreamt of by his simple followers,
Dark in his soul as midnight! If—but no—
He fears her though he hates!
What shall I do?
Rehearse to listening woods, or ask these oaks
What thoughts they have, what knowledge of the past?
They dwarf me with their greatness, but shall come
A meaner and a mightier than they,
And cut them down. Yet rather would I dwell
With them, with wildness and its stealthy forms—
Yea, rather with wild men, wild beasts and birds,
Than in the sordid town that here may rise.
For here I am a part of Nature's self,
And not divorced from her like men who plod

The weary streets of care in search of gain.
And here I feel the friendship of the earth:
Not the soft cloying tenderness of hand
Which fain would satiate the hungry soul
With household honey combs and parloured sweets,
But the strong friendship of primeval things—
The rugged kindness of a giant heart,
And love that lasts.

I have a poem made
Which doth concern Earth's injured majesty—
Be audience, ye still untroubled stems!

(Recites.)

There was a time on this fair continent
When all things throve in spacious peacefulness.
The prosperous forests unmolested stood,
For where the stalwart oak grew there it lived
Long ages, and then died among its kind.
The hoary pines—those ancients of the earth—
Brimful of legends of the early world,
Stood thick on their own mountains unsubdued.
And all things else illumined by the sun,
Inland or by the lifted wave, had rest.
The passionate or calm pageants of the skies
No artist drew; but in the auburn west
Innumerable faces of fair cloud
Vanished in silent darkness with the day.
The prairie realm—vast ocean's paraphrase—
Rich in wild grasses numberless, and flowers
Unnamed save in mute Nature's inventory,
No civilized barbarian trenched for gain.
And all that flowed was sweet and uncorrupt.
The rivers and their tributary streams,
Undammed, wound on forever, and gave up
Their lonely torrents to weird gulfs of sea,
And ocean wastes unshadowed by a sail.
And all the wild life of this western world
Knew not the fear of man; yet in those woods,
And by those plenteous streams and mighty lakes,
And on stupendous steppes of peerless plain,
And in the rocky gloom of canyons deep,
Screened by the stony ribs of mountains hoar
Which steeped their snowy peaks in purging cloud,
And down the continent where tropic suns

> Warmed to her very heart the mother earth,
> And in the congeal'd north where silence self
> Ached with intensity of stubborn frost,
> There lived a soul more wild than barbarous;
> A tameless soul—the sunburnt savage free—
> Free, and untainted by the greed of gain:
> Great Nature's man content with Nature's food.

But hark! I hear her footsteps in the leaves—
And so my poem ends.

Enter IENA, *downcast.*

My love! my love!
What! Iena in tears! Your looks, like clouds,
O'erspread my joy which, but a moment past,
Rose like the sun to high meridian.
Ah, how is this? She trembles, and she starts,
And looks with wavering eyes through oozing tears,
As she would fly from me. Why do you weep?
IENA. I weep, for I have come to say—farewell.
LEFROY. Farewell! I have fared well in love till now;
For you are mine, and I am yours, so say
Farewell, farewell, a thousand times farewell.
IENA. How many meanings has the word? since yours
Is full of joy, but mine, alas, of pain.
The pale-face and the Shawanoe must part.
LEFROY. Must part? Yes, part—we parted yesterday—
And shall to-day—some dream disturbs my love.
IENA. Oh, that realities were dreams! 'Tis not
A dream that parts us, but a stern command.
Tecumseh has proclaimed it as his law—
Red shall not marry white; so must you leave;
And therefore I have come to say farewell.
LEFROY. That word is barbed, and like an arrow aimed.
The maid who saved my life would mar it too!
IENA. Speak not of that! Your life's in danger now.
Tecumseh has returned, and—knowing all—
Has built a barrier betwixt our loves,
More rigid than a palisade of oak.

LEFROY. What means he? And what barrier is this?
IENA. The barrier is the welfare of our race—
Wherefore his law—"Red shall not marry white."
His noble nature halts at cruelty,
So fear him not! But in the Prophet's hand,
Dark, dangerous and bloody, there is death,
And, sheltered by Tecumseh's own decree,
He who misprizes you, and hates, will strike—
Then go at once! Alas for Iena,
Who loves her race too well to break its law.
LEFROY. I love you better than I love my race;
And could I mass my fondness for my friends,
Augment it with my love of noble brutes,
Tap every spring of reverence and respect,
And all affections bright and beautiful—
Still would my love for you outweigh them all.
IENA. Speak not of love! Speak of the Long-Knife's hate!
Oh, it is pitiful to creep in fear
O'er lands where once our fathers stept in pride!
The Long-Knife strengthens, whilst our race decays,
And falls before him as our forests fall.
First comes his pioneer, the bee, and soon
The mast which plumped the wild deer fats his swine.
His cattle pasture where the bison fed;
His flowers, his very weeds, displace our own—
Aggressive as himself. All, all thrust back!
Destruction follows us, and swift decay.
Oh, I have lain for hours upon the grass,
And gazed into the tenderest blue of heaven—
Cleansed as with dew, so limpid, pure and sweet—
All flecked with silver packs of standing cloud
Most beautiful! But watch them narrowly!
Those clouds will sheer small fleeces from their sides,
Which, melting in our sight as in a dream,
Will vanish all like phantoms in the sky.
So melts our heedless race! Some weaned away,
And wedded to rough-handed pioneers,

Who, fierce as wolves in hatred of our kind,
Yet from their shrill and acid women turn,
Prizing our maidens for their gentleness.
Some by outlandish fevers die, and some—
Caught in the white man's toils and vices mean—
Court death, and find it in the trader's cup.
And all are driven from their heritage,
Far from our fathers' seats and sepulchres,
And girdled with the growing glooms of war;
Resting a moment here, a moment there,
Whilst ever through our plains and forest realms
Bursts the pale spoiler, armed, with eager quest,
And ruinous lust of land. I think of all—
And own Tecumseh right. 'Tis he alone
Can stem this tide of sorrows dark and deep;
So must I bend my feeble will to his,
And, for my people's welfare, banish love.

LEFROY. Nay, for your people's welfare keep your love!
My heart is true: I know that braggart nation,
Whose sordid instincts, cold and pitiless,
Would cut you off, and drown your Council Fires.
I would defend you, therefore keep me here!
My love is yours alone, my hand I give,
With this good weapon in it, to your race.

IENA. Oh, heaven help a weak untutored maid,
Whose head is warring 'gainst a heart that tells,
With every throb, I love you. Leave me! Fly!

LEFROY. I kneel to you—it is my leave-taking,
So, bid me fly again, and break my heart!

(IENA *sings.*)

Fly far from me,
  Even as the daylight flies,
And leave me in the darkness of my pain!
Some earlier love will come to thee again,
  And sweet new moons will rise,
And smile on it and thee.

Fly far from me,
  Even whilst the daylight wastes—
Ere thy lips burn me in a last caress;

Ere fancy quickens, and my longings press,
  And my weak spirit hastes
For shelter unto thee !

Fly far from me,
  Even whilst the daylight pales—
So shall we never, never meet again !
Fly ! for my senses swim—Oh, Love ! Oh, Pain !—
  Help ! for my spirit fails—
I cannot fly from thee !

[IENA *sinks into* LEFROY'S *arms*.

LEFROY. No, Iena ! You cannot fly from me—
My heart is in your breast, and yours in mine ;
Therefore our love—

Enter TECUMSEH, *followed by* MAMATEE.

TECUMSEH. False girl ! Is this your promise ?
Would that I had a pale-face for a niece—
Not one so faithless to her pledge ! You owe
All duty and affection to your race,
Whose interest—the sum of our desires—
Traversed by alien love, drops to the ground.
IENA. Tecumseh ne'er was cruel until now.
Call not love alien which includes our race—
Love for our people, pity for their wrongs !
He loves our race because his heart is here—
And mine is in his breast. Oh, ask him there,
And he will tell you—
LEFROY. Iena, let me speak !
Tecumseh, we as strangers have become
Strangely familiar through sheer circumstance,
Which often breeds affection or disdain,
Yet, lighting but the surface of the man,
Shows not his heart. I know not what you think
And care not for your favour or your love,
Save as desert may crown me. Your decree,
" Red shall not marry white," is arbitrary,
And off the base of nature ; for if they

Should marry not, then neither should they love.
Yet Iena loves me, and I love her.
Be merciful! I ask not Iena
To leave her race; I rather would engage
These willing arms in her defence and yours.
Heap obligation up, conditions stern—
But send not your cold "Nay" athwart our lives.

IENA. Be merciful! Oh, uncle, pity us!

TECUMSEH. My pity, Iena, goes with reproach,
Blunting the edge of anger; yet my will
Is fixed, and the command to be obeyed—
This stranger must depart—you to your lodge!

MAMATEE. Tecumseh, I am in the background here,
As ever I have been in your affection.
For I have ne'er known what good women prize—
Earth's greatest boon to them—a husband's love.

TECUMSEH. My nation has my love, in which you share,
With special service rendered to yourself;
So that your cabin flows with mouffles sweet,
And hips of wapiti and bedded robes.
Teach me my duty further if you will!
My love is wide, and broods upon my race.

MAMATEE. The back is clad—the heart, alas! goes bare.
Oh, I would rather shiver in the snow—
My heart downed softly with Tecumseh's love—
Than sleep unprized in warmest couch of fur.
I know your love is wide, and, for that I
Share but a millionth part of it, and feel
Its meagreness, I plead most eagerly
For this poor white, whose heart is full of love,
And gives it all to her.

TECUMSEH. It cannot be!
You know not what you ask, 'Tis 'gainst our law,
Which, breached, would let our untamed people through.

LEFROY. I care not for your cruel law! The heart
Has statutes of its own which make for love.

TECUMSEH. You'd cross me too! This child's play of the heart,

Which sterner duty has repressed in me,
Makes even captives bold. (*Aside.*) I like his courage!
MAMATEE. If duty makes Tecumseh's heart grow cold,
Then shame on it! and greater shame on him
Who ever yet showed mercy to his foes,
Yet, turning from his own, in pity's spite
Denies it to a girl. See, here I kneel!
IENA. And I! O uncle, frown not on our love!
TECUMSEH. By the Great Spirit this is over much!
My heart is made for pity, not for war,
Since women's tears unman me. Have your will!
I shall respect your love, (*To* LEFROY.) your safety too.
I go at once to sound the Wyandots
Concerning some false treaties with the whites.
The Prophet hates you, therefore come with me.

[*The* PROPHET *rushes in with a band of Braves.*

PROPHET. She's here! Take hold of her and bear her off!
TECUMSEH. Beware! Lay not a finger on the girl!

[*The Braves fall back.*

PROPHET. There is no law Tecumseh will not break,
When women weep, and pale-face spies deceive.
MAMATEE. Ah, wretch! not all our people's groans could wring
A single tear from out your murderous eye.
PROPHET. (*Lifting his axe.*) This is my captive, and his life is mine!
IENA. (*Rushing to* LEFROY.) Save him! Save him!

[TECUMSEH *interferes.*

END OF FIRST ACT.

ACT II.

SCENE FIRST.—BEFORE THE PROPHET'S TOWN.

Enter TECUMSEH *and* LEFROY.

TECUMSEH. No guard or outlook here! This is most strange.
Chance reigns where prudence sleeps.

Enter a BRAVE.

Here comes a brave
With frenzy in his face. Where is the Prophet?
BRAVE. He fasts alone within the medicine-lodge,
And talks to our Great Spirit. All our braves,
Huddling in fear, stand motionless without,
Thrilled by strange sounds, and voices not of earth.
TECUMSEH. How long has it been thus?
BRAVE. Four nights have passed
And none have seen his face; but all have heard
His dreadful tongue, in incantations deep,
Fetch horrors up—vile beings flashed from hell,
Who fought as devils fight, until the lodge
Shook to its base with struggling, and the earth
Quaked as, with magic strength, he flung them down.
These strove with him for mastery of our fate;
But, being foiled, Yohewa has appeared,
And, in the darkness of our sacred lodge,
Communes with him.
TECUMSEH. Our Spirit great and good!
He comes not here for nought. What has he promised?
BRAVE. Much! for henceforth we are invulnerable.
The bullets of the Long-Knives will rebound,
Like petty hailstones, from our naked breasts;

And, in the misty morns of our attack,
Strange lights will shine on them to guide our aim,
Whilst clouds of gloom will screen us from their sight.
TECUMSEH. The Prophet is a wise interpreter,
And all his words, by valour backed, will stand;
For valour is the weapon of the soul,
More dreaded by our vaunting enemies
Than the plumed arrow, or the screaming ball.
What wizardry and witchcraft has he found
Conspiring 'gainst our people's good?
BRAVE. Why, none!
Wizard and witch are weeded out, he says;
Not one is left to do us hurt.
TECUMSEH. (*Aside.*) 'Tis well!
My brother has the eyeball of the horse,
And swerves from danger. (*To* BRAVE.) Bid our warriors come!
I wait them here.

[*Exit* BRAVE.

The Prophet soon will follow.
LEFROY. Now opportunity attend my heart,
Which waits for Iena! True love's behest,
Outrunning war's, will bring her to my arms
Ere cease the braves from gasping wonderment.
TECUMSEH. First look on service ere you look on love;
You shall not see her here.
LEFROY. My promises
Are sureties of my service—
TECUMSEH. But your deeds,
Accomplishments; our people count on deeds.
Be patient! Look upon our warriors
Roped round with scars and cicatrizèd wounds,
Inflicted in deep trial of their spirit.
Their skewered sides are proofs of manly souls,
Which, had one groan escaped from agony,
Would all have sunk beneath our women's heels,
Unfit for earth or heaven. So try your heart,
And let endurance swallow all love's sighs.

Yoke up your valour with our people's cause,
And I, who love your nation, which is just,
When deeds deserve it, will adopt you here,
By ancient custom of our race, and join
Iena's hand to yours.

LEFROY. Your own hand first
In pledge of this!

TECUMSEH. It ever goes with truth!

LEFROY. Now come some wind of chance and show me her
But for one heavenly moment! as when leaves
Are blown aside in summer, and we see
The nested oriole.

[*Enter Chiefs and warriors—The warriors cluster around* TECUMSEH, *shouting and discharging their pieces.*

TECUMSEH. My chiefs and braves!

MIAMI CHIEF. Fall back! Fall back! Ye press too close on him.

TECUMSEH. My friends! our joy is like to meeting streams,
Which draw into a deep and prouder bed.

[*Shouts from the warriors.*

DELAWARE CHIEF. Silence, ye braves! let great Tecumseh speak!

[*The warriors fall back.*

TECUMSEH. Comrades, and faithful warriors of our race!
Ye who defeated Harmar and St. Clair,
And made their hosts a winter's feast for wolves!
I call on you to follow me again,
Not now for war, but as forearmed for fight.
As ever in the past so is it still:
Our sacred treaties are infringed and torn;
Laughed out of sanctity, and spurned away;
Used by the Long-Knife's slave to light his fire,
Or turned to kites by thoughtless boys, whose wrists

Anchor their father's lies in front of heaven.
And now we're asked to Council at Vincennes;
To bend to lawless ravage of our lands,
To treacherous bargains, contracts false, wherein
One side is bound, the other loose as air!
Where are those villains of our race and blood
Who signed the treaties that unseat us here;
That rob us of rich plains and forests wide;
And which, consented to, will drive us hence
To stage our lodges in the Northern Lakes,
In penalties of hunger worse than death?
Where are they? that we may confront them now
With your wronged sires, your mothers, wives and babes,
And, wringing from their false and slavish lips
Confession of their baseness, brand with shame
The traitor hands which sign us to our graves.

MIAMI CHIEF. Some are age-bent and blind, and others sprawl,
And stagger in the Long-Knife's villages;
And some are dead, and some have fled away,
And some are lurking in the forest here,
Sneaking, like dogs, until resentment cools.

KICKAPOO CHIEF. We all disclaim their treaties. Should they come,
Forced from their lairs by hunger, to our doors,
Swift punishment will light upon their heads.

TECUMSEH. Put yokes upon them! let their mouths be bound!
For they are swine who root with champing jaws
Their fathers' fields, and swallow their own offspring.

Enter the PROPHET *in his robe—his face discoloured.*

Welcome, my brother, from the lodge of dreams!
Hail to thee, sagest among men—great heir
Of all the wisdom of Pengasega!

PROPHET. (*Aside.*) This pale-face here again! this hateful snake,

Who crawls between our people and their laws!
(*To* TECUMSEH.) Your greeting, brother, takes the chill from mine,
When last we parted you were not so kind.
TECUMSEH. The Prophet's wisdom covers all. He knows
Why Nature varies in her handiwork,
Moulding one man from snow, the next from fire—
PROPHET. Which temper is your own, and blazes up,
In winds of passion like a burning pine.
TECUMSEH. 'Twill blaze no more unless to scorch our foes.
My brother, there's my hand—for I am grieved
That aught befell to shake our proper love.
Our purpose is too high, and full of danger;
We have too vast a quarrel on our hands
To waste our breath on this.
[*Steps forward and offers his hand.*
PROPHET. My hand to yours.
SEVERAL CHIEFS. Tecumseh and the Prophet are rejoined!
TECUMSEH. Now, but one petty cloud distains our sky.
My brother, this man loves our people well.
(*Pointing to* LEFROY.)
LEFROY. I know he hates me, yet I hope to win
My way into his heart.
PROPHET. There—take my hand!
(*Aside.*) I must dissemble. Would this palm were poison!
(*To* TECUMSEH.) What of the Wyandots? And yet I know!
I have been up among the clouds, and down
Into the entrails of the earth, and seen
The dwelling-place of devils. All my dreams
Are from above, and therefore favour us.
TECUMSEH. With one accord the Wyandots disclaim
The treaties of Fort Wayne, and burn with rage.
Their tryst is here, and some will go with me
To Council at Vincennes. Where's Winnemac?
MIAMI CHIEF. That recreant has joined our enemies,
And with the peace-pipe sits beside their fire,
And whiffs away our lives.

KICKAPOO CHIEF. The Deaf-Chief, too,
With head awry, who cannot hear us speak
Though thunder shouted for us from the skies,
Yet hears the Long-Knives whisper at Vincennes;
And, when they jest upon our miseries,
Grips his old leathern sides, and coughs with laughter.

DELAWARE CHIEF. And old Kanaukwa—famed when we were young—
Has hid his axe, and washed his honours off.

TECUMSEH 'Tis honour he has parted with, not honours;
Good deeds are ne'er forespent, nor wiped away.
I know these men; they've lost their followers,
And, grasping at the shadow of command,
Where sway and custom once had realty,
By times, and turn about, follow each other.
They count for nought—but Winnemac is true,
Though over-politic; he will not leave us.

PROPHET. Those wizened snakes must be destroyed at once!

TECUMSEH. Have mercy, brother—those poor men are old.

PROPHET. Nay, I shall tease them till they sting themselves;
Their rusty fangs are doubly dangerous.

TECUMSEH. What warriors are ready for Vincennes?

WARRIORS. All! All are ready.
Tecumseh leads us on—we follow him.

TECUMSEH. Four hundred warriors will go with me,
All armed, yet only for security
Against the deep designs of Harrison.
For 'tis my purpose still to temporize,
Not lightly break with him till once again
I scour the far emplacements of our tribes.
Then shall we close at once on all our foes.
They claim our lands, but we shall take their lives;
Drive out their thievish souls, and spread their bones
To bleach upon the misty Alleghanies;
Or make death's treaty with them on the spot,

And sign our bloody marks upon their crowns
For lack of schooling—ceding but enough
Of all the lands they covet for their graves.

MIAMI CHIEF. Tecumseh's tongue is housed in wisdom's cheeks;
His valour and his prudence march together.

DELAWARE CHIEF. 'Tis wise to draw the distant nations on.
This scheme will so extend the Long-Knife force,
In lines defensive stretching to the sea,
Their bands will be but morsels for our braves.

PROPHET. How long must this bold project take to ripen?
Time marches with the foe, and his surveyors
Already smudge our forests with their fires.
It frets my blood and makes my bowels turn
To see those devils blaze our ancient oaks,
Cry "Right!" and drive their rascal pickets down.
Why not make war on them at once?

TECUMSEH. Not now!
Time will make room for weightier affairs.
Be this the disposition for the hour:
Our warriors from Vincennes will all return,
Save twenty—the companions of my journey—
And this brave white, who longs to share our toil,
And win his love by deeds in our defence.
You, brother, shall remain to guard our town,
Our wives, our children, all that's dear to us—
Receive each fresh accession to our strength;
And from the hidden world, which you inspect,
Draw a divine instruction for their souls.
Go, now, ye noble chiefs and warriors!
Make preparation—I'll be with you soon.
To-morrow we shall make the Wabash boil,
And beat its current, racing to Vincennes.

[*Exeunt all but* TECUMSEH *and the* PROPHET.

PROPHET. I shall return unto our sacred lodge,
And there invoke the Spirit of the Wind

To follow you, and blow good tidings back.
TECUMSEH. Our strait is such we need the help of heaven.
Use all your wisdom, brother, but—beware!
Pluck not our enterprise while it is green,
And breed no quarrel here till I return.
Avoid it as you would the rattling snake;
And, when you hear the sound of danger, shrink,
And face it not, unless with belts of peace.
White wampum, not the dark, till we can strike
With certain aim. Can I depend on you?
PROPHET. Trust you in fire to burn, or cold to freeze?
So may you trust in me. The heavy charge
Which you have laid upon my shoulders now
Would weigh the very soul of rashness down.
[*Exit the* PROPHET.
TECUMSEH. I think I can depend on him—I must!
Yet do I know his crafty nature well—
His hatred of our foes, his love of self,
And wide ambition. What is mortal man?
Who can divine this creature that doth take
Some colour from all others? Nor shall I
Push cold conclusions 'gainst my brother's sum
Of what is good—so let dependence rest!
[*Exit.*

SCENE SECOND—VINCENNES—A STREET.

Enter GERKIN, SLAUGH and TWANG.

GERKIN. Ain't it.about time Barron was back, Jedge?
TWANG. I reckon so. Our Guvner takes a crazy sight more pains than I would to sweeten that ragin' devil Tecumseh's temper. I'd sweeten it with sugar o' lead if I had *my* way.
SLAUGH. It's a reekin' shame—dang me if it ain't. And that two-faced one-eyed brother o' his, the Prophet —I'll be darned if folks don't say that the Shakers in them 'ere parts claims him for a disciple!

TWANG. Them Shakers is a queer lot. They dance jest like wild Injuns, and thinks we orter be kind to the red rascals, and use them honestly.

GERKIN. Wall! That's what our Guvner ses too. But I reckon he's shammin' a bit. Twixt you and me, he's on the make like the rest o' us. Think o' bein' kind to a red devil that would lift your har ten minutes arter! And as for honesty—I say "set 'em up" every time, and then rob 'em. That's the way to clar them out o' the kentry. Whiskey's better 'n gunpowder, and costs less than fightin' 'em in the long run.

Enter CITIZEN BLOAT.

TWANG. That's so! Hello, Major, what's up? You look kind o' riled to-day.

BLOAT. Wall, Jedge, I do feel right mad—have you heerd the news?

TWANG. No! Has old Sledge bust you at the kyards again?

BLOAT. Old Sledge be darned! I had jest clar'd him out o' continentals—fifty to the shillin'—at his own game, when in ript Roudi—the Eyetalian that knifed the Muskoe Injun for peekin' through his bar-room winder last spring—jest down from Fort Knox. You know the chap, General; you was on his jury.

SLAUGH. I reckon I do! The Court was agin him, but we acquitted him afore the Chief-Justice finished his charge, and gave him a vote o' thanks to boot. There's a heap o' furriners creepin' inter these parts—poor down-trodden cusses from Europe—and, if they're all like Roudi, they'll do—a'most as hendy with the knife as our own people. But what's up?

BLOAT. Roudi saw Barron at Fort Knox, restin' thar on his way back from the Prophet's Town, and he sez that red assassin Tecumseh's a-cumin' down with four hundred o' his painted devils to convarse with our Guvner. They're all armed, he sez, and will be here afore mid-day.

SLAUGH. Wall! our Guvner notified him to come—he's only gettin' what he axed for. There'll be a deal o' loose har flitterin' about the streets afore night, I reckon. Harrison's a heap too soft with them red roosters; he hain't got cheek enough.

GERKIN. I've heerd say the Guvner, and the Chief Justice too, thinks a sight o' this tearin' red devil. They say he's a great man. They say, too, that our treaty Injuns air badly used—that they shouldn't be meddled with on their resarves, and should hev skoolin'.

BLOAT. Skoolin'! That gits me! Dogoned if I wouldn't larn them jest one thing—what them regler officers up to the Fort larns their dogs—"to drap to shot," only in a different kind o' way like; and, as for their resarves, I say, give our farmers a chance—let them locate!

TWANG. That's so, Major! What arthly use air they—plouterin' about their little bits o' fields, with their little bits o' cabins, and livin' half the time on mush-rats? I say, let them move out, and give reliable citizens a chance.

SLAUGH. Wall, I reckon our Guvner's kind's about played out. They call themselves the old stock—the clean pea—the rale gentlemen o' the Revolooshun. But, gentlemen, ain't we the Revolooshun? Jest wait till the live citizens o' these United States and Territories gits a chance, and we'll show them gentry what a free people, with our institooshuns, *kin* do. There'll be no more talk o' skoolin for Injuns, you bet! I'd give them Kernel Crunch's billet.

GERKIN. What was that, General?

SLAUGH. Why, they say he killed a hull family o' redskins, and stuck 'em up as scar'-crows in his wheat-fields. Gentlemen, there's nothin' like original idees!

TWANG. That war an original idee! The Kernel orter hev tuk out a patent. I think I've heerd o' Crunch. Warn't he with Kernel Crawford, o' the melish', at one time?

SLAUGH. Whar?

TWANG. Why over to the Muskingum. You've heerd o' them Delaware Moravians over to the Muskingum, surely?

SLAUGH. Oh, them convarted chaps! but I a'most forgit the carcumstance.

TWANG. Wall, them red devils had a nice resarve thar —as yieldin' a bit o' sile as one could strike this side o' the Alleghanies. They was all convarted by the Moravians, and pertended to be as quiet and peaceable as the Shakers hereabout. But Kernel Crawford—who knew good sile when he sot his eyes on it—diskivered that them prayin' chaps had helped a war-party from the North with provisions—or thort they did, which was the same thing. So—one fine Sunday—he surrounds their church with his melish'—when the Injuns was all a-prayin' —and walks in himself, jest for a minute or two, and prays a bit so as not to skeer them too soon, end then walks out, and locks the door. The Kernel then cutely—my heart kind o' warms to that man—put a squad o' melish' at each winder with their bayonets pinted, and sot fire to the Church, and charred up the hull kit, preacher and all! The heft o' them was burnt; but some that warn't thar skinned out o' the kentry, and got lands from the British up to the Thames River in Canady, and founded what they call the Moravian Town thar; and thar they is still—fur them Britishers kind o' pampers the Injuns, so they may git at our scalps.

SLAUGH. I reckon we'll hev a tussle with them gentry afore long. But for Noo England we'd a hed it afore now; but them Noo Englanders kind o' curries to the Britishers. A war would spile their shippin', and so they're agin it. But we hain't got no ships to spile in this western kentry, and so I reckon we'll pitch in.

GERKIN. We'd better get out of this Injun fry-pan fust, old hoss! I could lick my own weight in wild-cats, but this ruck o' Injuns is jest a little too hefty.

BLOAT. Maybe they want to come to skool, and start store and sich!

GERKIN. Gentlemen, I mean to send my lady down stream, and I reckon you'd better do the same with your 'uns—jest for safety like. My time's limited—will you liquor?

ALL. You bet!

BLOAT. (*Meditatively.*) Skoolin'! Wall, I'll be darned!

[*Exeunt.*

SCENE THIRD. THE SAME. A ROOM IN GENERAL HARRISON'S HOUSE.

Enter GENERAL HARRISON, *and some Officers of the American Army.*

HARRISON. What savage handiwork keeps Barron back?

Enter BARRON.

Ah, here he comes, his looks interpreting
Mischief and failure! It is as I feared.
What answer do you bring?

BARRON. Tecumseh comes
To council, with four hundred men at back,
To which, with all persuasion, I objected—
As that it would alarm our citizens,
Whose hasty temper, by suspicion edged,
Might break in broils of quarrel with his braves;
But, sir, it was in vain—so be prepared!
Your Council records may be writ in blood.

HARRISON. Will he attack us, think you?

BARRON. No, not now.
His present thought is to intimidate.
But, lest some rash and foul-mouthed citizen
Should spur his passion to the run, fore-arm!

HARRISON. Tut! Arms are scarce as soldiers in our town,
And I am sick of requisitioning.
Nay, we must trust to something else than arms.
Tecumseh is a savage but in name—
Let's trust to him! What says he of our treaties?

BARRON. Oh, he discharges them as heavy loads,
Which, borne by red men only, break their backs.
All lands, he says, are common to his race;
Not to be sold but by consent of all.

HARRISON. Absurd! This proposition would prevent
All purchase and all progress. No, indeed;
We cannot tie our hands with such conditions.
What of the Prophet? Comes he with the rest?

BARRON. The Prophet stays behind.

HARRISON. He is a foil
Used by Tecumseh to augment his greatness;
And, by good husbandry of incantation,
And gloomy charms by night, this Prophet works
So shrewdly on their braves that every man,
Inflamed by auguries of victory,
Would rush on death.

1ST OFFICER. Why, General, I heard
He over-trumpt you once and won the trick.

HARRISON. How so?

1ST OFFICER. Well, once, before his braves, 'tis said,
You dared him to a trial of his spells,
Which challenge he accepted, having heard
From white men of a coming sun-eclipse.
Then, shrewdly noting day and hour, he called
Boldly his followers round him, and declared
That he would hide the sun. They stood and gazed,
And, when the moon's colossal shadow fell,
They crouched upon the ground, and worshipped him.

HARRISON. He caught me there, and mischief came of it.
Oh, he is deep. How different those brothers!
One dipt in craft, the dye of cruelty,
The other frank and open as the day.

Enter an ORDERLY.

ORDERLY. Tecumseh and his braves have reached the landing!

[*Excitement. All rise hastily.*

HARRISON. This room is smaller than our audience:
Take seats and benches to the portico—
There we shall treat with him.

[*Exeunt all but* GENERAL HARRISON.

Could I but strain
My charge this chief might be my trusty friend.
Yet I am but my nation's servitor;
Gold is the king who overrides the right,
And turns our people from the simple ways
And fair ideal of their fathers' lives.

[*Exit.*

SCENE FOURTH.—THE SAME. THE PORTICO OF GENERAL HARRISON'S HOUSE. AN OPEN GROVE AT A LITTLE DISTANCE IN FRONT.

[*Curtain rises and discovers* GENERAL HARRISON, *army officers and citizens, of various quality, including* TWANG, SLAUGH, GERKIN *and* BLOAT, seated *in the portico. A sergeant and guard of soldiers near by.*

Enter TECUMSEH *and his followers with* LEFROY *in Indian dress. They all stop at the grove.*

HARRISON. Why halts he there?
Go tell him he is welcome to our house.

[*An Orderly goes down with message.*

1ST OFFICER. How grave and decorous they look—"the mien
Of pensive people born in ancient woods."
But look at him! Look at Tecumseh there—
How simple in attire! that eagle plume
Sole ornament, and emblem of his spirit.
And yet, far-scanned, there's something in his face
That likes us not. Would we were out of this!

HARRISON. Yes; even at a distance I can see
His eyes distilling anger. 'Tis no sign
Of treachery, which ever drapes with smiles

The most perfidious purpose. Our poor strength
Would fail at once should he break out on us ;
But let us hope 'tis yet a war of wits
Where firmness may enact the part of force.

[*Orderly returns.*

What answer do you bring ?

ORDERLY. Tecumseh says :
" Houses are built for whites—the red man's house,
Leaf-roofed, and walled with living oak, is there—

[*Pointing to the grove.*

Let our white brother meet us in it ! "

2ND OFFICER. Oh !
White brother ! So he levels to your height,
And strips your office of its dignity.

3RD OFFICER. 'Tis plain he cares not for your dignity,
And touchingly reminds us of our tenets.
Our nation spurns the outward shows of state,
And ceremony dies for lack of service.
Pomp is discrowned, and throned regality
Dissolved away in our new land and laws.
Man is the Presence here !

1ST OFFICER. Well, for my part,
I like not that one in particular.

[*Pointing toward* TECUMSEH.

3RD OFFICER. No more do I ! I wish I were a crab,
And had its courtly fashion of advancing.

HARRISON. Best yield to him, the rather that he now
Invites our confidence. His heavy force
Scants good opinion somewhat, yet I know
There's honour, aye, and kindness in this Chief.

[*Rising.*

3RD OFFICER. Yes, faith, he loves us all, and means to keep
Locks of our hair for memory. Here goes !

[*All rise.*

Servants and soldiers carry chairs and benches to the grove, followed by GENERAL HARRISON *and others, who seat themselves*—TECUMSEH *and his followers still standing in the lower part of the grove.*

HARRISON. We have not met to bury our respect,
Or mar our plea with lack of courtesy.
The Great Chief knows it is his father's wish
That he should sit by him.

TECUMSEH. My father's wish!
My father is the sun; the earth my mother,
[*Pointing to each in turn.*
And on her mighty bosom I shall rest.

[TECUMSEH *and his followers seat themselves on the grass.*

HARRISON. (*Rising.*) I asked Tecumseh to confer with me,
Not in war's hue, but for the ends of peace.
Our own intent—witness our presence here,
Unarmed save those few muskets and our swords.
How comes it, then, that he descends on us
With this o'erbearing and untimely strength?
Tecumseh's virtues are the theme of all;
Wisdom and courage, frankness and good faith—
To speak of these things is to think of him!
Yet, as one theft makes men suspect the thief—
Be all his life else spent in honesty—
So does one breach of faithfulness in man
Wound all his after deeds. There is a pause
In some men's goodness like the barren time
Of those sweet trees which yield each second year,
Wherein what seems a niggardness in nature
Is but good husbandry for future gifts.
But this tree bears, and bears most treacherous fruit!
Here is a gross infringement of all laws
That shelter men in council, where should sit
No disproportioned force save that of reason—
Our strong dependence still, and argument,
Of better consequence than that of arms,
If great Tecumseh should give ear to it.

TECUMSEH. (*Rising.*) You called upon Tecumseh and he came!
You sent your messenger, asked us to bring

Our wide complaint to you—and it is here!
[*Pointing to his followers.*
Why is our brother angry at our force,
Since every man but represents a wrong?
Nay! rather should our force be multiplied!
Fill up your streets and overflow your fields,
And crowd upon the earth for standing room;
Still would our wrongs outweigh our witnesses,
And scant recital for the lack of tongues.
I know your reason, and its bitter heart,
Its form of justice, clad with promises—
The cloaks of death! That reason was the snare
Which tripped our ancestors in days of yore—
Who knew not falsehood and so feared it not:
Men who mistook your fathers' vows for truth,
And took them, cold and hungry, to their hearts,
Filled them with food, and shared with them their homes,
With such return as might make baseness blush.
What tree e'er bore such treacherous fruit as this?
But let it pass! let wrongs die with the wronged!
The red man's memory is full of graves.
But wrongs live with the living, who are here—
Inheritors of all our fathers' sighs,
And tears, and garments wringing wet with blood.
The injuries which you have done to us
Cry out for remedy, or wide revenge.
Restore the forests you have robbed us of—
Our stolen homes and vales of plenteous corn!
Give back the boundaries, which are our lives,
Ere the axe rise! aught else is reasonless.

HARRISON. Tecumseh's passion is a dangerous flood
Which sweeps away his judgment. Let him lift
His threatened axe to hit defenceless heads!
It cannot mar the body of our right,
Nor graze the even justice of our claim:
These still would live, uncancelled by our death.
Let reason rule us, in whose sober light
We read those treaties which offend him thus:

What nation was the first established here,
Settled for centuries, with title sound?
You know that people, the Miami, well.
Long ere the white man tripped his anchors cold,
To cast them by the glowing western isles,
They lived upon these lands in peace, and none
Dared cavil at their claim. We bought from them,
For such equivalent to largess joined,
That every man was hampered with our goods,
And stumbled on profusion. But give ear!
Jealous lest aught might fail of honesty—
Lest one lean interest or poor shade of right
Should point at us—we made the Kickapoo
And Delaware the sharer of our gifts,
And stretched the arms of bounty over heads
Which held but by Miami sufferance.
But, you! whence came you? and what rights have you?
The Shawanoes are interlopers here—
Witness their name! mere wanderers from the South!
Spurned thence by angry Creek and Yamasee—
Now here to stir up strife, and tempt the tribes
To break the seals of faith. I am surprised
That they should be so led, and more than grieved
Tecumseh has such ingrates at his back.

TECUMSEH. Call you those ingrates who but claim their own,
And owe you nothing but revenge? Those men
Are here to answer and confront your lies.

[*Turning to his followers.*

Miami, Delaware and Kickapoo!
Ye are alleged as signers of those deeds—
Those dark and treble treacheries of Fort Wayne.
Ye chiefs, whose cheeks are tanned with battle-smoke,
Stand forward, then, and answer if you did it!

KICKAPOO CHIEF. (*Rising.*) Not I! I disavow them! They were made
By village chiefs whose vanity o'ercame
Their judgment, and their duty to our race.

DELAWARE CHIEF. (*Rising.*) And I reject the treaties in the name
Of all our noted braves and warriors.
They have no weight save with the palsied heads
Which dote on friendly compacts in the past.

MIAMI CHIEF. (*Rising.*) And I renounce them also. They were signed
By sottish braves—the Long-Knife's tavern chiefs—
Who sell their honour like a pack of fur,
Make favour with the pale-face for his fee,
And caper with the hatchet for his sport.
I am a chief by right of blood, and fling
Your false and flimsy treaties in your face.
I am my nation's head, and own but one
As greater than myself, and he is here!

[*Pointing to* TECUMSEH.

TECUMSEH. You have your answer, and from those whose rights
Stand in your own admission. But from me—
The Shawanoe—the interloper here—
Take the full draught of meaning, and wash down
Their dry and bitter truths. Yes! from the South
My people came—fall'n from their wide estate
Where Altamaha's uncongealing springs
Kept a perpetual summer in their sight,
Sweet with magnolia blooms, and dropping balm,
And scented breath of orange and of pine.
And from the East the hunted Delawares came,
Flushed from their coverts and their native streams;
Your old allies, men ever true to you,
Who, resting after long and weary flight,
Are by your bands shot sitting on the ground.

HARRISON. Those men got ample payment for their land,
Full recompense, and just equivalent.

TECUMSEH. They flew from death to light upon it here!
And many a tribe comes pouring from the East,
Smitten with fire—their outraged women, maimed,

Screaming in horror o'er their murdered babes,
Whose sinless souls, slashed out by white men's swords,
Whimper in Heaven for revenge. O God!
'Tis thus the pale-face prays,. then cries "Amen";—
He clamours, and his Maker answers him,
Whilst our Great Spirit sleeps! Oh, no, no, no—
He does not sleep! He will avenge our wrongs!
That Christ the white men murdered, and thought dead—
Who, if He died for mankind, died for us—
He is alive, and looks from heaven on this!
Oh, we have seen your baseness and your guile;
Our eyes are opened and we know your ways!
No longer shall you hoax us with your pleas,
Or with the serpent's cunning wake distrust,
Range tribe 'gainst tribe—then shoot the remnant down,
And in the red man's empty cabin grin,
And shake with laughter o'er his desolate hearth.
No, we are one! the red men all are one
In colour as in love, in lands and fate!

HARRISON. Still, with the voice of wrath Tecumseh speaks,
And not with reason's tongue.

TECUMSEH. Oh, keep your reason!
It is a thief which steals away our lands.
Your reason is our deadly foe, and writes
The jeering epitaphs for our poor graves.
It is the lying maker of your books,
Wherein our people's vengeance is set down,
But not a word of crimes which led to it.
These are hushed up and hid, whilst all our deeds,
Even in self-defence, are marked as wrongs
Heaped on your blameless heads.
But to the point!
Just as our brother's Seventeen Council Fires
Unite for self-protection, so do we.
How can you blame us, since your own example
Is but our model and fair precedent?
The Long-Knife's craft has kept our tribes apart,

Nourished dissensions, raised distinctions up,
Forced us to injuries which, soon as done,
Are made your vile pretexts for bloody war.
But this is past. Our nations now are one—
Ready to rise in their imbanded strength.
You promised to restore our ravaged lands
On proof that they are ours—that proof is here,
And by the tongues of truth has answered you.
Redeem your sacred pledges, and no more
Our "leaden birds" will sing amongst your corn;
But love will shine on you, and startled peace
Will come again, and build by every hearth.
Refuse—and we shall strike you to the ground!
Pour flame and slaughter on your confines wide,
Till the charred earth, up to the cope of Heaven,
Reeks with the smoke of smouldering villages,
And steam of awful fires half quenched with blood.

TWANG. Did you ever hear the like? If I hed my shootin'-iron, darn me if I wouldn't draw a bead on that barkin' savage. The hungry devil gits under-holts on our Guvner every time.

SLAUGH. You bet! I reckon he'd better put a lump o' bacon in his mouth to keep his bilin' sap o' passion down.

BLOAT. That's mor'n I'd do. This is jest what we git for allowin' the skulkin' devils to live. I'd vittle 'em on lead pills if I was Guvner.

TWANG. That's so! Our civilizashun is jest this—we know what's what. If I hed *my* way—

HARRISON. Silence, you fools! If you provoke him here your blood be on your heads.

GERKIN. Right you air, Guvner! We'll close our dampers.

TECUMSEH. My brother's ears have heard. Where is his tongue?

HARRISON. My honest ears ache in default of reason.
Tecumseh is reputed wise, yet now
His fuming passions from his judgment fly,
Like roving steeds which gallop from the catch,

And kick the air, wasting in wantonness
More strength than in submission. His threats fall
On fearless ears. Knows he not of our force,
Which in the East swarms like mosquitoes here?
Our great Kentucky and Virginia fires?
Our mounted men and soldier-citizens?
These all have stings—let him beware of them!

TECUMSEH. Who does not know your vaunting citizens!
Well drilled in fraud and disciplined in crime;
But in aught else—as honour, justice, truth—
A rabble, and a base disordered herd.
We know them; and our nations, knit in one,
Will challenge them, should this, our last appeal,
Fall on unheeding ears. My brother, hearken!
East of Ohio you possess our lands,
Thrice greater than your needs, but west of it
We claim them all; then, let us make its flood
A common frontier, and a sacred stream
Of which our nations both may drink in peace.

HARRISON. Absurd! The treaties of Fort Wayne must stand.
Your village chiefs are heads of civil rule,
Whose powers you seek to centre in yourself,
Or vest in warriors whose trade is blood.
We bought from those, and from your peaceful men—
Your wiser brothers—who had faith in us.

TECUMSEH. Poor, ruined brothers, weaned from honest lives!

HARRISON. They knew our wisdom, and preferred to sell
Their cabins, fields, and wilds of unused lands
For rich reserves and ripe annuities.
As for your nations being one like ours—
'Tis false—else would they speak one common tongue.
Nay, more! your own traditions trace you here—
Widespread in lapse of ages through the land—
From o'er the mighty ocean of the West.
What better title have you than ourselves,

Who came from o'er the ocean of the East,
And meet with you on free and common ground?
Be reasonable, and let wisdom's words
Displace your passion, and give judgment vent.
Think more of bounty, and talk less of rights—
Our hands are full of gifts, our hearts of love.

TECUMSEH. My brother's love is like the trader's warmth—
O'er with the purchase. Oh, unhappy lives—
Our gifts which go for yours! Once we were strong.
Once all this mighty continent was ours,
And the Great Spirit made it for our use.
He knew no boundaries, so had we peace
In the vast shelter of His handiwork,
And, happy here, we cared not whence we came.
We brought no evils thence—no treasured hate,
No greed of gold, no quarrels over God;
And so our broils, to narrow issues joined,
Were soon composed, and touched the ground of peace.
Our very ailments, rising from the earth,
And not from any foul abuse in us,
Drew back, and let age ripen to death's hand.
Thus flowed our lives until your people came,
Till from the East our matchless misery came!
Since then our tale is crowded with your crimes,
With broken faith, with plunder of reserves—
The sacred remnants of our wide domain—
With tamp'rings, and delirious feasts of fire,
The fruit of your thrice-cursèd stills of death,
Which make our good men bad, our bad men worse,
Ay! blind them till they grope in open day,
And stumble into miserable graves.
Oh, it is piteous, for none will hear!
There is no hand to help, no heart to feel,
No tongue to plead for us in all your lànd.
But every hand aims death, and every heart,
Ulcered with hate, resents our presence here;
And every tongue cries for our children's land

To expiate their crime of being born.
Oh, we have ever yielded in the past,
But we shall yield no more! Those plains are ours!
Those forests are our birth-right and our home!
Let not the Long-Knife build one cabin there—
Or fire from it will spread to every roof,
To compass you, and light your souls to death!

HARRISON. Dreams he of closing up our empty plains?
Our mighty forests waiting for the axe?
Our mountain steeps engrailed with iron and gold?
There's no asylumed madness like to this!
Mankind shall have its wide possession here;
And these rough assets of a virgin world
Stand for its coming, and await its hand.
The poor of every land shall come to this,
Heart-full of sorrows, and shall lay them down.

LEFROY. (*Springing to his feet.*) The poor! What care your rich thieves for the poor?
Those graspers hate the poor, from whom they spring,
More deeply than they hate this injured race.
Much have they taken from it—let them now
Take this prediction, with the red man's curse!
The time will come when that dread power—the Poor—
Whom, in their greed and pride of wealth, they spurn—
Will rise on them, and tear them from their seats;
Drag all their vulgar splendours down, and pluck
Their shallow women from their lawless beds,
Yea, seize their puling and unhealthy babes,
And fling them as foul pavement to the streets.
In all the dreaming of the Universe
There is no darker vision of despairs!

1ST OFFICER. What man is this? 'Tis not an Indian.

HARRISON. Madman, you rave!—you know not what you say.

TECUMSEH. Master of guile, this axe should speak for him!

[*Drawing his hatchet as if to hurl it at* HARRISON.

2ND OFFICER. This man means mischief! Quick! Bring up the guard!

[GENERAL HARRISON *and officers draw their swords. The warriors spring to their feet and cluster about* TECUMSEH, *their eyes fixed intently upon* HARRISON, *who stands unmoved.* TWANG *and his friends disappear. The soldiers rush forward and take aim, but are ordered not to fire.*

END OF SECOND ACT.

ACT III.

SCENE FIRST.—VINCENNES.—A COUNCIL CHAMBER IN GENERAL HARRISON'S HOUSE.

Enter HARRISON *and five* COUNCILLORS.

HARRISON. Here are despatches from the President,
As well as letters from my trusted friends,
Whose tenor made me summon you to Council.
[*Placing papers on table.*
1ST COUNCILLOR. Why break good news so gently? Is it true
War is declared 'gainst England?
HARRISON. Would it were!
That war is still deferred. Our news is draff,
And void of spirit, since New England turns
A fresh cheek to the slap of Britain's palm.
Great God! I am amazed at such supineness.
Our trade prohibited, our men impressed,
Our flag insulted—still her people bend,
Amidst the ticking of their wooden clocks,
Bemused o'er small inventions. Out upon 't!
Such tame submission yokes not with my spirit,
And sends my southern blood into my cheeks,
As proxy for New England's sense of shame.
2ND COUNCILLOR. We all see, save New England, what to do;
But she has eyes for her one interest—
A war might sink it. So the way to war
Puzzles imagining.
HARRISON. There is a way
Which lies athwart the President's command.

The reinforcements asked for from Monroe
Are here at last, but with this strict injunction,
They must not be employed save in defence,
Or in a forced attack. [*Taking up a letter.*
Now, here is news,
Fresh from the South, of bold Tecumseh's work:
The Creeks and Seminolés have conjoined,
Which means a general union of the tribes,
And ravage of our Southern settlements.
Tecumseh's master hand is seen in this,
And these fresh tidings tally with his threats
Before he left Vincennes.

3RD COUNCILLOR. You had a close
Encounter with him here.

HARRISON. Not over close,
Nor dangerous—I saw he would not strike.
His thoughts outran his threats, and looked beyond
To wider fields and trials of our strength.

4TH COUNCILLOR. Our tree is now too bulky for his axe.

HARRISON. Don't underrate his power! But for our States
This man would found an empire to surpass
Old Mexico's renown, or rich Peru.
Allied with England, he is to be feared
More than all other men.

1ST COUNCILLOR. You had some talk
In private, ere he vanished to the South?

HARRISON. Mere words, yet ominous. Could we restore
Our purchases, and make a treaty line,
All might be well; but who would stand to it?

2ND COUNCILLOR. It is not to be thought of.

OTHER COUNCILLORS. No, no, no.

HARRISON. In further parley at the river's edge,
Scenting a coming war, he clapped his hands,
And said the English whooped his people on,
As if his braves were hounds to spring at us;
Compared our nation to a whelming flood,

And called his scheme a dam to keep it back—
Then proffered the old terms; whereat I urged
A peaceful mission to the President.
But, by apt questions, gleaning my opinion,
Ere I was ware, of such a bootless trip,
He drew his manly figure up, then smiled,
And said our President might drink his wine
In safety in his distant town, whilst we—
Over the mountains here—should fight it out;
Then entering his bark, well manned with braves,
Bade me let matters rest till he returned
From his far mission to the distant tribes,
Waved an adieu, and in a trice was gone.

2ND COUNCILLOR. Your news is but an earnest of his work.

4TH COUNCILLOR. This Chief's despatch should be our own example.
Let matters rest, forsooth, till he can set
Our frontier in a blaze! Such cheap advice
Pulls with the President's, not mine.

HARRISON. Nor mine!
The sum of my advice is to attack
The Prophet ere Tecumseh can return.

5TH COUNCILLOR. But what about the breach of your instructions?

HARRISON. If we succeed we need not fear the breach—
In the same space we give and heal the wound.

Enter a Messenger, who hands letters to HARRISON.

Thank you, Missouri and good Illinois—
Your governors are built of western clay.
Howard and Edwards both incline with me,
And urge attack upon the Prophet's force.
This is the nucleus of Tecumseh's strength—
His bold scheme's very heart. Let's cut it out!

1ST COUNCILLOR. Yes! yes! and every other part will fail.

2ND COUNCILLOR. Let us prepare to go at once!

3RD COUNCILLOR. Agreed.
4TH COUNCILLOR. I vote for it.
5TH COUNCILLOR. But should the Prophet win?
4TH COUNCILLOR. Why, then, the Prophet, not Tecumseh, kills us—
Which has the keener axe?
1ST COUNCILLOR. Breech-clouted dogs!
Let us attack them, and, with thongs of fire,
Whip their red bodies to a deeper red.
HARRISON. This feeling bodes success, and with success
Comes war with England; for a well-won fight
Will rouse a martial spirit in the land
To emulate our deeds on higher ground.
Now hasten to your duties and prepare!
Bronzed autumn comes, when copper-coloured oaks
Drop miserly their stiff leaves to the earth;
And ere the winter's snow doth silver them,
Our triumph must be wrought.

[*Exeunt.*

SCENE SECOND.—TECUMSEH'S CABIN IN THE PROPHET'S TOWN.

Enter IENA *and* MAMATEE, *agitated.*

IENA. My heart is sad, and I am faint with fear.
My friend, my more than mother, go again—
Plead with the Prophet for a single day!
Perchance within his gloomy heart will stir
Some sudden pulse of pity for a girl.
MAMATEE. Alas, my Iena, it is in vain!
He swore by Manitou this very morn,
That thou shouldst wed the chief, Tarhay, to-night.
IENA. Nay, try once more, oh, Mamatee, once more!
I had a dream, and heard the gusty breeze
Hurtle from out a sea of hissing pines,
Then dwindle into voices, faint and sweet,
Which cried—we come! It was my love and yours!

They spoke to me—I know that they are near,
And waft their love to us upon the wind.

MAMATEE. Some dreams are merely fancies in our sleep;
I'll make another trial, but I feel
Your only safety is in instant flight.

IENA. Flight! Where and how—beset by enemies?
My fear sits like the partridge in the tree,
And cannot fly whilst these dogs bark at me.

SCENE THIRD.—AN ELEVATED PLATEAU, DOTTED WITH HEAVY OAKS, WEST OF THE PROPHET'S TOWN.

Enter three of HARRISON'S *staff Officers.*

1ST OFFICER. Well, here's the end of all our northward marching!

2ND OFFICER. A peaceful end, if we can trust those chiefs
Who parleyed with us lately.

3RD OFFICER. Yes, for if
They mean to fight, why point us to a spot
At once so strong and pleasant for our camp?

1ST OFFICER. Report it so unto our General.

[*Exit* 3RD OFFICER.

'Tis worth our long march through the forest wild
To view these silent plains! The Prophet's Town,
Sequestered yonder like a hermitage,
Disturbs not either's vast of solitude,
But rather gives, like graveyard visitors,
To deepest loneliness a deeper awe.

Re-enter 3RD OFFICER.

3RD OFFICER. I need not go, for Harrison is here.

Enter GENERAL HARRISON, *his force following.*

1ST OFFICER. Methinks you like the place; some thanks we owe

Unto the Prophet's chiefs for good advice.

HARRISON. (*Looking around keenly.*) These noble oaks, the streamlet to our rear,
This rank wild grass—wood, water and soft beds!
The soldier's luxuries are here together.

1ST OFFICER. Note, too, the place o'erlooks the springy plain
Which lies betwixt us and the Prophet's Town.
I think, sir, 'tis a very fitting place.

HARRISON. A fitting place if white men were our foes;
But to the red it gives a clear advantage.
Sleep like the weasel here, if you are wise!

1ST OFFICER. Why, sir, their chiefs, so menacing at first,
Became quite friendly at the last. They fear
A battle, and will treat on any terms.
The Prophet's tide of strength will ebb away,
And leave his stranded bark upon the mire.

HARRISON. 'Tis the mixed craft of old dissembling Nature!
If I could look upon her smallest web,
And see in it but crossed and harmless hairs,
Then might I trust the Prophet's knotted seine.
I did not like the manner of those chiefs
Who spoke so fairly. What but highest greatness
Plucks hatred from its seat, and in its stead
Plants friendship in an instant? This our camp
Is badly placed; each coulee and ravine
Is dangerous cover for approach by night;
And all the circuit of the spongy plain
A treacherous bog to mire our cavalry.
They who directed us so warmly here
Had other than our comfort in their eye.

2ND OFFICER. Fear you a night-attack, sir?

HARRISON. Fear it! No!
I but anticipate, and shall prepare.
'Tis sunset, and too late for better choice,
Else were the Prophet welcome to his ground.
Pitch tents and draw our baggage to the centre;

Girdle the camp with lynx-eyed sentinels;
Detail strong guards of choice and wakeful men
As pickets in advance of all our lines;
Place mounted riflemen on both our flanks;
Our cavalry take post in front and rear,
But still within the lines of infantry,
Which, struck at any point, must hold the ground
Until relieved. Cover your rifle pans—
The thick clouds threaten rain. I look to you
To fill these simple orders to the letter.
But stay! Let all our camp-fires burn
Till, if attacked, we form—then drown them out.
The darkness falls—make disposition straight;
Then, all who can, to sleep upon their arms.
I fear me, ere night yields to morning pale,
The warriors' yell will sound our wild reveille.

SCENE FOURTH.—Tecumseh's Cabin.

Enter Iena.

Iena. 'Tis night, and Mamatee is absent still!
Why should this sorrow weigh upon my heart,
And other lonely things on earth have rest?
Oh, could I be with them! The lily shone
All day upon the stream, and now it sleeps
Under the wave in peace—in cradle soft
Which sorrow soon may fashion for my grave.
Ye shadows which do creep into my thoughts—
Ye curtains of despair! what is my fault,
That ye should hide the happy earth from me?
Once I had joy of it, when tender Spring,
Mother of beauty, hid me in her leaves;
When Summer led me by the shores of song,
And forests and far-sounding cataracts
Melted my soul with music. I have heard
The rough chill harpings of dismantled woods,
When Fall had stripped them, and have felt a joy

Deeper than ear could lend unto the heart;
And when the Winter from his mountains wild
Looked down on death, and, in the frosty sky,
The very stars seemed hung with icicles,
Then came a sense of beauty calm and cold,
That weaned me from myself, yet knit me still
With kindred bonds to Nature. All is past,
And he who won from me such love for him,
And he, my valiant uncle and my friend,
Come not to lift the cloud that drapes my soul,
And shield me from the fiendish Prophet's power.

Enter MAMATEE.

Give me his answer in his very words!
MAMATEE. There is a black storm raging in his mind—
His eye darts lightning like the angry cloud
Which hangs in woven darkness o'er the earth.
Brief is his answer—you must go to him.
The Long-Knife's camp-fires gleam among the oaks
Which dot yon western hill. A thousand men
Are sleeping there cajoled to fatal dreams
By promises the Prophet breaks to night.
Hark! 'tis the war-song!
IENA. Dares the Prophet now
Betray Tecumseh's trust, and break his faith?
MAMATEE. He dares do anything will feed ambition.
His dancing braves are frenzied by his tongue,
Which prophesies revenge and victory.
Before the break of day he will surprise
The Long-Knife's camp, and hang our people's fate
Upon a single onset.
IENA. Should he fail?
MAMATEE. Then all will fail;—Tecumseh's scheme will fail.
IENA. It shall not! Let us go to him at once!
MAMATEE. And risk your life?
IENA. Risk hovers everywhere
When night and man combine for darksome deeds.

I'll go to him, and argue on my knees—
Yea, yield my hand—would I could give my heart!
To stay his purpose and this act of ruin.

MAMATEE. He is not in the mood for argument.
Rash girl! they die who would oppose him now.

IENA. Such death were sweet as life—I go! But, first—
Great Spirit! I commit my soul to Thee.

[*Kneels.*

SCENE FIFTH—AN OPEN SPACE IN THE FOREST NEAR THE PROPHET'S TOWN. A FIRE OF BILLETS BURNING. WAR-CRIES ARE HEARD FROM THE TOWN.

Enter the PROPHET.

PROPHET. My spells do work apace! Shout yourselves hoarse,
Ye howling ministers by whom I climb!
For this I've wrought until my weary tongue,
Blistered with incantation, flags in speech,
And half declines its office. Every brave,
Inflamed by charms and oracles, is now
A vengeful serpent, who will glide ere morn
To sting the Long-Knife's sleeping camp to death.
Why should I hesitate? My promises!
My duty to Tecumseh! What are these
Compared with duty here? Where I perceive
A near advantage, there my duty lies;
Consideration strong which overweighs
All other reason. Here is Harrison—
Trapanned to dangerous lodgment for the night—
Each deep ravine which grooves the prairie's breast
A channel of approach; each winding creek
A screen for creeping death. Revenge is sick
To think of such advantage flung aside.
For what? To let Tecumseh's greatness grow,
Who gathers his rich harvest of renown
Out of the very fields that I have sown!

By Manitou, I will endure no more!
Nor, in the rising flood of our affairs,
Fish like an osprey for this eagle longer.

But, soft!

It is the midnight hour when comes
Tarhay to claim his bride, (*calls*) Tarhay! Tarhay!

Enter TARHAY *with several braves.*

TARHAY. Tarhay is here!
PROPHET. The Long-Knives die to-night.
The spirits which do minister to me
Have breathed this utterance within my ear.
You know my sacred office cuts me off
From the immediate leadership in fight.
My nobler work is in the spirit-world,
And thence come promises which make us strong.
Near to the foe I'll keep the Magic Bowl,
Whilst you, Tarhay, shall lead our warriors on.
TARHAY. I'll lead them; they are wild with eagerness.
But fill my cold and empty cabin first
With light and heat! You know I love your niece,
And have the promise of her hand to-night.
PROPHET. She shall be yours! (*To the braves.*)
Go bring her here at once—
But, look! Fulfilment of my promise comes
In her own person.

Enter IENA *and* MAMATEE.

Welcome, my sweet niece!
You have forestalled my message by these braves,
And come unbidden to your wedding place.
IENA. Uncle! you know my heart is far away—
PROPHET. But still your hand is here! this little hand!
(*Pulling her forward.*)
IENA. Dare you enforce a weak and helpless girl,
Who thought to move you by her misery?
Stand back! I have a message for you too.

What means the war-like song, the dance of braves,
And bustle in our town?
  PROPHET.   It means that we
Attack the foe to-night.
  IENA.   And risk our all?
O that Tecumseh knew! his soul would rush
In arms to intercept you. What! break faith,
And on the hazard of a doubtful strife
Stake his great enterprise and all our lives!
The dying curses of a ruined race
Will wither up your wicked heart for this!
  PROPHET. False girl! your heart is with our foes;
Your hand I mean to turn to better use.
  IENA. Oh, could it turn you from your mad intent
How freely would I give it! Drop this scheme,
Dismiss your frenzied warriors to their beds;
And, if contented with my hand, Tarhay
Can have it here.
  TARHAY.   I love you, Iena!
  IENA. Then must you love what I do! Love our race!
'Tis this love nerves Tecumseh to unite
Its scattered tribes—his fruit of noble toil,
Which you would snatch unripened from his hand
And feed to sour ambition. Touch it not—
Oh, touch it not, Tarhay! and though my heart
Breaks for it, I am yours.
  PROPHET.   His anyway,
Or I am not the Prophet!
  TARHAY.   For my part
I have no leaning to this rash attempt,
Since Iena consents to be my wife.
  PROPHET. Shall I be thwarted by a yearning fool!
(*Aside.*)
This soft, sleek girl, to outward seeming good,
I know to be a very fiend beneath—
Whose sly affections centre on herself,
And feed the gliding snake within her heart.

TARHAY. I cannot think her so—
MAMATEE. She is not so!
There is the snake that creeps among our race,
Whose venomed fangs would bite into our lives,
And poison all our hopes.
PROPHET. She is the head—
The very neck of danger to me here,
Which I must break at once! (*Aside.*) Tarhay—attend!
I can see dreadful visions in the air;
I can dream awful dreams of life and fate;
I can bring darkness on the heavy earth;
I can fetch shadows from our fathers' graves,
And spectres from the sepulchres of hell.
Who dares dispute with me disputes with death!
Dost hear, Tarhay?
[TARHAY *and braves cower before the* PROPHET.
TARHAY. I hear, and will obey.
Spare me! Spare me!
PROPHET. As for this foolish girl,
The hand she offers you on one condition,
I give to you upon a better one;
And, since she has no mind to give her heart—
Which, rest assured, is in her body still—
There,—take it at my hands!
(*Flings* IENA *violently toward* TARHAY, *into whose arms she falls fainting, and is then borne away by* MAMATEE.)
(*To* TARHAY.) Go bring the braves to view the Mystic Torch
And belt of Sacred Beans grown from my flesh—
One touch of it makes them invulnerable—
Then creep, like stealthy panthers, on the foe!

SCENE SIXTH.—MORNING. THE FIELD OF TIPPECANOE AFTER THE BATTLE. THE GROUND STREWN WITH DEAD SOLDIERS AND WARRIORS.

Enter HARRISON, *Officers and Soldiers and* BARRON.

HARRISON. A costly triumph, reckoned by our slain!
Look how some lie still clenched with savages
In all-embracing death, their bloody hands
Glued in each other's hair! Make burial straight
Of all alike in deep and common graves:
Their quarrel now is ended.

1ST OFFICER. I have heard
The red man fears our steel—'twas not so here!
From the first shots, which drove our pickets in,
Till daylight dawned, they rushed upon our lines,
And flung themselves upon our bayonet points
In frenzied recklessness of bravery.

BARRON. They trusted in the Prophet's rites and spells,
Which promised them immunity from death.
All night he sat on yon safe eminence,
Howling his songs of war and mystery,
Then fled, at dawn, in fear of his own braves.

Enter an AIDE.

HARRISON. What tidings bring you from the Prophet's Town?

AIDE. The wretched women with their children flee
To distant forests for concealment. In
Their village is no living thing save mice
Which scampered as we oped each cabin door.
Their pots still simmered on the vacant hearths,
Standing in dusty silence and desertion.
Naught else we saw, save that their granaries
Were crammed with needful corn.

HARRISON. Go bring it all—
Then burn their village down!

[*Exit* AIDE.

2ND OFFICER. This victory
Will shake Tecumseh's project to the base.
Were I the Prophet I should drown myself
Rather than meet him.
BARRON. We have news of him—
Our scouts report him near in heavy force.
HARRISON. 'Twill melt, or draw across the British line,
And wait for war. But double the night watch,
Lest he should strike, and give an instant care
To all our wounded men : to-morrow's sun
Must light us on our backward march for home.
Thence Rumor's tongue will spread so proud a story
New England will grow envious of our glory ;
And, greedy for renown so long abhorred,
Will on old England draw the tardy sword !

SCENE SEVENTH.—THE RUINS OF THE PROPHET'S TOWN.

Enter the PROPHET, *who gloomily surveys the place.*

PROPHET. Our people scattered, and our town in ashes !
To think these hands could work such madness here—
This envious head devise this misery !
Tecumseh, had not my ambition drawn
Such sharp and fell destruction on our race,
You might have smiled at me ! for I have matched
My cunning 'gainst your wisdom, and have dragged
Myself and all into a sea of ruin.

Enter TECUMSEH.

TECUMSEH. Devil ! I have discovered you at last !
You sum of treacheries, whose wolfish fangs
Have torn our people's flesh—you shall not live !
(*The* PROPHET *retreats, facing and followed by* TECUMSEH.)
PROPHET. Nay—strike me not ! I can explain it all !
It was a woman touched the Magic Bowl,
And broke the brooding spell.

TECUMSEH. Impostor ! Slave !
Why should I spare you ?
[*Lifts his hand as if to strike.*
PROPHET. Stay, stay, touch me not !
One mother bore us in the self-same hour.
TECUMSEH. Then good and evil came to light together.
Go to the corn-dance, change your name to villain !
Away ! Your presence tempts my soul to mischief.
[*Exit the* PROPHET.
Would that I were a woman, and could weep,
And slake hot rage with tears ! O spiteful fortune,
To lure me to the limit of my dreams,
Then turn and crowd the ruin of my toil
Into the narrow compass of a night.
My brother's deep disgrace—myself the scorn
Of envious harriers and thieves of fame,
Oh, I could bear it all ! But to behold
Our ruined people hunted to their graves—
To see the Long-Knife triumph in their shame—
This is the burning shaft, the poisoned wound
That rankles in my soul ! But why despair ?
All is not lost—the English are our friends.
My spirit rises—Manhood, bear me up !
I'll haste to Malden, join my force to theirs,
And fall with double fury on our foes.
Farewell, ye plains and forests, but rejoice !
Ye yet shall echo to Tecumseh's voice.

Enter LEFROY.

LEFROY. What tidings have you gleaned of Iena ?
TECUMSEH. My brother meant to wed her to Tarhay—
The chief who led his warriors to ruin ;
But, in the gloom and tumult of the night,
She fled into the forest all alone !
LEFROY. Alone ! In the wide forest all alone !
Angels are with her now, for she is dead.
TECUMSEH. You know her to be skilful with the bow.
'Tis certain she would strike for some great lake—

Erie or Michigan. At the Detroit
Are people of our nation, and perchance
She fled for shelter there. I go at once
To join the British force.

[*Exit* TECUMSEH.

LEFROY. But yesterday
I climbed to Heaven upon the shining stairs
Of love and hope, and here am quite cast down.
My little flower amidst a weedy world,
Where art thou now? In deepest forest shade?
Or onward, where the sumach stands arrayed
In autumn splendour, its alluring form
Fruited, yet odious with the hidden worm?
Or, farther, by some still sequestered lake,
Loon-haunted, where the sinewy panthers slake
Their noon-day thirst, and never voice is heard,
Joyous of singing waters, breeze or bird,
Save their wild wailings. (*A halloo without.*) 'Tis Tecumseh calls!
Oh, Iena! If dead, where'er thou art—
Thy saddest grave will be this ruined heart! [*Exit.*

END OF THIRD ACT.

ACT IV.

Enter CHORUS.

War is declared, unnatural and wild,
By Revolution's calculating sons!
So leave the home of mercenary minds,
And wing with me, in your uplifted thoughts,
Away to our unyielding Canada!
There to behold the Genius of the Land,
Beneath her singing pine and sugared tree,
Companioned with the lion, Loyalty.

SCENE FIRST.—A ROOM IN FORT GEORGE.

Enter GENERAL BROCK *reading a despatch from Montreal.*

BROCK. Prudent and politic Sir George Prevost!
Hull's threatened ravage of our western coast
Hath more breviloquence than your despatch.
Storms are not stilled by reasoning with air,
Nor fires quenched by a syrup of sweet words.
So to the wars, Diplomacy, for now
Our trust is in our arms and arguments
Delivered only from the cannon's mouth!

[*Rings.*

Enter an ORDERLY.

ORDERLY. Your Exc'llency?
BROCK. Bid Colonel Proctor come!

[*Exit* ORDERLY.

Now might the head of gray Experience
Shake o'er the problems that surround us here.

I am no stranger to the brunt of war,
But all the odds so lean against our side
That valour's self might tremble for the issue.
Could England stretch its full assisting hand
Then might I smile though velvet-footed Time
Struck all his claws at once into our flesh;
But England, noble England, fights for life,
Couching the knightly lance for liberty
'Gainst a new dragon that affrights the world.
And, now, how many noisome elements
Would plant their greed athwart this country's good!
How many demagogues bewray its cause!
How many aliens urge it to surrender!
Our present good must match their present ill,
And, on our frontiers, boldest deeds in war
Dismay the foe, and strip the loins of faction.

Enter COLONEL PROCTOR.

Time waits not our conveniency; I trust
Your preparations have no further needs.
PROCTOR. All is in readiness, and I can leave
For Amherstburg at once.
BROCK. Then tarry not,
For time is precious to us now as powder.
You understand my wishes and commands?
PROCTOR. I know them and shall match them with obedience.
BROCK. Rest not within the limit of instructions
If you can better them, for they should bind
The feeble only; able men enlarge
And shape them to their needs. Much must be done
That lies in your discretion. At Detroit
Hull vaunts his strength, and meditates invasion,
And loyalty, unarmed, defenceless, bare,
May let this boaster light upon our shores
Without one manly motion of resistance.
So whilst I open Parliament at York,

Close it again, and knit our volunteers,
Be yours the task to head invasion off.
Act boldly, but discreetly, and so draw
Our interest to the balance, that affairs
May hang in something like an even scale,
Till I can join you with a fitting force,
And batter this old Hull until he sinks.
So fare-you-well—success attend your mission!

PROCTOR. Farewell, sir! I shall do my best in this,
And put my judgment to a prudent use
In furtherance of all.

[*Exit* PROCTOR.

BROCK. Prudent he will be—'tis a vice in him.
For in the qualities of every mind
There's one o'ergrows, and prudence in this man
Tops all the rest. 'Twill suit our present needs.
But, boldness, go with me! for, if I know
My nature well, I shall do something soon
Whose consequence will make the nation cheer,
Or hiss me to my grave.

Re-enter ORDERLY.

ORDERLY. Your Exc'llency,
Some settlers wait without.

BROCK. Whence do they come?

Enter COLONEL MACDONELL.

ORDERLY. From the raw clearings of Lake Erie, sir.

BROCK. Go bring them here at once. (*Exit* ORDERLY.)
The very men
Who meanly shirk their service to the Crown!
A breach of duty to be remedied;
For disaffection like an ulcer spreads
Until the caustic ointment of the law,
Sternly applied, eats up and stays corruption.

Enter DEPUTATION OF YANKEE SETTLERS.

Good morrow, worthy friends; I trust you bear
Good hopes in loyal hearts for Canada.

1ST SETTLER. That kind o' crop's a failure in our county.
Gen'ral, we came to talk about this war
With the United States. It ain't quite fair
To call out settlers from the other side.

BROCK. From it yet on it too! Why came you thence?
Is land so scarce in the United States?
Are there no empty townships, wilds or wastes
In all their borders but you must encroach
On ours? And, being here, how dare you make
Your dwelling-places harbours of sedition,
And furrow British soil with alien ploughs
To feed our enemies? There is not scope,
Not room enough in all this wilderness
For men so base.

2ND SETTLER. Why, General, we thought
You wanted settlers here.

BROCK. Settlers indeed!
But with the soldier's courage to defend
The land of their adoption. This attack
On Canada is foul and unprovoked;
The hearts are vile, the hands are traitorous,
That will not help to hurl invasion back.
Beware the lariat of the law! 'Tis thrown
With aim so true in Canada it brings
Sedition to the ground at every cast.

1ST SETTLER. Well, General, we're not your British sort,
But if we were we know that Canada
Is naught compared with the United States.
We have no faith in her, but much in them.

BROCK. You have no faith! Then take a creed from me!
For I believe in Britain's Empire, and
In Canada, its true and loyal son,
Who yet shall rise to greatness, and shall stand

At England's shoulder helping her to guard
True liberty throughout a faithless world.
Here is a creed for arsenals and camps,
For hearts and heads that seek their country's good;
So, go at once, and meditate on it!
I have no time to parley with you now—
But think on this as well! that traitors, spies,
And aliens who refuse to take up arms,
Forfeit their holdings, and must leave this land,
Or dangle nearer Heaven than they wish.
So to your homes, and ponder your condition.

[*Exeunt Settlers ruefully.*

This foreign element will hamper us.
Its alien spirit ever longs for change,
And union with the States.

MACDONELL. O fear it not,
Nor magnify the girth of noisy men!
Their name is faction, and their numbers few.
While everywhere encompassing them stands
The silent element that doth not change;
That points with steady finger to the Crown—
True as the needle to the viewless pole,
And stable as its star!

BROCK. I know it well,
And trust to it alone for earnestness,
Accordant counsels, loyalty and faith.
But give me these—and let the Yankees come!
With our poor handful of inhabitants
We can defend our forest wilderness,
And spurn the bold invader from our shores.

Re-enter ORDERLY.

ORDERLY. Your boat is ready, sir!

BROCK. Man it at once—
I shall forthwith to York.

[*Exeunt.*

SCENE SECOND.—YORK, THE CAPITAL OF UPPER CANADA. THE SPACE IN FRONT OF OLD GOVERNMENT HOUSE.

Enter two U. E. LOYALISTS, *separately.*

1ST U. E. LOYALIST. Well met, my friend! A stirrer like myself.
2ND U. E. LOYALIST. Yes, affairs make me so. Such stirring times
Since Brock returned and opened Parliament!
Read you his speech?
1ST U. E. LOYALIST. That from the Throne?
2ND U. E. LOYALIST. Ay, that!
1ST U. E. LOYALIST. You need not ask, since 'tis on every tongue,
Unstaled by repetition. I affirm
Words never showered upon more fruitful soil
To nourish valour's growth.
2ND U. E. LOYALIST. That final phrase—
Oh, it struck home: a sentence to be framed
And hung in every honourable heart
For daily meditation.

"*We are engaged in an awful and eventful contest. By unanimity and despatch in our councils, and by vigour in our operations, we may teach the enemy this lesson, that a country defended by free men, enthusiastically devoted to the cause of their king and constitution, can never be conquered.*"

1ST U. E. LOYALIST. That reaches far; a text to fortify
Imperial doctrine and Canadian rights.
Sedition skulks, and feels its blood a-cold,
Since first it fell upon the public ear.
2ND U. E. LOYALIST. There is a magic in this soldier's tongue.
Oh, language is a common instrument;
But when a master touches it—what sounds!

1ST U. E. LOYALIST. What sounds indeed! But Brock can use his sword
Still better than his tongue. Our state affairs,
Conned and digested by his eager mind,
Draw into form, and even now his voice
Cries, Forward! To the Front!

2ND U. E. LOYALIST. Look—here he comes!

1ST U. E. LOYALIST. There's matter in the wind; let's draw-a-near.

Enter GENERAL BROCK, *accompanied by* MACDONELL, NICHOL, ROBINSON *and other Canadian Officers and friends conversing.*

BROCK. 'Tis true our Province faces heavy odds:
Of regulars but fifteen hundred men
To guard a frontier of a thousand miles;
Of volunteers what aidance we can draw
From seventy thousand widely scattered souls.
A meagre showing 'gainst the enemy's
If numbers be the test. But odds lie not
In numbers only, but in spirit too—
Witness the might of England's little isle!
And what made England great will keep her so—
The free soul and the valour of her sons;
And what exalts her will sustain you now
If you contain her courage and her faith.
So not the odds so much are to be feared
As private disaffection, treachery—
Those openers of the door to enemies—
And the poor crouching spirit that gives way
Ere it is forced to yield.

ROBINSON. No fear of that!

BROCK. I trust there is not: yet I speak of it
As what is to be feared more than the odds.
For like to forests are communities—
Fair at a distance, entering you find
The rubbish and the underbrush of states.

'Tis ever the mean soul that counts the odds,
And, where you find this spirit, pluck it up—
'Tis full of mischief.
MACDONELL. It is almost dead.
England's vast war, our weakness, and the eagle
Whetting his beak at Sandwich, with one claw
Already in our side, put thought to steep
In cold conjecture for a time, and gave
A text to alien tongues. But, since you came,
Depression turns to smiling, and men see
That dangers well opposed may be subdued
Which, shunned, would overwhelm us.
BROCK. Hold to this!
For since the storm has struck us we must face it.
What is our present count of volunteers?
NICHOL. More than you called for have assembled, sir—
The flower of York and Lincoln.
BROCK. Some will go
To guard our frontier at Niagara,
Which must be strengthened even at the cost
Of York itself. The rest to the Detroit,
Where, with Tecumseh's force, our regulars,
And Kent and Essex loyal volunteers,
We'll give this Hull a taste of steel so cold
His teeth will chatter at it, and his scheme
Of easy conquest vanish into air.

Enter a Company of Militia with their Officers, unarmed. They salute, march across the stage, and make their exit.

What men are those? Their faces are familiar.
ROBINSON. Some farmers whom you furloughed at Fort George,
To tend their fields, which still they leave half reaped
To meet invasion.
BROCK. I remember it!
The jarring needs of harvest-time and war,
'Twixt whose necessities grave hazards lay.

ROBINSON. They only thought to save their children's bread,
And then return to battle with light hearts.
For, though their hard necessities o'erpoised
Their duty for the moment, they are men
Who draw their pith from loyal roots, their sires,
Dug up by revolution, and cast out
To hovel in the bitter wilderness,
And wring, with many a tussle, from the wolf
Those very fields which cry for harvesters.
BROCK. Oh, I observed them closely at Fort George—
Red-hot for action in their summer-sleeves,
And others drilling in their naked feet—
Our poor equipment (which disgraced us there)
Too scanty to go round. See they get arms,
An ample outfit and good quarters too.
NICHOL. They shall be well provided for in all.

Enter COLONELS BABY* *and* ELLIOTT.

BROCK. Good morning both; what news from home, Baby?
BABY. None, none, your Exc'llency—whereat we fear
This Hull is in our rear at Amherstburg.
BROCK. Not yet; what I unsealed last night reports
Tecumseh to have foiled the enemy
In two encounters at the Canard bridge.
A noble fellow, as I hear, humane,
Lofty and bold, and rooted in our cause.
BABY. I know him well; a chief of matchless force.
If Mackinaw should fall—that triple key
To inland seas and teeming wilderness—
The bravest in the West will flock to him.
BROCK. 'Twere well he had an inkling of affairs.
My letter says he chafes at my delay—
Not mine, but thine, thou dull and fatuous House—

* Pronounced Baw-bée.

Which, in a period that whips delay,
When men should spur themselves and flash in action,
Letst idly leak the unpurchasable hours
From our scant measure of most precious time!

BABY. 'Tis true, your Exc'llency, some cankered minds
Have been a daily hindrance in our House.
No measure so essential, bill so fair,
But they would foul it by some cunning clause,
Wrenching the needed statute from its aim
By sly injection of their false opinion.
But this you cannot charge to us whose hearts
Are faithful to our trust; nor yet delay;
For, Exc'llency, you hurry on so fast
That other men wheeze after, out of breath,
And haste itself, disparaged, lags behind.

BROCK. Friends, pardon me, you stand not in reproof.
But haste, the evil of the age in peace,
Is war's auxiliary, confederate
With Time himself in urgent great affairs.
So must we match it with the flying hours!
I shall prorogue this tardy Parliament,
And promptly head our forces for Detroit.
Meanwhile, I wish you, in advance of us,
To speed unto your homes. Spread everywhere
Throughout the West broad tidings of our coming,
Which, by the counter currents of reaction,
Will tell against our foes and for our friends.
As for the rest, such loyal men as you
Need not our counsel; so, good journey both!

BABY. We shall not spare our transport or ourselves.

Enter a travel-stained MESSENGER.

ELLIOTT. Good-bye.

BABY. Tarry a moment, Elliott!
Here comes a messenger—let's have his news.

MESSENGER. It is his Excellency whom I seek.
I come, sir, with despatches from the West.

BROCK. Tidings, I trust, to strengthen all our hopes.

MESSENGER. News of grave interest, this not the worst.
[*Handing a letter to* GENERAL BROCK.

BROCK. No, by my soul, for Mackinaw is ours!
That vaunted fort, whose gallant capture frees
Our red allies. This is important news!
What of Detroit?

MESSENGER. Things vary little there.
Hull's soldiers scour our helpless settlements,
Our aliens join them, but the loyal mass—
Sullen, yet overawed—longs for relief.

BROCK. I hope to better this anon. You, sirs,
(*To his aides.*)
Come with me; here is matter to despatch
At once to Montreal. Farewell, my friends.
(*To* BABY *and* ELLIOTT.)

BABY. We feel now what will follow this, farewell!
[*Exeunt* BABY, ELLIOTT *and* MESSENGER.

BROCK. Now, gentlemen, prepare against our needs,
That no neglect may check us at the start,
Or mar our swift advance. And, for our cause,
As we believe it just in sight of God,
So should it triumph in the sight of man,
Whose generous temper, at the first, assigns
Right to the weaker side, yet coldly draws
Damning conclusions from its failure. Now
Betake you to your tasks with double zeal;
And, meanwhile, let our joyful tidings spread!
[*Exeunt.*

SCENE THIRD.—THE SAME.

Enter two OLD MEN *of York, separately.*

1ST OLD MAN. Good morrow, friend! a fair and fitting time
To take our airing, and to say farewell.
'Tis here, I think, we bid our friends God-speed,
A waftage, peradventure, to their graves.

2ND OLD MAN. 'Tis a good cause they die for, if they fall.
By this gray pate, if I were young again,
I would no better journey. Young again!
This hubbub sets old pulses on the bound
As I were in my teens.

Enter a CITIZEN.

What news afoot?

CITIZEN. Why everyone's afoot and coming here.
York's citizens are turned to warriors,
And gentle hearts beat high for Canada!
For, as you pass, on every hand you see,
Through the neglected openings of each house—
Through doorways, windows—our Canadian maids
Strained by their parting lovers to their breasts;
And loyal matrons busy round their lords,
Buckling their arms on, or, with tearful eyes,
Kissing them to the war!

1ST OLD MAN. The volunteers
Will pass this way?

CITIZEN. Yes, to the beach, and there
Embark for Burlington, whence they will march
To Long Point, taking open boats again
To plough the shallow Erie's treacherous flood.
Such leaky craft as farmers market with:
Rare bottoms, one sou-wester-driven wave
Would heave against Lake Erie's wall of shore,
And dash to fragments. 'Tis an awful hazard—
A danger which in apprehension lies,
Yet palpable unto the spirit's touch
As earth to finger.

1ST OLD MAN. Let us hope a calm
May lull this fretful and ill tempered lake
Whilst they ascend.

[*Military music is heard.*

CITIZEN. Hark! here our soldiers come.

Enter GENERAL BROCK, *with his aides*, MACDONELL *and* GLEGG, NICHOL, *and other Officers, followed by the Volunteers in companies. A concourse of Citizens.*

MACDONELL. Our fellows show the mark of training, sir,
And many, well-in-hand, yet full of fire,
Are burning for distinction.
BROCK. This is good:
Love of distinction is the fruitful soil
From which brave actions spring; and, superposed
On love of country, these strike deeper root,
And grow to greater greatness. Cry a halt—
A word here—then away!
[*Flourish. The volunteers halt, form line, and order arms.*
Ye men of Canada!
Subjects with me of that Imperial Power
Whose liberties are marching round the earth:
I need not urge you now to follow me,
Though what befalls will try your stubborn faith
In the fierce fire and crucible of war.
I need not urge you, who have heard the voice
Of loyalty, and answered to its call.
Who has not read the insults of the foe—
The manifesto of his purposed crimes?
That foe, whose poison-plant, false liberty,
Runs o'er his body politic and kills
Whilst seeming to adorn it, fronts us now!
Threats our poor Province to annihilate,
And should he find the red men by our side—
Poor injured souls, who but defend their own—
Calls black Extermination from its hell
To stalk abroad, and stench your land with slaughter.
These are our weighty arguments for war,
Wherein armed Justice will enclasp her sword,
And sheath it in her bitter adversary;
Wherein we'll turn our bayonet-points to pens,
And write in blood:—*Here lies the poor invader;*

Or be ourselves struck down by hailing death;
Made stepping-stones for foes to walk upon—
The lifeless gangways to our country's ruin.
For now we look not with the eye of fear;
We reck not if this strange mechanic frame
Stop in an instant in the shock of war.
Our death may build into our country's life,
And failing this, 'twere better still to die
Than live the breathing spoils of infamy.
Then forward for our cause and Canada!
Forward for Britain's Empire—peerless arch
Of Freedom's raising, whose majestic span
Is axis to the world! On, on, my friends!
The task our country sets must we perform—
Wring peace from war, or perish in its storm!

[*Excitement and leave-taking. The volunteers break into column and sing:*

O hark to the voice from the lips of the free!
O hark to the cry from the lakes to the sea!
Arm! arm! the invader is wasting our coasts,
And tainting the air of our land with his hosts.
Arise! then, arise! let us rally and form,
And rush like the torrent, and sweep like the storm,
On the foes of our King, of our country adored,
Of the flag that was lost, but in exile restored!

And whose was the flag? and whose was the soil?
And whose was the exile, the suffering, the toil?
Our Fathers'! who carved in the forest a name,
And left us rich heirs of their freedom and fame.
Oh, dear to our hearts is that flag, and the land
Our Fathers bequeathed—'tis the work of their hand!
And the soil they redeemed from the woods with renown
The might of their sons will defend for the Crown!

Our hearts are as one, and our spirits are free,
From clime unto clime, and from sea unto sea!
And chaos may come to the States that annoy,
But our Empire united what foe can destroy?
Then away! to the front! march! comrades away!
In the lists of each hour crowd the work of a day!
We will follow our leader to fields far and nigh,
And for Canada fight, and for Canada die!

[*Exeunt with military music.*

SCENE FOURTH.—FORT DETROIT.—THE AMERICAN CAMP.

Enter GENERAL HULL, COLONEL CASS *and other Officers.*

CASS. Come, General, we must insist on reasons!
Your order to withdraw from Canada
Will blow to mutiny, and put to shame
That proclamation which I wrote for you,
Wherein 'tis proudly said, "*We are prepared*
To look down opposition, our strong force
But vanguard of a mightier still to come!"
And men have been attracted to our cause
Who now will curse us for this breach of faith.
Consider, sir, again!

HULL. I am not bound
To tack my reasons to my orders; this
Is my full warrant and authority—

[*Pointing to his Instructions.*

Yet, I have ample grounds for what I do.

CASS. What are they, then?

HULL. First, that this proclamation
Meets not with due response, wins to our side
The thief and refugee, not honest men.
These plainly rally round their government.

1ST OFFICER. Why, yes; there's something lacking in this people,
If we must conquer them to set them free.

HULL. Ay, and our large force must be larger still
If we would change these Provinces to States.
Then, Colonel Proctor's intercepted letter—
Bidding the captor of Fort Mackinaw
Send but five thousand warriors from the West,
Which, be it artifice or not, yet points
To great and serious danger. Add to this
Brock's rumoured coming with his volunteers,
All burning to avenge their fathers' wrongs,
And our great foe, Tecumseh, fired o'er his;

These are the reasons ; grave enough, I think,
Which urge me to withdraw from Canada,
And wait for further force ; so, go at once,
And help our soldiers to recross the river.

CASS. But I see——

HULL. No "buts"! You have my orders.

CASS. No solid reason here, naught but a group
Of flimsy apprehensions——

HULL. Go at once!
Who kicks at judgment, lacks it.

CASS. I——

HULL. No more!
I want not wrangling but obedience here.

[*Exeunt* CASS *and other officers, incensed.*

Would I had ne'er accepted this command!
Old men are out of favour with the time,
And youthful folly scoffs at hoary age.
There's not a man who executes my orders
With a becoming grace ; not one but sulks,
And puffs his disapproval with a frown.
And what am I? A man whom Washington
Nodded approval of, and wrote it too!
Yet here, in judgment and discretion both,
Ripe to the dropping, scorned and ridiculed.
Oh, Jefferson, what mischief have you wrought—
Confounding Nature's order, setting fools
To prank themselves, and sit in wisdom's seat
By right divine, out-Heroding a King's!
But I shall keep straight on—pursue my course,
Responsible and with authority,
Though boasters gird at me, and braggarts frown.

[*Exit.*

SCENE FIFTH.—SANDWICH, ON THE DETROIT.—A ROOM IN THE BABY MANSION.

Enter GENERAL BROCK, COLONELS PROCTOR, GLEGG, BABY, MACDONELL, NICHOL, ELLIOTT *and other Officers.*

BABY. Welcome! thrice welcome!
Brave Brock, to Sandwich and this loyal roof!
Thank God, your oars, those weary levers bent
In many a wave, have been unshipped at last;
And, now, methinks those lads who stemmed the flood
Would boldly face the fire.

BROCK. I never led
Men of more cheerful and courageous heart,
But for whose pluck foul weather and short seas,
'Twere truth to say, had made an end of us.
Another trial will, I think, approve
The manly strain this Canada hath bred.

PROCTOR. 'Tis pity that must be denied them now,
Since all our enemies have left our shores.

BROCK. No, by my soul, it shall not be denied!
Our foe's withdrawal hath a magnet's power
And pulls my spirit clean into his fort.
But I have asked you to confer on this.
What keeps Tecumseh?

ELLIOTT. 'Tis his friend, Lefroy,
Who now rejoins him, after bootless quest
Of Iena, Tecumseh's niece.

BROCK. Lefroy!
I had a gentle playmate of that name
In Guernsey, long ago.

BABY. It may be he.
I know him, and, discoursing our affairs,
Have heard him speak of you, but in a strain
Peculiar to the past.

BROCK. He had in youth
All goods belonging to the human heart,

But fell away to Revolution's side—
Impulsive ever, and o'er prompt to see
In kings but tyrants, and in laws but chains.
I have not seen or heard of him for years.

BABY. The very man!

BROCK. 'Tis strange to find him here!

ELLIOTT. He calls the red men freedom's last survival;
Says truth is only found in Nature's growth—
Her first intention, ere false knowledge rose
To frame distinctions, and exhaust the world.

BROCK. Few find like him the substance of their dreams.
But, Elliott, let us seek Tecumseh now.
Stay, friends, till we return.

[*Exeunt* BROCK *and* ELLIOTT.

GLEGG. How odd to find
An old friend in this fashion!

PROCTOR. Humph! a fool
Who dotes on forest tramps and savages.
Why, at the best, they are the worst of men;
And this Tecumseh has so strained my temper,
So over-stept my wishes, thrid my orders,
That I would sooner ask the devil's aid
Than such as his.

NICHOL. Why, Brock is charmed with him!
And, as you saw, at Amherstburg he put
Most stress upon opinion when he spoke.

MACDONELL. Already they've determined on assault.

PROCTOR. Then most unwisely so! There are no bounds
To this chief's rashness, and our General seems
Swayed by it too, or rashness hath a twin.

NICHOL. Well, rashness is the wind of enterprise,
And blows its banners out. But here they come
Who dig beneath their rashness for their reasons.

Re-enter GENERAL BROCK *and* COLONEL ELLIOTT, *accompanied by* TECUMSEH, *conversing.*

TECUMSEH. We have been much abused! and have abused
Our fell destroyers too—making our wrongs
The gauge of our revenge. And, still forced back
From the first justice and the native right,
Ever revenge hath sway. This we would void,
And, by a common boundary, prevent.
So, granting that a portion of our own
Is still our own, then let that portion be
Confirmed by sacred treaty to our tribes.
This is my sum of asking—you have ears!

BROCK. Nay, then, Tecumseh, speak of it no more!
My promise is a pledge, and from a man
Who never turned his back on friend or foe.
The timely service you have done our cause,
Rating not what's to come, would warrant it.
So, if I live, possess your soul of this—
No treaty for a peace, if we prevail,
Will bear a seal that doth not guard your rights.
Here, take my sash, and wear it for my sake—
Tecumseh can esteem a soldier's gift.

TECUMSEH. Thanks, thanks, my brother, I have faith in you;
My life is at your service!

BROCK. Gentlemen,
Have you considered my proposal well
Touching the capture of Detroit by storm?
What say you, Colonel Proctor?

PROCTOR. I object!
'Tis true, the enemy has left our shores,
But what a sorry argument is this!
For his withdrawal, which some sanguine men,
Jumping all other motives, charge to fear,
Prudence, more deeply searching, lays to craft.
Why should a foe, who far outnumbers us,
Retreat o'er this great river, save to lure
Our poor force after him? And, having crossed—
Our weakness seen, and all retreat cut off—

What would ensue but absolute surrender,
Or sheer destruction? 'Tis too hazardous!
Discretion balks at such a mad design.

BROCK. What say the rest?

1ST OFFICER. I fear 'tis indiscreet.

2ND OFFICER. 'Twould be imprudent with our scanty force.

BROCK. What say you, Nichol, to my foolish scheme?

NICHOL. I think it feasible and prudent too.
Hull's letters, captured by Tecumseh, prove
His soldiers mutinous, himself despondent.
And dearly Rumour loves the wilderness,
Which gives a thousand echoes to a tongue
That ever swells and magnifies our strength.
And in this flux we take him, on the hinge
Of two uncertainties—his force and ours.
So, weighed, objections fall; and our attempt,
Losing its grain of rashness, takes its rise
In clearest judgment, whose effect will nerve
All Canada to perish, ere she yield.

BROCK. My very thoughts! What says Tecumseh now?

TECUMSEH. I say attack the fort! This very night
I'll cross my braves, if you decide on this.

BROCK. Then say no more! Glegg, take a flag of truce,
And bear to Hull this summons to surrender.
Tell him Tecumseh and his force are here—
A host of warriors brooding on their wrongs,
Who, should resistance flush them to revenge,
Would burst from my control like wind-borne fire,
And match on earth the miseries of hell.
But, should he yield, his safety is assured.
Tell him Tecumseh's word is pledged to this,
Who, though his temperate will in peace is law,
Yet casts a loose rein to enforcèd rage.
Add what your fancy dictates; but the stress
Place most on what I speak of—this he fears,
And these same fears, well wrought upon by you,
May prove good workers for us yet.

GLEGG. I go,
And shall acquit myself as best I can.

[*Exit* GLEGG.

BROCK. Tecumseh, wonder not at such a message!
The guilty conscience of your foes is judge
Of their deserts, and hence 'twill be believed.
The answer may be "nay," so to our work—
Which perfected, we shall confer again,
Then cross at break of morn.

[*Exeunt all but* TECUMSEH.

TECUMSEH. This is a man!
And our Great Father, waking from his sleep,
Has sent him to our aid. Master of Life,
Endue my warriors with double strength!
May the wedged helve be faithful to the axe,
The arrow fail not, and the flint be firm!
That our great vengeance, like the whirlwind fell,
May cleave through thickets of our enemies
A broad path to our ravaged lands again.

[*Exit.*

SCENE SIXTH.—MOONLIGHT. THE BANK OF THE DETROIT RIVER, NEAR THE BABY MANSION.

Enter CAPTAIN ROBINSON.

ROBINSON. I thought to find my brother here—poor boy,
The day's hard labour woos him to his rest.
How sweet the night! how beautiful the place!
Who would not love thee, good old Sandwich town!
Abode of silence and sweet summer dreams—
Let speculation pass, nor progress touch
Thy silvan homes with hard, unhallowed hand!
The light wind whispers, and the air is rich
With vapours which exhale into the night;
And, round me here, this village in the leaves
Darkling doth slumber. How those giant pears
Loom with uplifted and high-ancient heads,

Like forest trees! A hundred years ago
They, like their owner, had their roots in France—
In fruitful Normandy—but here refuse,
Unlike, to multiply, as if their spirits
Grieved in their alien home. The village sleeps,
So should I seek that hospitable roof
Of thine, thou good old loyalist, Baby!
Thy mansion is a shrine, whereto shall come
On pilgrimages, in the distant days,
The strong and generous youths of Canada,
And, musing there in rich imaginings,
Restore the balance and the beaver-pack
To the wide hall; see forms of savagery,
Vanished for ages, and the stately shades
Of great Tecumseh and high-hearted Brock.
So shall they profit, drinking of the past,
And, drinking loyally, enlarge the faith
Which love of country breeds in noble minds.
But now to sleep—good-night unto the world!

[*Exit.*

Enter IENA, *in distress.*

IENA. Oh, have I eaten of the spirit-plant!
My head swims, and my senses are confused,
And all grows dark around me. Where am I?
Alas! I know naught save of wanderings,
And this poor bosom's weight. What pang is here,
Which all my pressing cannot ease away?
Poor heart! poor heart! Oh, I have travelled far,
And in the forest's brooding place, or where
Night-shrouded surges beat on lonely shores,
Have sickened with my deep, dread, formless fears;
But, never have I felt what now I feel!
Great Spirit, hear me! help me!—this is death!

[*Staggers and swoons behind some shrubbery.*

Enter GENERAL BROCK *and* LEFROY.

BROCK. You may be right, Lefroy! but, for my part,
I stand by old tradition and the past.

My father's God is wise enough for me,
And wise enough this gray world's wisest men.
LEFROY. I tell you, Brock,
The world is wiser than its wisest men,
And shall outlive the wisdom of its gods,
Made after man's own liking. The crippled throne
No longer shelters the uneasy king,
And outworn sceptres and imperial crowns
Now grow fantastic as an idiot's dream.
These perish with the kingly pastime, war,
And war's blind tool, the monster, Ignorance!
Both hateful in themselves, but this the worst.
One tyrant will remain—one impious fiend
Whose name is Gold—our earliest, latest foe!
Him must the earth destroy, ere man can rise,
Rightly self-made, to his high destiny,
Purged of his grossest faults; humane and kind;
Co-equal with his fellows, and as free.
BROCK. Lefroy, such thoughts, let loose, would wreck the world.
The kingly function is the soul of state,
The crown the emblem of authority,
And loyalty the symbol of all faith.
Omitting these, man's government decays—
His family falls into revolt and ruin.
But let us drop this bootless argument,
And tell me more of those unrivalled wastes
You and Tecumseh visited.
LEFROY. We left
The silent forest, and, day after day,
Great prairies swept beyond our aching sight
Into the measureless West; uncharted realms,
Voiceless and calm, save when tempestuous wind
Rolled the rank herbage into billows vast,
And rushing tides which never found a shore.
And tender clouds, and veils of morning mist,
Cast flying shadows, chased by flying light,
Into interminable wildernesses,

Flushed with fresh blooms, deep perfumed by the rose,
And murmurous with flower-fed bird and bee.
The deep-grooved bison-paths like furrows lay,
Turned by the cloven hoofs of thundering herds
Primeval, and still travelled as of yore.
And gloomy valleys opened at our feet—
Shagged with dusk cypresses and hoary pine;
And sunless gorges, rummaged by the wolf,
Which through long reaches of the prairie wound,
Then melted slowly into upland vales,
Lingering, far-stretched amongst the spreading hills.

BROCK. What charming solitudes! And life was there!

LEFROY. Yes, life was there! inexplicable life,
Still wasted by inexorable death.
There had the stately stag his battle-field—
Dying for mastery among his hinds.
There vainly sprung the affrighted antelope,
Beset by glittering eyes and hurrying feet.
The dancing grouse, at their insensate sport,
Heard not the stealthy footstep of the fox;
The gopher on his little earthwork stood,
With folded arms, unconscious of the fate
That wheeled in narrowing circles overhead;
And the poor mouse, on heedless nibbling bent,
Marked not the silent coiling of the snake.
At length we heard a deep and solemn sound—
Erupted moanings of the troubled earth
Trembling beneath innumerable feet.
A growing uproar blending in our ears,
With noise tumultuous as ocean's surge,
Of bellowings, fierce breath and battle shock,
And ardour of unconquerable herds.
A multitude whose trampling shook the plains,
With discord of harsh sound and rumblings deep,
As if the swift revolving earth had struck,
And from some adamantine peak recoiled,
Jarring. At length we topped a high-browed hill—
The last and loftiest of a file of such—

And, lo! before us lay the tameless stock,
Slow wending to the northward like a cloud!
A multitude in motion, dark and dense—
Far as the eye could reach, and farther still,
In countless myriads stretched for many a league.
BROCK. You fire me with the picture! What a scene!
LEFROY. Nation on nation was invillaged there,
Skirting the flanks of that imbanded host;
With chieftains of strange speech and port of war,
Who, battle-armed, in weather-brawny bulk,
Roamed fierce and free in huge and wild content.
These gave Tecumseh greetings fair and kind,
Knowing the purpose havened in his soul.
And he, too, joined the chase as few men dare;
For I have seen him, leaping from his horse,
Mount a careering bull in foaming flight,
Urge it to fury o'er its burden strange,
Yet cling tenacious, with a grip of steel,
Then, by a knife-plunge, fetch it to its knees
In mid career, and pangs of speedy death.
BROCK. You rave, Lefroy! or saw this in a dream.
LEFROY. No, no; 'tis true—I saw him do it, Brock!
Then would he seek the old, and with his spoils
Restore them to the bounty of their youth,
Cheering the crippled lodge with plenteous feasts,
And warmth of glossy robes, as soft as down,
Till withered cheeks ran o'er with feeble smiles,
And tongues, long silent, babbled of their prime.
BROCK. This warrior's fabric is of perfect parts!
A worthy champion of his race—he heaps
Such giant obligations on our heads
As will outweigh repayment. It is late,
And rest must preface war's hot work to-morrow,
Else would I talk till morn. How still the night!
Here Peace has let her silvery tresses down,
And falls asleep beside the lapping wave.
Wilt go with me?
LEFROY. Nay, I shall stay awhile.

BROCK. You know my quarters and the countersign—
Good-night, Lefroy!
LEFROY. Good-night, good-night, good friend!
[*Exit* BROCK.
Give me the open sleep, whose bed is earth,
With airy ceiling pinned by golden stars,
Or vaultage more confined, plastered with clouds!
Your log-roofed barrack-sleep, 'twixt drum and drum,
Suits men who dream of death, and not of love.
Love cannot die, nor its exhausted life,
Exhaling like a breath into the air,
Blend with the universe again. It lives,
Knit to its soul forever. Iena!
Dead in the forest wild—earth cannot claim
Aught but her own from thee. Sleep on! sleep on!
IENA. (*Reviving.*) What place is this?
LEFROY. Who's there? What voice is that?
IENA. Where am I now?
LEFROY. I'll follow up that sound!
A desperate hope now ventures in my heart!
IENA. Help me, kind Spirit!
LEFROY. I could pick that voice
From out a choir of angels! Iena!
[*Finds her behind the shrubbery.*
'Tis she! 'tis she! Speak to me, Iena—
No earthly power can mar your life again,
For I am here to shield it with my own.
IENA. Lefroy!
LEFROY. Yes, he!
IENA. My friends! found, found at last!
LEFROY. Found, found, my love! I swear it on your lips,
And seal love's contract there! Again—again—
Ah, me! all earthly pleasure is a toil
Compared with one long look upon your face.
IENA. Oh, take me to my friends! A faintness came
Upon me, and no farther could I go.
LEFROY. What spirit led you here?
IENA. My little bark

Is yonder by the shore—but take me hence !
For I am worn and weak with wandering.
LEFROY. Come with me then.

Enter the PROPHET, *who stalks gloomily over the stage—scowling at* IENA *and* LEFROY *as he passes out.*

IENA. The Prophet ! I am lost !
LEFROY. This monster here ! But he is powerless now.
Fear him not, Iena ! Tecumseh's wrath
Burns 'gainst him still—he dare not do thee hurt.
IENA. Must I endure for ever this fiend's hate ?
He stabbed me with his eye—
LEFROY. Oh, horrible !
Let us but meet again, and I shall send
His curst soul out of this accursed world !
[*Exeunt.*

SCENE SEVENTH.—THE HIGHWAY THROUGH THE FOREST LEADING TO FORT DETROIT—THE FORT IN THE DISTANCE ; CANNON AND GUNNERS AT THE GATE.

Enter TECUMSEH, STAYETA, *and other Chiefs and Warriors.*

TECUMSEH. There is the Long-Knive's fort, within whose walls
We lose our lives or find our lands to-day.
Fight for that little space—'tis wide domain !
That small enclosure shuts us from our homes.
There are the victors in the Prophet's strife—
Within that fort they lie—those bloody men
Who burnt your town to light their triumph up,
And drove your women to the withered woods
To shudder through the cold slow-creeping night,
And help their infants to out-howl the wolf.
Oh, the base Long-Knife grows to head, not heart—
A pitiless and murdering minister
To his desires ! But let us now be strong,
And, if we conquer, merciful as strong !

Swoop like the eagles on their prey, but turn
In victory your taste to that of doves;
For ever it has been reproach to us
That we have stained our deeds with cruelty,
And dyed our axes in our captives' blood.
So, here, retort not on a vanquished foe,
But teach him lessons in humanity.
Now let the big heart, swelling in each breast,
Strain every rib for lodgment! Warriors!
Bend to your sacred task, and follow me.

STAYETA. Lead on! We follow you!

KICKAPOO CHIEF. Advance, ye braves!

TECUMSEH. Stay! make a circuit in the open woods—
Cross, and recross, and double on the path—
So shall the Long-Knives overcount our strength.
Do this, Stayeta, whilst I meet my friend—
My brave white brother, and confer with him.

Enter GENERAL BROCK, PROCTOR, NICHOL, MACDONELL *and other Officers and Forces, on the highway.* TECUMSEH *goes down to meet them.*

BROCK. Now by God's providence we face Detroit,
Either to sleep within its walls to-night
Or in deep beds dug by exulting foes.
Go, Nichol, make a swift reconnoissance—
We'll follow on.

NICHOL. I shall, but ere I go
I do entreat you, General, take the rear;
Those guns are shrewdly placed without the gate—
One raking fire might rob us of your life,
And, this lost, all is lost!

BROCK. Well meant, my friend!
But I am here to lead, not follow, men
Whose confidence has come with me thus far!
Go, Nichol, to your task!

[*Exit* NICHOL. TECUMSEH *advances.*

Tecumseh, hail!
Brave chieftain, you have made your promise good.

TECUMSEH. My brother stands to his! and I but wait
His orders to advance—my warriors
Are ripe for the assault.
BROCK. Deploy them, then,
Upon our landward flank, and skirt the woods,
Whilst we advance in column to attack.
[TECUMSEH *rejoins his warriors.*
Signal our batteries on the farther shore
To play upon the Fort! Be steady, friends—
Be steady! Now upon your country turn
Your multiplying thoughts, and strike for her!
Strike for your distant and inviolate homes,
Perfumed with holy prayer at this hour!
Strike! with your fathers' virtue in your veins
You must prevail—on, on, to the attack!
[BROCK *and forces advance towards the Fort. A heavy cannonading from the British batteries.*

Re-enter NICHOL *hastily.*

NICHOL. Stay, General! I saw a flag of truce
Cross from the Fort to the Canadian shore.
BROCK. Halt! There's another from yon bastion flung;
And, see! another waves adown the road—
Borne by an officer! What think you, Nichol?
NICHOL. Your threats are conquerors! The Fort is ours!
GLEGG. Yes, look! the gunners have been all withdrawn
Who manned the cannon at yon western gate.
PROCTOR. So many men to yield without a blow!
Why, this is wonderful! It cannot be!
BROCK. Say, rather, should not be, and yet it is!
'Tis plainly written on this captain's face.

[*Officer with flag of truce approaches.*

OFFICER. This letter from our General contains
Proposals to capitulate—pray send
An officer to ratify the terms.
[GENERAL BROCK *reads letter.*

7

BROCK. You have a wise and politic commander!
OFFICER. Our General, knowing your superior force—
NICHOL. (*Aside.*) Oh, this is good! 'tis barely half his own!
OFFICER. And, noting your demand of yesterday,
With clearer judgment, doth accede to it,
To bar effusion of much precious blood
By reasonable treaty of surrender.
BROCK. Why, this is excellent, and rare discretion!
OFFICER. He fears your Indians could not be restrained.
Our women's prayers—red visions of the knife—
We know not what—have melted his stout heart,
And brought him to this pass.
BROCK. Ay, ay, how good!
Great judgment and humanity combined.
Glegg and Macdonell, go at once and sign
Those happy stipulations which restore
Fair Michigan to empire and the crown.

[*Exeunt* GLEGG, MACDONELL *and Officer with flag.*

We shall await our officers' return—
But now prepare to occupy the Fort!
With colours flying we shall enter it,
And martial music, as befits the scene.
No Sunday ever saw a finer sight—
Three cheers for Canada and England's right!

[*Shouts and congratulations from the soldiery.*

SCENE EIGHTH.—FORT DETROIT.—A TUMULT OF AMERICAN SOLDIERS AND CITIZENS.

Enter GENERAL HULL *and one of his officers, accompanied by* BROCK'S *Aides,* GLEGG *and* MACDONELL.

HULL. Here is the paper! Tell your General
Divine humanity, which hath in me
A deeper root than fear of him, thus yields:
A sheer compunction lest the savage axe
Should drink too deeply in confused revenge.

GLEGG. Depend upon it, we shall tell him so,
And shall away at once.
[*Exeunt* GLEGG *and* MACDONELL.

HULL. 'Tis well I lived
To stop this bloody work! Deferment played
Into the hands of death.

OFFICER. Oh, sir, I think
That what begins in honour so should end—
First deeds, not stained, but dusted by the last;
For thus the long day of a useful life
Seems burnished by its close.

HULL. My friend, had all
Been trusty as the men of your command!
But—I am great in silence and shall speak
No more of this! What's done is for the best.
[*Retiring.*

OFFICER. A bleached and doting relic of stale time!
His best is bad for us.

[*A squad of Volunteer Militia insultingly surround the General, hooting and groaning.*

1ST VOLUNTEER. Hull! hold the fort!

2ND VOLUNTEER. Resist! We'll back you up!

HULL. Insolent ruffians!
Some men are here in whose sincerity
And courage I have perfect faith—but you!—
Untaught, unmannerly and mutinous—
Your muddy hearts would squirm within your ribs
If I but gave the order to resist!
You would command me! You who never learned
The simple first note of obedience!
Stand off, nor let me! I regard you not.
Fine Volunteers are you, who mutinied
O'er such privations as true soldiers laugh at!
Fine Volunteers! whom we were forced to coax
And almost drag upon the forest march.
Oh, if I had a thousand more of men,
A thousand less of things—which is your name—

I would defend this Fort, and keep it too.
Stand off, and let me pass!

[*Exit.*

1ST VOLUNTEER. The General
Talks well, boys, when he's mad!

Enter an OFFICER.

OFFICER. Fall in! Fall in!
Here come the British troops—the Fort's surrendered!

Enter GENERAL BROCK *and Forces, with Colours flying and military music. The American soldiers sullenly ground arms, and march out of the Fort.*

BROCK. This is a happy end! You, Nichol, make—
With Proctor—rough lists of our spoils of war,
Then join with us in grateful prayers to Heaven.

[*Exeunt* NICHOL *and* PROCTOR.

Enter TECUMSEH *and* STAYETA (*the latter wearing* BROCK'S *sash*) *with other Chiefs and Warriors, and* LEFROY.

TECUMSEH. My valiant brother is the rising sun—
Our foes the night, which disappears before him!
Our people thank him, and their hearts are his!
BROCK. Why, here is misdirection! For their thanks—
They fall to you, Tecumseh, more than me!
And, lest what lies in justice should too long
Stand in expectancy—till thanks seem cold—
Take mine, Tecumseh! for your services
Have won, with us, the honours of the day,
And you shall share its spoils.
TECUMSEH. Freedom I prize,
And my poor people's welfare, more than spoils!
No longer will they wander in the dark;
The path is open, and the sky is clear.
We thank you for it all!
BROCK. Nay, then, our thanks

We'll interchange—take mine, as I take thine!
But how is this? Is friendship's gift unused?
Where is my brother's sash?—
TECUMSEH. That gift I deemed
Conferred on me as on a warrior,
And, when I saw a worthier than myself,
I could not wear it. 'Tis Stayeta's now—
He keeps it till he finds a worthier still.
BROCK. Noble Tecumseh! thou art still the best!
Men envy their own merit in another—
Grudging e'en what's superfluous to themselves—
But thou, great valour's integer, wouldst share
Its very recompense with all the world!
Here are my pistols—take them from a friend—
Nay—take them! Would I had a richer gift!
LEFROY. This is a noble friendship.
BROCK. Ah, Lefroy!
What think you now of war?
LEFROY. If this war shield
Nature's most intimate and injured men,
I shall revoke my words and call it blest.

Re-enter GENERAL HULL.

HULL. You asked not for my sword—but here it is!
I wielded it in honour in my youth,
And now to yield it, tarnished, in old age,
Vexes me to the soul.
BROCK. Then keep it, sir!
HULL. Trenton and Saratoga speak for me! (*Aside.*)
I little thought that I should have to knead,
In my gray years, this lumpy world again.
But, when my locks were brown, my heart aflame
For liberty, believe me, sir, this sword
Did much to baffle your imperious King!
BROCK. That stands not in dispute, so keep the sword!
'Tis strange that those who fought for liberty
Should seek to wrench it from their fellowmen.
Impute not guilty war to Kings alone,

Since 'tis the pastime of Republics, too!
Yours has its dreams of glory, conquest, spoil—
Else should we not be here. But, General,
Wilt dine with us? We shall discuss this matter!

HULL. Nay, let me to my house; I cannot eat.

BROCK. Sir, as you will—but, prithee, be prepared!
I sail in six days for Niagara,
And you for Montreal.

HULL. Till then, adieu!
[*Exit* GENERAL HULL.

TECUMSEH. Why should my brother leave Detroit so soon?

BROCK. Our foes are massing at Niagara,
And I must meet them; Colonel Proctor stays
In this command.

TECUMSEH. I know him very well.
My brother's friend says "Go!" but you say "Come!"

BROCK. (*Aside.*) How am I straitened for good officers!
(*To* TECUMSEH.) Friend Proctor's prudence may be useful here.

TECUMSEH. I do misgive me o'er my brother's friend.

Re-enter NICHOL *and* PROCTOR.

NICHOL. Large stores, munitions, public properties;
A rare account of needed stands of arms;
A brig of war, and military chest—
These are the spoils of bloodless victory.
[*Handing* GENERAL BROCK *a list.*

BROCK. Nought is much prized that is not won with blood!

GLEGG. And yet I would old England's victories
Were all as bloodless, ample and complete.

MACDONELL. Oh, 'tis a victory fitly gained this day;
Great turning point of our Canadian fortunes!
This day forever should red-lettered stand
In all the calendars of our loved land!
[*Exeunt.*

END OF FOURTH ACT.

ACT V.

Enter CHORUS.

CHORUS. O Canada!
Bright youth among the graybeards of the earth,
Dark days have come upon thee! Brock is slain—
That spirit glorious who fired thy soul,
And led thee to renown and victory.
Alas! the rare advantages he won,
By weak successors (equals in command,
But, oh, of what inferior mould in greatness!)
Have been let slip unto the winds, thy hopes
By an untimely armistice destroyed,
Those fleets he would have captured from the foe,
But for a hateful truce on him enjoined,
Were, in a fataler still, equipped, and loosed
To lord it o'er thee on the lakes. One bore
Destruction to thy upper Capital—
The other meets thy poorly furnished hulls
On Erie's bosom, and with hosts of men
And weight of armament doth bear them down.
O lamentable hour, which paves the way
To sad remaining scenes—a coward's part,
And the last pulse-beat of a hero's heart.

[*Exit.*

SCENE FIRST.—THE INDIAN COUNCIL HOUSE, AMHERSTBURG.

Enter BABY *and* ELLIOTT.

BABY. Now, Elliott, what think you keeps our fleet?
We heard the crash of battle yesterday,
And still no tidings come.

ELLIOTT. I fear the worst.
BABY. I fear it, too! Worse still to think this worst
Owes to sheer folly—to an armistice
Astutely urged, and too politely granted.
Some chance politenesses obstruct themselves,
Like meeting men who shuffle in the street,
Each striving to give way; but this, of Sheaffe's,
Was of the stately kind! He stood aside;
Bowed, hat in hand, and let the foe pass by
To build his navy up.
ELLIOTT. Well, we have here
A fool who beats Sheaffe's folly at the game,
But for whose slackness we might still record
Some gains on land, 'gainst losses on the lake.
BABY. You speak of Proctor; hum! a prudent man,
Who loves his life, and will maintain his love.
'Tis a safe temper.
ELLIOTT. Ay, for peace, not war.
But what a damper to our volunteers!
They left their customable, proper toil
To fight, not for a wage, but for their freedom—
A thing to be achieved by instant ways,
Though they run blood. Thus, if they won and lived,
The sooner to their homes; and, if they died—
Fair end: their lives went for their country's good.
But how, by bootless and lame leadership,
Has Proctor soured the temper of our men;
Cooling them to contempt, till, in a pique,
He straight disarms, then sends them to their homes!
BABY. Unheard-of folly! All this is a text
From which I often preach unto myself.
ELLIOTT. Would that by preaching we could mend the matter!
Even Tecumseh he insults, whose cause
Lies close to ours; and, saving him and us,
(Whose aid he would dispense with if he dared,)
What force is left him but his regulars,
Whose sickly frames and broken confidence
Would scarcely face the effigies of foes!

BABY. True! true! it breeds fear but to think of it.
ELLIOTT. Then hear him prate about the charge he bears
Upon his individual shoulders—his!
Oh, it is galling! while he boasts withal
What he would do were things fortuitous,
And in a fairer plight; and this fudged stuff
Goes down with some. But, not to spin it out,
We know that, at Sandusky, Harrison
(Who is as good a substitute for Hull
As ours a poor one for immortal Brock)
Waits transport to invade us in large force.
So—lest our General means to beat retreat,
Or ruinously yield—'tis time to stir.
BABY. What can we do? We are not in command.
ELLIOTT. Force him who is to face our enemies—
First calling back our volunteers.
BABY. Force him,
Who would not face yourself, to face five thousand!
Why, Elliott, we might as well expect
Light from a cave, as leadership from him.

Enter MCKEE.

What news, McKee?
MCKEE. It could not well be worse.
Our fleet is captured, and the General
Has issued orders to retreat.
BABY. Ay, ay;
We had already lost our fleet in thought,
Which ofttimes pre-digests calamities.
But this retreat—how looks Tecumseh at it?
MCKEE. I never saw him in so strange a temper—
Calm on the surface, but convulsed beneath,
Just poising on the edge of whirling rage.
He now harangues his chiefs and warriors,
And has demanded conference with Proctor,
Wherein I look for deep outbursts of wrath.
For Proctor, fearing him, pretends our fleet
Is absent for repairs—a foolish lie,
Which yet will deepen what it but prorogues.

BABY. We must compose this threatened broil, McKee;
Dissension now would ruin everything.
McKEE. Tecumseh thinks there's ruin in retreat.
Proctor can't thumb his temper to the point,
Nor rove him through his plans.
BABY. Well, certainly,
Had we but power and time enough to mass
Our people's strength 'twould be the nobler part
To risk a battle here. But, pshaw! this counts
In mere conjecture as to what might be
Had we command; for Proctor will retreat!
He feels endangered in a special sense.
The savage massacre of prisoners
At Old Miami and at Raisin River
Has made him hated by the enemy,
Who, right or wrong, put all the blame on him,
And this he knows.

Enter GENERAL PROCTOR.

McKEE. Would Brock were still alive!
PROCTOR. Pardon my overhearing ears!—what then?
McKEE. (*Turning sharply.*) Then we should fight!
Some bold, some daring plan,
Would still forefend retreat.
PROCTOR. Some strange exploit!
Some headlong rashness which would find you graves.
'Twas prologue to his own: a fault in him
I would not emulate.
ELLIOTT. A fault in him!
His death was of the parcel of the man.
In him example, striving to excel
The precept, made him reckless of his life.
'Twas thus he lost it: his main force behind—
With but a handful, taken by surprise,
Rather than flee he charged! and, with the words,
"*Push on, my brave York Volunteers!*" he fell.
Oh, such a fall atoned for such a fault;

For by that fall he lashed his followers
Up to a sure and terrible revenge.
It was a fearful victory! Our foes,
Flying from death to death, sprang o'er the cliffs
And precipices of Niagara,
And, on the rocks, or in the swirling flood,
Made expiation of their foul invasion.
Let this dwell in our minds! and let not death,
Or, rather, fear of death, repel us now,
Nor turn us to a base retreat from it.

PROCTOR. Let wisdom dwell, too, in our minds, I urge.
Bethink you: Harrison is on the wing—
Thousands to hundreds is his argument!
Our fleet is captured; our supplies are scant;
And winter may be scented in the air.
We must retreat, since men must eat or die;
So, winding up these threads of sense, prepare!
Lest time desert our opportunity.

BABY. What will Tecumseh say to this?

PROCTOR. That dog,
Who barks at all I do, must come with us,
And guard our rear—else were his absence best.

McKEE. Should he refuse?

PROCTOR. Then tell him we retire
But further east to make a desperate stand.
'Tis well to say it lest he cross my plans.
As for his prate, not all the forest's combs
Could sweeten such a tongue.

BABY. I think you lack
The fair idea of this chief; his mind
Has greatness in it—but here comes the man:
Confer with him yourself!

Enter TECUMSEH *and a concourse of Chiefs and Warriors.*

PROCTOR. Nay, I must go,
And push our preparations—

TECUMSEH. (*Confronting* PROCTOR.) Stay, my friend!

PROCTOR. I cannot stay; speak to him, gentlemen.
[*Going.*

TECUMSEH. (*Touching his hatchet.*) I am Tecumseh.
You are Proctor—stay!

PROCTOR. What means this madman? He is insolent.
(*Aside.*)

TECUMSEH. Brother! My people are before you now!
In the last war, the British father gave
Our chiefs the hatchet, and they fought for him;
But in that bloody strife the Long-Knife laid
The King upon his back; whereat he took
Our foes, without our knowledge, by the hand.
Again the Long-Knife warred upon the King;
Again our father handed us the axe,
With promise that our lands would be restored.
We have not shrunk from battle. We have fought,
And many of our people have been slain!
Our promise is redeemed! but what of his?
Oft have we heard you, boasting of him, say
He never would withdraw from British ground.
Yet, neither asking nor advising us,
We mark you now preparing to retreat—
Afraid to even see his enemies!
My brother, you are like a lusty dog
Which proudly curls its tail upon its back,
But, when affrighted, whips it 'tween its legs,
And runs for life! Why should you meanly flee?
The Long-Knives have not yet defeated us
By land, nor is it certain that your ships
Are captured on the lake; but, even so,
First fight, and, if defeated, then retreat!
But, brother, if you will not fight, you hold
The arms our father furnished for our use.
Give these to us, and you may go in peace.
My people are in our Great Spirit's care!
We are determined to defend our lands,
Or, if He wills it, strew them with our bones.

BABY. Why, this is manliness, and pathos, too!

PROCTOR. We must retreat. We cannot spare the arms
You now demand of us.

TECUMSEH. Not spare them, brother?
Do I hear aright?

PROCTOR. We cannot spare them.

TECUMSEH. By Manitou, you shall! Those arms are ours.
I would not quarrel lightly with my friend,
Nor cut the bands which bind me to his cause
Upon a small occasion; but those arms,
Useless to him, are precious life to us,
And we shall have them.

PROCTOR. Yes, if you retreat!
We cannot spare them else.

TECUMSEH. And why retreat?
The timid woman and the child will stand
And struggle when assaulted by their kind;
Nay, hares resist, and gnats and flies will fight.
One thing alone runs from its sort in fear,
And thou art it!

PROCTOR. The wildest talk in sleep
Outmeasures this in sense. We must retreat!

TECUMSEH. Must! must! Oh, could my kindred spirit, Brock,
But live again—be here—would he retreat?
Yours his command—but why should I compare
The king-bird with the crow? Brave Brock retreat!
Oh, when that badger was abroad, dogs hid
And gave the lie to nature! Here we stay.
Give us the arms, and we shall act like him,
Whilst you make off in peace.

PROCTOR. This man would breed
A deadly quarrel—prudence bear me through! (*Aside.*)
I mean to give those arms, but for a use
More wise than you would put them to. Retreat
Is but to find some vantage in the woods—
Some footing for defence; so, come with us;
I would not ask you else.

TECUMSEH. Seek your own kind!
Go boom in festering swales, or, like a frog,
Croak your dull night-song in the standing pool—
Your voice is not a man's.

PROCTOR. This chief is fevered.
Explain the why and wherefore of retreat,
Then let him come with us or stay; I care not.
[*Going.*

TECUMSEH. Ha! There are cares my brother never cared for;
Duties to which he never paid his duty;
Sacred agreements, oaths and covenants
Which he would break like twigs. Coward and liar!
There's something here that whispers to my hand
[*Drawing his hatchet.*
To set you free from all.
[BABY, ELLIOTT *and* MCKEE *interpose.*

ELLIOTT. Tecumseh, hold!

BABY. This is unworthy of you. Be a man!

TECUMSEH. A man! Oh, if to honour words by deeds;
To look on truth as on the healthful air,
Without which I should suffocate and die;
To love my injured people, and oppose
My constant spirit 'gainst tumultuous wrongs—
If this is lack of manhood mark me down.
But to be over-reached and thrown aside—
Our mighty sacrifices and our service
Rated as nothing in this coward's plans—
It rends my soul. Back! I shall chop his own
From out its frame, and send the mould of lies
Down to his people's hell! Away!

MCKEE. No! no!

ELLIOTT. Stay, be advised by us!
[PROCTOR *retires.*

BABY. Do nothing rash!
We are your friends—you know us to be true,
And we, like you, despise this General.
Fear bares the coward's heart. The gaudy acts

Whereby unsoundness shores its credit up
Are at its touch exposed. 'Tis so with him—
And thus far we are with you. But retreat
Hath a discreetness too. This Harrison,
Once landed (for our long and liberal shores
We cannot well defend), might circle us,
And, with o'erwhelming numbers, hem us in.
But, by retreat, we have the choice of place,
And Harrison—you know the man—will follow.
The forest will befriend us—we can stand
Where'er we please, and shall whene'er you please.

TECUMSEH. So! Proctor's promises deceive you, too!

BABY. Nay, 'tis my promise, and you know the stuff
My word is built on. Deal with me, Tecumseh,
As you had dealt with Proctor, if I lie.

TECUMSEH. My friend, your reason breaks a spirit's wing
That ne'er touched ground before. Oh, I grow weak—
Cast from my thoughts, and banished from my dream!
The plumed hope droops—fate's shadow covers it;
And dim forebodings peer into my soul.
I am not what I was—there—there—I'll go!

BABY. I hope to see you smile at this ere long.

[*Exeunt.*

SCENE SECOND.—A WOOD NEAR AMHERSTBURG.—TECUMSEH'S CAMP.—A VISTA TO THE EAST, THE SUN'S UPPER RIM JUST RISING ABOVE THE HORIZON.

Enter WARRIORS *and* JOSAKEEDS. *The warriors extend their weapons towards the sun. The* JOSAKEEDS *advance facing it.*

1ST JOSAKEED. He comes! Yohewah! the Great Spirit, comes
Up from his realm—the place of Breaking Light!
Hush, nations! Worship, in your souls, the King,
Above all Spirits! Master of our lives!

I-ge-zis ! He that treads upon the day,
And makes the light !

2ND JOSAKEED. He comes ! he comes ! he comes !
The ever-dying, ever-living One !
He hears us, and he speaks thus to mine ears !
I wipe once more the darkness from the earth ;
I look into the forest, and it sings—
The leaves exult ; the waters swim with joy.
I look upon the nations, and their souls
Strengthen with courage to resist their foes.
I will restore them to their fathers' lands ;
I will pour laughter on the earth, like rain,
And fill the forest with its ancient food.
Corn will be plenteous in the fields as dust,
And fruits, moved to their joy, on every bough
Will glow and gleam like ardent fire and gold.

3RD JOSAKEED. O Mighty Spirit ! Guardian of our Breath !
We see thy body, and yet see thee not.
The spirits in our forms, which no man sees,
Breathe forth to thee, for they are born of thee.
Hear us, thy children, and protect our lives !
Our warriors retreat—it is thy will !
Declare the way—the fateful time to stand !
Then, if in battle they decline in death,
Take them, O Master, to thy Mighty Heart—
Thy Glorious Ground and Shining Place of Souls !
Yohewa ! Master of Breath ! Yohewa !
Hear us ! Hear us !

ALL. Master of Breath—hear us !

[*Exeunt.*

SCENE THIRD.—THE SAME.

A girl's voice singing without, then enter IENA, WINONA, WEETAMORE *and other Indian maidens—some at quill-work, others embroidering.*

IENA. There is within my heart, I know not why,
An apprehension I ne'er felt before.
WINONA. The night-sun set in cloud, and curling mists
Hid the plumed star from sight. Mayhap, those signs
Bode danger to our loves. Sing, Weetamore—
Your tender voice will charm away our fears.
IENA. Nay, sing no more in strains so sorrowful!
Why is it all our people's songs are sad?

[*A bird's note is heard.*

WINONA. I know not why; no more than yon poor bird
Knows why it mourns.
IENA. It is the wood pewee,
That haunts the deepest forest. 'Tis the bird
Yohewa gave to solitude for voice—
The lonely heart within the lonely heart!
Why comes this feathered sadness from its wilds,
To thrill us with its pain?

Enter MAMATEE.

O Mamatee!
MAMATEE. Alas, alas, the Long-Knife's big canoes
Are on the lake, and sweeping to our shores!
Fort Malden burns; our warriors retreat;
And we, poor souls! must fly to densest woods,
And wait till they return?
IENA. Till they return—
Ah! when shall they return?

Enter LEFROY.

Here comes my love,
With parting in his eyes.
LEFROY. You speak the word!
But, if we part, we part to meet again.
And, thus, to leave you for love's sake makes sweet
The bitter word, and will uphold my heart.
Tecumseh is already gone—farewell.
IENA. Farewell, and we shall meet again—here? where?
Yes, yes, I know—there's something tells me where.
Farewell! my love will follow you on wings
High-flighted as the swan's—my soul! my soul!
[LEFROY *places* IENA *in* MAMATEE'S *arms.*
LEFROY. In loving arms I place this precious charge.
Oh, cherish her! for she is dear to me
As is the Intercessor to your race.
[*Exit* LEFROY.
IENA. Now let me go—see—I am well again!
An impulse rises from the seat of dreams—
Love's apprehension may be cured by love.
Winona, will you help me?
WINONA. Sister, how?
IENA. Your brother, Chaska, is a slender youth,
With features softly fashioned. 'Tis a boy
Some say resembles me; and like me, too,
His gentle form contains a venturous soul.
You make a young brave's suit for him, I think.
WINONA. Yes, for his huskenaw; you call it that—
We have another name. Look, this completes it!
[*Holding up an ornamented moccasin.*
'Tis from the self-piece cut, and quill'd all o'er—
Your gathered edges show not half so well.
IENA. Oh, if you love me, let me have this dress.
WINONA. With all my heart: but tell me, Iena,
What means this strange request?
IENA. Come to your lodge!
I there shall tell you all I have in mind.
[*Exeunt* IENA *and* WINONA.

MAMATEE. The girl conceives some folly. To my cares!
O weary woman, thine the weary work !

[*Exit* MAMATEE.

1ST MAIDEN. Iena asked, and I do marvel why,
Our songs are all so sad. We forest maids
Should sing as lightly as our forest leaves.
'Tis strange !

WEETAMORE. You are too happy-young to think
'Tis else than strange. Now I shall answer you
Ere Iena can come to chide the strain.

(WEETAMORE *sings.*)

Who would not be a forest-maid,
And ever spend at ease
The flowery season in the shade
Of sighing summer's sweetest trees?
But who would be a forest-maid,
Beset by foes and fears?
To see in every flash a blade,
To start at every sound she hears !

We flit—we fly—no home have we,
And terror is the tale !
A fate is whispered by the tree—
A doom is uttered by the gale.
Short season of delight have we,
But that of pain is long ;
And, so, 'tis sorrow, and not glee,
That gives the burden to our song.

Re-enter IENA, *dressed as a young Indian Brave.*

IENA. Now for my bow ! my quiver ! here it is !
This quiver slung, I'm ready for the field.

1ST MAIDEN. Why, this is Iena !

IENA. Yes, Iena.
But, sisters, lock this secret in your hearts.
Love's Spirit whispered in a dream—" *Go, shield*
Your lover in the fight !"

2ND MAIDEN. A dream, a dream !

3RD MAIDEN. A sacred dream !

ALL. We promise to be true,

[*The* MAIDENS *join hands and move in a circle round* IENA, *chanting:*

Spirit of Love! Spirit of Love!
  That in Great Nature's heart doth dwell:
Spirit of Love! Spirit of Love!
  Go with our sister—shield her well!

SCENE FOURTH.—THE RUINS OF FORT MALDEN AT AMHERSTBURG.

Enter GENERAL HARRISON *and other American Officers.*

HARRISON. All gone! all gone! Naught here but smoking ruins!
Now would I give this Province for one man,
Were that man only Proctor. Perfidy!
Thy manager has fled; and we are balked
In our just vengeance.
1ST OFFICER. Let us follow him!
There are no ties 'twixt mercy and this man
That we should spare him.
HARRISON. No, his ruthless axe,
Stayed only by Tecumseh's noble rage,
Has lit upon too many helpless heads.
Their blood cries, "*After him!*" and with our force
We can o'erwhelm his if we overtake him.
2ND OFFICER. 'Tis strange Tecumseh hugs his flying fortunes!
3RD OFFICER. Think you he is gone?
HARRISON. No doubt of it, else would he face us here.
2ND OFFICER. Had he remained we might perchance have made
Our peace with him, and ended this long feud.
HARRISON. Made peace with him! There is no peace on earth
For him, save in it. We are what we are;
And if some miracle will work a change
In us, then shall we find him, as we would,

Contented but with peace. This much I say,
Knowing the man—but this is not the point!
'Tis Proctor, not Tecumseh, we discuss,
And Proctor we must capture if we can.

Enter a SCOUT.

What tidings have you gathered?
SCOUT. Proctor's force
Is making for the Heights of Burlington.
'Tis said Tecumseh made him pledge his word
To stand, and fight at the Moravian Town,
Should we pursue.
HARRISON. Will hounds pursue the hare?
'Tis boot-and-saddle, and quick marches now,
If we would catch the foe.
[*Exeunt.*

SCENE FIFTH.—THE HIGHWAY THROUGH THE FOREST ON THE RIVER THAMES, NEAR THE MORAVIAN TOWN.

Enter TECUMSEH *and his Chiefs*, GENERAL PROCTOR, COLONEL BABY *and other Officers*, *and* PROCTOR'S ORDERLY.

TECUMSEH. I'll go no further.
PROCTOR. A little further—
Toward the heights—'twere well!
TECUMSEH. No, not a step,
Were they the Alleghanies! Here we stand!
The enemy draws near, and we must fight.
PROCTOR. Well, here we stand—here shall I lay my bones,
If so God wills it. Ha—I like the spot!
A river to protect us on our left;
Swamps to the north, and forest everywhere.
What a gigantic panoply of woods!

Why, here are maples scarce three men could girth
With their encircling arms. What trees!

TECUMSEH. Yes, yes—
Would they were soldiers, brother; they are strong,
And, being rooted to their place, would ne'er
Give way as we have done. But to affairs—

PROCTOR. Ay, to the proper ordering of our force.
Do you direct! What think you now is best?

TECUMSEH. Two swamps are here o'ergrown with swollen trunks
Of black and moss-hung ash. Their underbrush,
Thick-set, and tangled with the blistering vine,
No cavalry can pass. Between them lies
A neck of open woods and turfy soil,
Where I shall plant my braves; but this straight path—
This highway by the river—is your ground.
Here place your cannon, and await attack,
Whilst I oppose it there.

Enter a SCOUT.

SCOUT. Make ready, sirs!
The enemy approaches—we can hear
His trumpet-calls resounding through the woods.

[*Exit* SCOUT.

PROCTOR. Then, briefly, my opinion sides with yours.
The trial hour is come—farewell, my friend!
We two shall stand or fall upon this field,
And fame it to all time.

TECUMSEH. Keep a stout heart,
I pray you, brother; all will thus be well.

[*Exeunt* TECUMSEH *and his Chiefs.*

BABY. I think this disposition excellent.

PROCTOR. It is, it is. Now let us fight it out!
There are occasions when the spirit mounts,
Uplifted by what threats it; this is one.
Go, gentlemen, and marshal up our force—

I shall await you here. Stay you with me,
(*To his* ORDERLY.)
I have instructions for you.
[*Exeunt all but* PROCTOR *and his* ORDERLY.
Come hither!
We may be beaten here—
ORDERLY. I think we shall.
PROCTOR. What right have you to think?
ORDERLY. You said it, sir.
PROCTOR. I said we may—(*aside*) tut! this is less than prudent.
Go, put my fleetest horses to my carriage;
Have others ready-saddled in our rear,
And, with some trusty fellows, stay by them—
They may be useful in emergency.
[*Exit* ORDERLY.
If there are seasons in the soul of man,
As in the year, it is my bleakest now.
How many rail at me, and call me coward,
Because with prudent outlook I foresee
What can be done and what can not be done!
One must endure! though to be misconceived;
To find one's actions and one's qualities
Framed in misapprehension; to be deemed
The thing that one is not, might well offend.
But that which guides my life enables me
To bear against the rub of false opinion;
So, prudence, miscalled cowardice by those
Who count their rashness virtue, tend me still!
Tecumseh foolishly resolves to die—
For who, against such odds, can hope to live?
And, if there be a virtue in mere death,
Then is he welcome to his grave and all
The honour and the glory death can give.
But those who have some business still on earth—
Something to do that cannot else be done—
Look on this matter with a different eye.

It is our trumpet call; my soldiers come.
In the adieu to death the quick resolve
Must spur calm judgment on to execution.

[*Exit.*

SCENE SIXTH.—TECUMSEH'S PART OF THE FIELD.

Enter TECUMSEH.

TECUMSEH. This is our summer—when the painted wilds,
Like pictures in a dream, enchant the sight.
The forest bursts in glory like a flame!
Its leaves are sparks; its mystic breath the haze
Which blends in purple incense with the air.
The Spirit of the Woods has decked his home,
And put his wonders like a garment on,
To flash, and glow, and dull, and fade, and die.
Oh, let not manhood fade within my soul!
And thou, pale doubt, that hast distracted me—
Ye forecasts that would drag my spirit down—
Hence and forever flee! Ye have no place,
No business in this breast. My field is here!
Here must my people's cause be lifted up,
Or sink to rise no more. [*Exit.*

Enter three American SCOUTS, *looking cautiously about them.*

1ST SCOUT. This is their spot.
2ND SCOUT. I see them coming. Look! away—away—
[*Exeunt.*

(*Firing, and other sounds of conflict, are heard from* PROCTOR'S *part of the field, and then suddenly stop.*)

Re-enter TECUMSEH, *with* STAYETA *and his other Chiefs and Warriors.*

STAYETA. The noise of battle rose, and then it ceased
Almost upon beginning. This is strange.

TECUMSEH. It is; ah, Proctor, how my soul mistrusts thee!
Go, some of you, see what this silence means—
But stay—here comes a witness of the fight.

Enter LEFROY, *out of breath, and excited.*

LEFROY. The line was broken by a charge of horse,
And, in the British quarter, all is lost.
TECUMSEH. And Proctor—he who meant to leave his bones,
If so God willed it—
LEFROY. Willed it otherwise!
Upon the instant of attack he fled;
And, seeing this, the line gave way at once.
TECUMSEH. 'Twas this I feared. He loves his wretched life
Too well to leave his vile bones anywhere.
Dastard and coward! Oh, the heavens should crack,
And dart their lightning down upon this slave!
How come such creatures 'mongst the breed of men
To make their nation blush?
LEFROY. I cannot tell.
Like sulphur in rain-channels after storms,
Or little frogs, one marvels how they come.
But some fought well; Baby, among the rest,
Who now is prisoner. Myself was saved
Most strangely by a boy—a youthful brave,
Whose arrows helped me in a dangerous spot.
I never saw so sweet a lad before.
His face! I started when I saw it first—
It seemed so like to Iena's! Think you,
Could she be here?
TECUMSEH. Impossible!
DAHCOTA CHIEF. No, no.
'Twas Chaska, of our nation; one who longs
For plumes before his time. He has been seen,
Yet is so active that we cannot catch him.

LEFROY. Ah, then, 'twas he! This way he ran before me,
Round the rough angle of the lower swamp,
Then darted into it. I followed fast,
And sought, but could not find him—he was gone.

(*A flourish of trumpets without, sounding the advance of the American Force.*)

STAYETA. Hark! Now the Long-Knives come!

TECUMSEH. Yes, now they come.
Courage! Warriors, courage! Let our deeds
Take colour from the scene. Now must we fight
Like men; not run like slaves. What matters it
To those who fled, and left us, if they flee?
They can join palms, make peace, draw treaties up,
And son and father, reconciled again,
Will clap their hands, and glory in their race
Which hath despoiled our own. For us, no peace
Save what our axes gain, or, in our graves.
Therefore—as men fore-doomed to war or death—
Let valour make excuse that we shall live,
And, breathing vengeance, shake our spoilers so
That they will reel in terror to the East,
From whence they came, and cry—"*The West is yours!*"
Oh, warriors, think of all, and strike like men
Whose homes are in their hands, whose souls are free.
The voice that calls you now will call no more,
For something whispers to this fearless heart—
Here must I fight, and for my people die!

DELAWARE CHIEF. Then shall we fight and die with you like men.

DAHCOTA CHIEF. Or live to see you Chief of all our race.

(*A flourish without, then enter the American Forces. A fierce hand-to-hand conflict begins.*)

TECUMSEH. Our foes are turning! Strike them! beat them back!

STAYETA. Pursue! pursue!

(*The American Troops retreat fighting. Exeunt omnes.*)

Enter IENA, *from behind.*

IENA. I hear, yet cannot see,
The dreadful fray! My arrows all are spent.
There are a thousand in my quivered heart
Could I but match them to this useless bow.
What shall I do? Ah, this is our own tree!
It will protect me whilst I wait the end.

[*Retires behind a large sugar maple.*

Re-enter a small band of Braves, driven back by Soldiers, who chase them out and then return.

1ST SOLDIER. Ha, ha, those red-skins fled like hunted wolves!
Away, and start another pack!

[*Exeunt forward.*

IENA. (*Looking out.*) Alas!
Our people 'gin to flee—I fear—I fear.
Here comes my love! Oh, for one arrow more!

Enter LEFROY *and an* AMERICAN OFFICER *fighting with swords. In the struggle they draw abreast of* IENA'S *tree, and pause.*

OFFICER. You are a white man.
LEFROY. I *am* a white man.
OFFICER. And what a soulless one are you who leave
Your place in civil, good society
To herd with savages; from one extreme
Falling away unto the basest side—
The furthest from the humanizèd world.
LEFROY. Nay, I deny it! Further, I would say,
My genius leans, like Nature, to all sides,
Can love them all at once, and live with all.
OFFICER. So! so! you are a poet, painter, what?
Well, that is nothing; I must try and kill you.

[*They fight again, and* LEFROY *disarms the* OFFICER.

LEFROY. Now might I kill you if I had the heart.
Be prisoner instead; I cannot kill
A man thus, in cold blood.

Re-enter two SOLDIERS.

OFFICER. 'Tis more than kind.
1ST SOLDIER. Why, that's our captain there, disarmed—let fly!
My carbine is unloaded.

(*Second* SOLDIER *aims at* LEFROY. IENA, *with a cry, leaps from her shelter and intercepts the shot.*)

LEFROY. Who is this?
Not Chaska! Oh, no, no—'tis Iena!
I see her now, who could not see my love—
Love clear and incorruptible as glass,
Love that had dared a monster, wilds and floods—
Dare fire, and draw the bow that shielded me.
Speak to me, Iena! No voice—she's dead!
OFFICER. This is the strangest chapter of my life—
Soldiers, stand off, and rest upon your arms.
LEFROY. Silent for ever! Oh, my girl! my girl!
Those rich eyes melt; those lips are sun-warm still—
They look like life, yet have no semblant voice.
Millions of creatures throng, and multitudes
Of heartless beings flaunt upon the earth:
There's room enough for them; but thou, dull Fate—
Thou cold and partial tender of life's field,
That pluck'st the flower, and leav'st the weed to thrive—
Thou hadst not room for her! Oh, I must seek
A way out of the rack—I need not live.
OFFICER. The world grows less familiar every hour:—
Is that a girl?
LEFROY. Yes, yes, but she is dead—
And love is left upon the earth to starve.
My object's gone, and I am but a shell,
A husk, an empty case, or anything
That may be kicked about the world.
[*Exit* LEFROY, *carrying* IENA.

OFFICER. I see!
I have a tear or two behind these eyes,
And they are coming. If he need a friend
I know of one.

2ND SOLDIER. Now, dang me, who'd 'a thought
That was a girl!

OFFICER. (*Turning aside.*) What strange and selfless paths
Do skirt the world's hard highway! I have seen
What gives me sight. The tide of battle rolls
Back, and our people win, as win they must:
But, now, methinks, I'll strive with different heart.
Come, soldiers, let's away and join the fight.
[*Exeunt through a by-entrance.*

Re-enter TECUMSEH'S *warriors driven back, and then re-enter* TECUMSEH, STAYETA, *and other Chiefs.*

TECUMSEH. Has death died out, that no one now can die?
Or are you driven back by fear of it?
Oh, slaves or men, determine which you are!

Re-enter the American troops, in pursuit.

STAYETA. Tecumseh calls! On, warriors, strike them down!

(TECUMSEH *and his warriors, by a fierce onslaught, again drive their opponents back. The fight continues without —then re-enter* TECUMSEH *mortally wounded.*)

TECUMSEH. Great Spirit, hadst thou spared me but one hour—
Yet thy behest rules all.

Re-enter DELAWARE CHIEF, *also wounded.*

DELAWARE CHIEF. What! wounded too?

TECUMSEH. Yes, I am shot. Recall some warriors
To bear my body hence. Give no alarm,

Lest our poor braves lose courage; but make haste—
I have not long to live. Yet hear my words!
Bury me in the deep and densest forest,
And let no white man know where I am laid.
Promise this ere you go.

DELAWARE CHIEF. I promise it.
Alas, alas, our bravest and our best!

[*Exit* DELAWARE CHIEF.

TECUMSEH. The hour is come! these weary hands and feet
Draw to the grave. Oh, I have loved my life,
Not for my own but for my people's cause.
Who now will knit them? who will lead them on?
Lost! lost! lost! The pale destroyer triumphs!
I see my people flee—I hear their shrieks—
And none to shield or save! My axe! my axe—
Ha—it is here! No, no—the power is past.
O Mighty Spirit, shelter—save—my people!

[*Dies.*

SCENE SEVENTH.—ANOTHER PART OF THE FIELD.

Enter GENERAL HARRISON *and other American Officers, and* COLONEL BABY, *a prisoner.*

HARRISON. You were too brave a man, Baby, to swell
The craven Proctor's flight of followers.

BABY. Speak not of him! I mourn the death of one—
A soldier—and a savage if you will—
Able and honourable, valiant, pure,
As ever graced the annals of the earth.

HARRISON. You mean Tecumseh; search is made for him.
I hope to give him fitting burial.

BABY. Oh, sir, he loved his people! They are men
Much hated by the small and greedy mind—
The mind that is not gentle, and that jeers
And laughs at all forlorn and broken fortune.

And some there be who coldly pass them by
As creatures ruled by appetite, not law;
Yet, though to such they seem but human beasts,
They are to those who know, or study them,
A world of wonders! I entreat you, sir,
To make right use of your authority,
And shield them if you can.

HARRISON. I shall, I shall.
Right feeling tends this way, though 'tis a course
Not to be smoothly steered.

Enter a party of soldiers.

1ST SOLDIER. Tecumseh's body
Cannot be found; 'twas borne away and buried
By faithful friends who would not name the place,
If they were tortured.

1ST OFFICER. He is well content
Without our honours. This man's race hath lost
A lofty spirit.

2ND OFFICER. All will mourn for him!
No need had he of schools or learned books—
His soul his mentor, his keen lion-looks
Pierced to the heart of things. Nor needed he
Counsels of strength and goodness. To be free
Required no teacher, no historic page,
No large examples sought from age to age.
For such things were himself, and, as his breath,
Instinctive, pleaders 'gainst the fears of death.

HARRISON. Sleep well, Tecumseh, in thy unknown grave,
Thou mighty savage, resolute and brave!
Thou, master and strong spirit of the woods,
Unsheltered traveller in sad solitudes,
Yearner o'er Wyandot and Cherokee,
Couldst tell us now what hath been and shall be!

[*Exeunt.*

THE END.

CANADIAN POEMS

THE LEGEND OF CHILEELI.

(A Transposition from "Schoolcraft.")

WHIR! what glad tidings! what delicious din!
Throw up the windows! Let the songtide in!
The mid-May sky is dapple-gray, earth sere,
And the woods leafless, but the birds are here!

So then I sighed for summer. When it came,
With all its rose-fed reveries, and flame
Of honeyed sunflowers, and the scented thorn,
I wandered out into the woods at morn.
A fair young morn, in which a shower had been,
So all the world was in its deepest green,
And every spot whereon the cool rain fell
Breathed soothing odours. Yet it seemed a spell
Inthralled the woods, for not a leaflet stirred,
And, save the murmurs of a piney herd,
Which sighed aloft, although the nether air
Was still as death,—'twas silence everywhere.

'Twas silence save when sudden voices made
A momentary descant in the shade.
The small birds of the forest were unseen,
Yet ofttimes from their lofty coverts green
Would fall a little trickling melody,
Which leapt at intervals from spray to spray
Like rills from rock to rock. And through the bush
There stole the mournful "Faraway!" of the thrush—
The song of songs! Who hearkens unto it
Soon finds a swarm of old-love memories flit
In dreamy guise about his painèd heart,
And, if he ponder long, then tears will start,

Remembering the pageant of the past,
And thinking how the days which fly so fast
Seem thin and naked, and of little girth,
Compared with old, old vanished days and mirth.

And, as I strolled, there came into my mind,
Out of the lost lore of the savage kind,
Out of the wreck of years, a tale oft told
By Indian maidens to their swains of old.
For, here, a lounger in this woodland world,
Thrilled through with song, each dewy bloom unfurled,
Might feed his spirit, roaming on the brink
Of Fairyland, with fantasies, or drink
At memory's fount. So fictions read in youth,
And parables which hide some deathless truth,
And tales and histories of vanished times,
Traditions dim, and half-forgotten rhymes
Stole in and out of mind as steals some brook
From shade to sunshine, and from nook to nook.
And thus it chanced to stray into my thought,
This quaint old legend of the forest, fraught
With love and loss—this story of a man,
Inspired, but built on Nature's savage plan.

A chief hight Wawanosh, of high renown,
But cruel, proud and stern—a man whose frown
Smote all with fear; whose very smile was cold
As winter's sun when ramping clouds unfold,
And let him look a moment through, then close—
Had one fair child, the paragon, the rose
Of all his tribe; a tender creature, born
To sweeten to the world that bitter thorn
Upon a parent stem, his savage heart.
He could not look on her but he would smart
With inner consciousness (quite out of ken
Whene'er he looked on common maids or men)
Of something there—a soul which he misprized,
So pure and good it was, yet recognized

As infinitely finer than his own.
So would he turn from her with inward groan,
And scowl upon his people till they quailed,
In ignorance that his dark spirit failed
At sight of her. Yet they withstood him not,
And bore it meekly, since he had begot
This loving creature who was all men's praise.
For as a wretch sometimes, by wondrous ways,
Wins a true woman's love, and friends demur,
At first, then chance him for the sake of her,
So could no sire have such a child as she,
A maid so infinitely kind, and be
Outlawed from human liking. Hence they shook
Before him, yet endured, nay, even took
A pleasure in his frowns at thought of her;
But, as for him, there was no blasted fir
More bleached in feeling, dry at heart, and dead.

So when the youth, Chileeli, sought to wed,
And asked him for his daughter, he uprose,
And stared, as if the meanest of his foes
Affronted him. "What! wed her to a boy—
An idler ignorant of war's employ!
A coward who has never fleshed a spear,
Not even in the timid jumping deer!
Begone! lest with a puff of manly breath
I blow thee from my sight. Begone! 'tis death
To ask again. Away! my wrath is hot."
So this young swain, who was a poet, not
A vengeful man by nature, in despair
Fled to the wilds to nurse his passion there.

A mighty promontory, gray and bold,
O'erhung a lonely lake, which lay unrolled
A hill-girt league beneath the summer sun.
Its dreaming waters few e'er looked upon
Save young Chileeli; for dark spirits met,
And whispered round its shores, and so beset

Its pleasant places that his people feared,
And shunned it. Hence upon this height he reared
A bower of living leaves, whereto he stole
To sigh alone, and marvel in his soul
Why he so differed from his fellowmen.
For all were ruthless warriors, and, when
The hatchet was unearthed, all took delight
In the fierce dance, the war-path, and the fight.
And all were keen as eagles in the chase;
Could sight the stealthy fox afar, and trace
The cunning carcajou unto his lair;
Could track the moose, and trap the horrid bear,
And kill sweet birds without a moment's pain,
Or simply wound, nor think of them again.
And all were traders keen, who knew the price
And value of the white man's merchandise;
And, boasting of the gew-gaws they had bought,
Could match him at his very game, they thought.
All fond of gawds, all fond of spoil and blood,
They flew from chase to chase, from feud to feud:
A restless tribe, redeemed by one deep trait,
Their love of her—his dream by night and day.

So he bewailed his fate, for that his life
Jarred, and was out of keeping with the rife,
Rude manhood round him. Why had he been born,
And forced by Nature to endure the scorn
Of Wawanosh and every common brave?
To feel there was no heart this side the grave
Which beat for him? No heart! Ah, there was one,
The sweetest and the fondest 'neath the sun!
One soul who loved, whoever else might jibe
And jeer at this lone poet of his tribe.
Blest thought! Again the flowers looked, as of old,
Companionable, and the woods less cold.
Again those wards of Nature, summer-bright,
Seemed sentient creatures lapt in self-delight.
And o'er the lake some fairy hand had drawn

An amethystine glory, like the dawn
Of some far morn in heaven; a haze which blent
The solemn waters with the firmament
In charmed suffusion, rifted by the day
With dreamy lights, which faded far away
In infinite perspective. Long he gazed
On this entrancing scene, his soul upraised,
Each intuition keener than the last,
Till consciousness into his being passed
Of Nature, and of Nature's final cause:
How the Great Spirit, working through his laws,
Sheds beauty from him as the endless need
Of his supernal essence; hence the breed
Of artist minds, wherein reflected lie
The emanations of his deity.

But what of these? and wherein served they now
The needs of present love? His chieftain's brow
Frowned on his suit because he hated war,
And haunted spirit-lakes and cliffs afar,
And shunned the common looks of common men.
These understood him not, laughed long, and then
Grew cold as death. There was no comfort nigh;
Earth seemed to gloom again, its grace to fly,
And his large heart grow empty as the air.
There seemed no edge, no end, to his despair;
No promise, save in dreams by love distilled,
And longings which might never be fulfilled.

There seemed, in truth, one only way to win;
But to put out the inner light, to sin
Against his better self, to warp, and bend
His nature, even for so great an end,
Cut conscience to the core. He pondered long,
But reason kicks the beam where love is strong;
Nay, turns love's advocate, and smooths away
Its own misgivings and perplexity.

So, step by step, our lover reached resolve:
He, too, would seek the nearest way, and solve
Love's problem with the axe; by paths untried
Win savage Wawanosh unto his side,
Or bear his fate alone.

There is a goal,
In the horizon of each living soul,
By noble toil attained, or cunning plan;
The starting place is naught—all's in the man.
But woe betide the love, the fame, or pelf,
Grasped by a soul unfaithful to itself.
Such love, when won, is dust, such fame a dream,
Such wealth unstable as a desert stream.
So runs the rede Time's ancient tomes unfold;
So runs the sequel of this legend old.

Chileeli's nature seemed to change outright.
He who had shunned the chase, and scorned the fight,
Now craved permission to be made a brave.
This gained, with ceremony due, he gave
Three days to fasting; neither ate nor slept,
Nor moved one muscle of his frame, but kept
The self-same posture all that time alone.
Then came the torture, borne without a groan,
In presence of his tribe; the sacred dance,
The profuse feast, the dreaming-lodge, the trance,
And the awaking to new life, renamed,
Armed like his fellows, and already famed.

Armed, and notorious! For in very truth
A thousand tongues were busy with the youth,
A thousand heads shook gravely. Was not this
The Solitary who thought war amiss,
And all the customs of his people wrong?
Yet now they heard this stripling's double-tongue
Urging them on to strife! What warrior keen
Could trust the changer? Yet, with haughty mien,

This whilom butt of every urchin's jibe
Now dared the foremost hunters of his tribe
To fetch their spoils upon a certain day
And match them with his own. These lounged away,
Smiling askance, and dreaming not of shame,
Till the appointed morn. Their trophies came—
But his! alack, what slaughter! Ears and paws
And tails of panther, wolf, and fox, the claws
Of monstrous bears, mouffles of moose, and wings
Of owls and eagles—in his wanderings
Nothing escaped him. From the innocent wren
To the poor moldwarp in its sinuous den,
All fared alike; the bittern from the brake,
Earth's primal brood, toad, lizard, turtle, snake—
All things that fly, or walk, or crawl, or creep
Were there, in whole or part, in this vast heap,
So that the hunters stared in blank surprise,
And all the people rent the air with cries—
"This is the Slayer!" and made loud acclaim.

This strange exploit so swelled Chileeli's fame
That, when he sought to raise a band for war,
The choicest spirits rallied from afar;
Experienced braves, and youngsters of his clan,
With, here and there, some wizened, wild old man
Who smelt the fray, and would not be denied.
Nay, even Wawanosh unbent his pride,
Coughed, eyed the sun, and sneezed, and then
Cried, "Good! Yet fools oft end where better men
Begin. Still you have chosen wisely. Go!
The way to love's delight lies through the foe."

Enough! Chileeli's soul was all on fire
With eagerness and unfulfilled desire!
He needed not his chief's ungracious praise,
Or any pressure from without, to raise
His spirit to its height. At his behest
The braves were painted, and each scalp-lock drest

All in a trice. The sacred war-song rose,
And swelled upon the night, but, at its close,
He grasped the instant purpose, bade each man
Fall into file, and so the march began.

His scheme was dangerous, the path unknown,
The enemy a race renowned, and blown
With countless triumphs. If he routed them
His purpose was attained—what chief could stem
His claim, or keep him longer from his love?
So, on he hasted in pursuit thereof,
His braves estranged, yet faithful; for an awe
Seemed to inspire their spirits when they saw
The unimaginable light that burned
In his impetuous eyes. Their course now turned
Eastward along a clamouring stream, which played
Its organ-tune amongst the hills, and made
Immortal music. Flowers of precious dye,
And birds of song, appealed as he passed by,
But all in vain. He saw but felt not; heard,
But no responsive sense of beauty stirred
Within his mind distraught. On, day by day,
He and his painted warriors made way.
By stream and hill, by slimy swamp and swale,
Through forests deep and many a sunless vale,
Silent as shadows, stealthily they passed,
And reached, unseen, their enemy at last.

The pathway ended where a tongue of land
O'erlookt the foeman's village. On each hand
The hamlet lay half hid by fruited trees,
And corn and vines and summer's greeneries.
And, nestling where a flower-fringed streamlet run,
Red with the radiance of the setting sun,
Each cabin in the dying lustre stood
Transfigured by romance and solitude.
And life was there, the savage life of old,
Of fine-limbed women and of warriors bold.

Unarmed they gambled by their evening fires,
Or listened to the legends of their sires.
And through the vale the tender echoes spread
Of soft sweet Indian laughter—maidenhead
And youth in dalliance sweet—the joyous cry
Of boys at play—the mother's lullaby.
And young Chileeli in his ambush knelt,
And looked on this, and, for an instant, felt
A spirit rise—his former self—which gave
One parting pang, then vanished in the wave
Of his intense resolve.

The sun went down,
Night's shadows fell upon the little town ;
And when each cabin lay in slumber deep—
As still as death—the very dogs asleep—
Then rose Chileeli from his hiding-place
With all his warriors, and stole apace,
Like phantoms in the darkness, to their ground.
This reached, they listened, but no cabined sound
Of waking life was there ; naught met the ear
Save Sleep's deep breathing, like the moaning drear
Of desert wind. Then rose the awful cry,
The war-whoop wild resounding to the sky !
Each cabin door upon its hinges spun,
And in a trice the savage fight begun !

Chileeli triumphed. Morn had come again
Ere the strife ceased and every foe was slain.
That summer sun showed heaven the direst sight—
Men, women, children, all had perished quite !
Nothing survived ; the very vines were killed,
The corn uprooted, and the fruit trees pilled.
So, when the ruin was complete, and fate
Had filled its measure to the brim ; when hate
Had nothing left to wreak itself upon,
When the hot fever of revenge was gone,
And the fell lust for blood no longer burned,
Chileeli and his warriors homeward turned.

That bourne regained, our lover quickly spread
His monstrous spoils before his nation's head—
Grim Wawanosh—who looked, at first, askance
At the array, then took a straiter glance,
And cried, "Why, this is strange! The youth has brought
Outlandish spoils, unheard of, out of thought!
Not scalps alone, but breasts of maidens fair,
And infants' arms wound in their mothers' hair,
And warriors' string-fingers, ears and toes,
And see! among the rest, this giant nose—
I know it well—'tis Honka's! he who thrust
His knife here once; he too has bit the dust!
Enough! This youth has won his choice of wives—
Go, bring my daughter here! Whoso contrives
A rarer wedding feast than ours to-day
Must range afar!"

Chileeli dared not stay
The messenger, for all things, life and death,
Were in the chieftain's hands, who, with a breath,
Could make or mar his fate. But, now, a thing—
A strange delay which set all wondering—
Took place. The messenger returned, and said
That he had sought, but could not find, the maid.
Then other, and still other men were sent,
But each came back in like bewilderment.
And soon the tribe was all astir, the ground
Ransacked for leagues, and yet she was not found;
Nor by her tribe, in forest or on plain,
Was that chief's daughter ever seen again.

The people mourned for her, by day and night,
But young Chileeli was distracted quite.
Once more he shunned his fellowmen, and now
Haunted the dreamy promontory's brow
Where stood his bower, and brooded there alone.
But all was changed; the mystic charm had flown,
The beauty perished. He had wrenched his heart,

And wrested to vain ends its better part;
Earth's grace had vanished, for his soul was blind.
One aim remained, one bootless aim, to find—
What seemed irrevocably lost—his love!
But how, or where? What spirit from above,
Or from earth's shadows under, good or ill,
Could waft her to his side, or work his will?
Haggard and spent with searching, here and there
His eye turned restlessly—the gloomy stare
Of one half-mad, who looks from this to that
By turns, as if mere longing had begat
The thing desired. Then all at last grew blank—
A dull, dead space wherein his spirit sank,
As sinks some drowned thing in the desolate wave.

For hours he sat in stupor thus, nor gave
One sign of life, till suddenly there came
Upon the air a voice which called his name
Midst wingings soft. Then, slowly opening wide
His listless eyes, he presently espied,
Above the neighbouring wood, a wondrous bird,
Which thrilled the air with voice till now unheard,
As if some flower had risen from its throng,
On shining wings, and burst into a song!
And ever was its tender voice the same—
Chileeli! still Chileeli! still his name!
So that his heart leapt up, and hopes and fears
Chased through his fevered soul, and burning tears
Oozed from his aching eyes. What spell was this
That lay on him? Her fond embrace, her kiss—
He felt such raptures now! What spell was it
Which caused that winged form to descend, and sit,
And gaze upon him from the neighbouring thorn?
Ah, me! What magic now was in the morn?
For, as he looked, the bird began to grow,
Its shape to change, its plumage, white as snow,
Or myriad-tinted, turned to floating hair,
And soon there stood, transformed before him there,

His very love! who, in his ravished sight,
Bent on him once again her looks of light.

Ah, such another vision ne'er was seen,
So fond a gaze yet passionless a mien!
Divinely featured, of seraphic hue—
Her face seemed not of earth, yet cherished, too,
An earthly beauty, for her upper lip
Was Cupid's bow, clear-cut, yet 'neath each tip
A little cherub nestled in a smile!
He rushed to clasp her glorious form, the while
It backward fled, and faded into air—
Then reappeared in shape supremely fair,
And waved him to his place with warning hand.
Then came her voice—"Approach not where I stand!
I am immortal, thou wast born for death!
Thy earthly love shall perish like thy breath;
For love's almighty Father neither asks
The baser service of the world, nor tasks,
Nor tempts the heart to win by ways unblest.
Not his the indirection, or behest,
Which ruled thy hand; for what is pure must be
Won by pure deeds—the Spirit's mastery
O'er lust and temporal fears. And since that thou
Wouldst win unwisely, and hast stained thy brow,
Bewrayed thy poet-function, thrust apart
Thy finer nature, and abused thy heart,
Therefore the Father of pure thoughts hath ta'en
Me from thy path, and from the bitter pain
Of thy unhallowed love. Yet do I feel
My woman-spirit yearn, and fain would steal—
For love is strong—into thy life forlorn;
Into thy sinful being, tempest-torn;
Away with thee unto thy destined shore,
Thy silence and thy darkness evermore!

"Alack, what have I said? Adieu! Adieu!"

Her form became a bird again, and flew
Far off unto the bourne of endless life.
And he? Alas, the unavailing strife—
The search for that which never could be found!
Crushed by despair, he swooned upon the ground,
And lay for long as dead; then rose again,
To feel love's hunger and undying pain
Still gnawing at his heart. He could not sleep;
So dry his life had grown he could not weep.
He sought his tribe, and found it still intent
On war and spoil. Old Wawanosh unbent
His sullen brow, and caught him by the hand,
Then, grinning fiercely, offered him command,
With a fresh choice of wives! Their very sport
Seemed drearier than death; and, all amort,
And spirit-sunk, like many a thing of yore,
He fled away, and ne'er was heard of more.

1885.

A BALLAD FOR BRAVE WOMEN.

A STORY worth telling our annals afford,
'Tis the wonderful journey of Laura Secord!
Her poor crippled spouse hobbled home with the news,
That Bœrstler was nigh! "Not a minute to lose,
Not an instant," said Laura, "for stoppage or pause—
I must hurry and warn our brave troops at Decaw's."
"What! you!" said her husband, "to famish and tire!"
"Yes, me!" said brave Laura, her bosom on fire.
"And how will you pass the gruff sentry," said he,
"Who is posted so near us?"

"Just wait till you see!
The foe is approaching, and means to surprise
Our troops, as you tell me. Oh, husband, there flies
No dove with a message so needful as this—
I'll take it, I'll bear it. Good-bye!" with a kiss.
Then a biscuit she ate, tucked her skirts well about,
And a bucket she slung on each arm, and went out.

'Twas the bright blush of dawn, when the stars melt from sight,
Dissolved by its breath like a dream of the night;
When Heaven seems opening on man and his pain,
Ere the rude day strengthens and shuts it again.
But Laura had eyes for her duty alone—
She marked not the glow and the gloom that were thrown
By the nurslings of morn, by the cloud-lands at rest,
By the spells of the East, and the weirds of the West.
Behind was the foe, full of craft and of guile;
Before her a long day of travel and toil.

" No time this for gazing," said Laura, as near
To the sentry she drew—

" Halt ! You cannot pass here ! "
" I cannot pass here ! Why, sirrah, you drowse !
Are you blind ? Don't you see I am off to my cows ? "
" Well, well, you can go ! " So she wended her way
To the pasture's lone side, where the farthest cow lay,
Got her up, caught a teat, and, with pail at her knees,
Made her budge, inch by inch, till she drew by degrees
To the edge of the forest : " I've hoaxed, on my word,
Both you and the sentry," said Laura Secord.

With a lingering look at her home, then away
She sped through the wild-wood—a wilderness gray—
Nature's privacy, haunt of a virgin sublime,
And the mother who bore her, as ancient as Time ;
Where the linden had space for its fans and its flowers,
The balsam its tents, and the cedar its bowers ;
Where the lord of the forest, the oak, had its realm,
The ash its domain, and its kingdom the elm ;
Where the pine bowed its antlers in tempests, and gave
To the ocean of leaves the wild dash of the wave ;
And the mystical hemlock—the forest's high-priest—
Hung its weird, raking top-gallant branch to the east.

And denser and deeper the solitude grew ;
The underwood thickened and drenched her with dew.
She tript over moss-covered logs, fell, arose,
Sped and stumbled again by the hour, till her clothes
Were rent by the branches and thorns, and her feet
Grew tender and way-worn and blistered with heat.
And on, ever on, through the forest she passed,
Her soul in her task, but each pulse beating fast ;
For shadowy forms seemed to flit through the glades,
And beckon her into their limitless shades ;
And mystical sounds—in the forest alone,
Ah, who has not heard them ?—the voices ! the moan

Or the sigh of mute nature which sinks on the ear,
And fills us with sadness, or thrills us with fear?
And who, lone and lost in the wilderness deep,
Has not felt the strange fancies, the tremours which creep
And assemble within, till the heart 'gins to fail,
The courage to flinch, and the cheek to grow pale,
Midst the shadows which mantle the Spirit that broods
In the sombre, the deep-haunted, heart of the woods?

She stopt—it was noonday. The wilds she espied
Seemed solitudes measureless. "Help me!" she cried;
Her piteous lips parched with thirst, and her eyes
Strained with gazing. The sun in his infinite skies
Looked down on no creature more hapless than she,
For woman is woman where'er she may be.
For a moment she faltered, then came to her side
The heroine's spirit—the Angel of Pride.
One moment she faltered. Beware! What is this?
The coil of the serpent! the rattlesnake's hiss!
One moment, then onward. What sounds far and near?
The howl of the wolf! yet she turned not in fear,
Nor bent from her course, till her eye caught a gleam,
From the woods, of a meadow through which flowed a
stream,
Pure and sweet with the savour of leaf and of flower,
By the night-dew distilled and the soft forest shower;
Pure and cold as its spring in the rock crystalline,
Whence it gurgled and gushed 'twixt the roots of the pine.

And blest above bliss is the pleasure of thirst,
Where there's water to quench it; for pleasure is nursed
In the cradle of pain, and twin marvels are they
Whose interdependence is born with our clay.
Yes, blessed is water, and blessed is thirst,
Where there's water to quench it; but this is the worst
Of this life, that we reck not the blessings God sends,
Till denied them. But Laura, who felt she had friends
In Heaven, as well as on earth, knew to thank
The Giver of all things, and gratefully drank.

Once more on the pathway, through swamp and through
mire,
Through covert and thicket, through bramble and brier,
She toiled to the highway, then over the hill,
And down the deep valley, and past the new mill,
And through the next woods, till, at sunset, she came
To the first British picket, and murmured her name;
Thence, guarded by Indians, footsore and pale,
She was led to FitzGibbon, and told him her tale.

For a moment her reason forsook her; she raved,
She laughed, and she cried—"They are saved! they are
saved!"
Then her senses returned, and, with thanks loud and deep
Sounding sweetly around her, she sank into sleep.
And Bœrstler came up; but his movements were known,
His force was surrounded, his scheme was o'erthrown.
By a woman's devotion—on stone be't engraved!—
The foeman was beaten, and Burlington saved.

Ah! faithful to death were our women of yore.
Have they fled with the past, to be heard of no more?
No, no! Though this laurelled one sleeps in the grave,
We have maidens as true, we have matrons as brave;
And should Canada ever be forced to the test—
To spend for our country the blood of her best—
When her sons lift the linstock and brandish the sword,
Her daughters will think of brave Laura Secord.

THE LAST BISON.

(Written in 1890.)

EIGHT years have fled since, in the wilderness,
I drew the rein to rest my comrade there—
My supple, clean-limbed pony of the plains.
He was a runner of pure Indian blood,
Yet in his eye still gleamed the desert's fire,
And form and action both bespoke the Barb.
A wondrous creature is the Indian's horse;
Degenerate now, but from the "Centaurs" drawn—
The apparitions which dissolved with fear
Montezuma's plumed Children of the Sun,
And throned rough Cortez in his realm of gold!

A gentle vale, with rippling aspens clad,
Yet open to the breeze, invited rest.
So there I lay, and watched the sun's fierce beams
Reverberate in wreathed ethereal flame;
Or gazed upon the leaves which buzzed o'erhead,
Like tiny wings in simulated flight.
Within the vale a lakelet, lashed with flowers,
Lay like a liquid eye among the hills,
Revealing in its depths the fulgent light
Of snowy cloud-land and cerulean skies.
And rising, falling, fading far around,
The homeless and unfurrowed prairies spread
In solitude and idleness eterne.

And all was silence save the rustling leaf,
The gadding insect, or the grebe's lone cry,
Or where Saskatchewan, with turbid moan,
Deep-sunken in the plain, his torrent poured.

Here Loneliness possessed her realm supreme,
Her prairies all about her, undeflowered,
Pulsing beneath the summer sun, and sweet
With virgin air and waters undefiled.
Inviolate still! Bright solitudes, with power
To charm the spirit—bruised where ways are foul—
Into forgetfulness of chuckling wrong,
And all the weary clangour of the world.

Yet, Sorrow, too, had here its kindred place,
As o'er my spirit swept the sense of change.
Here sympathy could sigh o'er man's decay;
For here, but yesterday, the warrior dwelt
Whose faded nation had for ages held,
In fealty to Nature, these domains.
Around me were the relics of his race—
The grassy circlets where his village stood,
Well-ruled by custom's immemorial law.
Along these slopes his happy offspring roved
In days gone by, and dusky mothers plied
Their summer tasks, or loitered in the shade.
Here the magician howled his demons up,
And here the lodge of council had its seat,
Once resonant, with oratory wild.
All vanished! perished in the swelling sea
And stayless tide of an encroaching power
Whose civil fiat, man-devouring still,
Will leave, at last, no wilding on the earth
To wonder at or love!

With them had fled
The bison-breed which overflowed the plains,
And, undiminished, fed uncounted tribes.
Its vestiges were here—its wallows, paths,
And skulls and shining ribs and vertebræ;
Gray bones of monarchs from the herds, perchance,
Descended, by De Vaca first beheld,
Or Coronado, in mad quest of gold.
Here hosts had had their home; here had they roamed,

Endless and infinite—vast herds which seemed
Exhaustless as the sea. All vanished now!
Of that wild tumult not a hoof remained
To scour the countless paths where myriads trod.

Long had I lain 'twixt dreams and waking, thus,
Musing on change and mutability,
And endless evanescence, when a burst
Of sudden roaring filled the vale with sound.
Perplexed and startled, to my feet I sprang,
And in amazement from my covert gazed,
For, presently, into the valley came
A mighty bison, which, with stately tread
And gleaming eyes, descended to the shore!
Spell-bound I stood. Was this a living form,
Or but an image by the fancy drawn?
But no—he breathed! and from a wound blood flowed,
And trickled with the frothing from his lips.
Uneasily he gazed, yet saw me not,
Haply concealed; then, with a roar so loud
That all the echoes rent their valley-horns,
He stood and listened; but no voice replied!
Deeply he drank, then lashed his quivering flanks,
And roared again, and hearkened, but no sound,
No tongue congenial answered to his call—
He was the last survivor of his clan!

Huge was his frame! the famed Burdash, so grown
To that enormous bulk whose presence filled
The very vale with awe. His shining horns
Gleamed black amidst his fell of floating hair—
His neck and shoulders, of the lion's build,
Were framed to toss the world! Now stood he there
And stared, with head uplifted, at the skies,
Slow-yielding to his deep and mortal wound.
He seemed to pour his mighty spirit out
As thus he gazed, till my own spirit burned,
And teeming fancy, charmed and overwrought

By all the wildering glamour of the scene,
Gave to that glorious attitude a voice,
And, rapt, endowed the noble beast with song.

THE SONG.

Hear me, ye smokeless skies and grass-green earth,
Since by your sufferance still I breathe and live !
Through you fond Nature gave me birth,
And food and freedom—all she had to give.
Enough ! I grew, and with my kindred ranged
Their realm stupendous, changeless and unchanged,
Save by the toll of nations primitive,
Who throve on us, and loved our life-stream's roar,
And lived beside its wave, and camped upon its shore.

They loved us, and they wasted not. They slew,
With pious hand, but for their daily need ;
Not wantonly, but as the due
Of stern necessity which Life doth breed.
Yea, even as earth gave us herbage meet,
So yielded we, in turn, our substance sweet
To quit the claims of hunger, not of greed.
So stood it with us that what either did
Could not be on the earth foregone, nor Heaven forbid.

And, so, companioned in the blameless strife
Enjoined upon all creatures, small and great,
Our ways were venial, and our life
Ended in fair fulfilment of our fate.
No gold to them by sordid hands was passed ;
No greedy herdsman housed us from the blast ;
Ours was the liberty of regions rife
In winter's snow, in summer's fruits and flowers—
Ours were the virgin prairies, and their rapture ours !

So fared it with us both ; yea, thus it stood
In all our wanderings from place to place,
Until the red man mixed his blood
With paler currents. Then arose a race—
The reckless hunters of the plains—who vied
In wanton slaughter for the tongue and hide,
To satisfy vain ends and longings base.
This grew ; and yet we flourished, and our name
Prospered until the pale destroyer's concourse came.

Then fell a double terror on the plains,
  The swift inspreading of destruction dire—
Strange men, who ravaged our domains
  On every hand, and ringed us round with fire ;
Pale enemies, who slew with equal mirth
The harmless or the hurtful things of earth,
    In dead fruition of their mad desire :
The ministers of mischief and of might,
Who yearn for havoc as the world's supreme delight.

So waned the myriads which had waxed before
  When subject to the simple needs of men.
As yields to eating seas the shore,
  So yielded our vast multitude, and then—
It scattered ! Meagre bands, in wild dismay,
Were parted and, for shelter, fled away
    To barren wastes, to mountain gorge and glen.
A respite brief from stern pursuit and care,
For still the spoiler sought, and still he slew us there.

Hear me, thou grass-green earth, ye smokeless skies,
  Since by your sufferance still I breathe and live !
The charity which man denies
  Ye still would tender to the fugitive !
I feel your mercy in my veins—at length
My heart revives, and strengthens with your strength—
    Too late, too late, the courage ye would give !
Naught can avail these wounds, this failing breath,
This frame which feels, at last, the wily touch of death.

Here must the last of all his kindred fall ;
  Yet, midst these gathering shadows, ere I die—
Responsive to an inward call,
  My spirit fain would rise and prophesy.
I see our spoilers build their cities great
Upon our plains—I see their rich estate :
    The centuries in dim procession fly !
Long ages roll, and then at length is bared
The time when they who spared not are no longer spared.

Once more my vision sweeps the prairies wide,
  But now no peopled cities greet the sight ;
All perished, now, their pomp and pride :
  In solitude the wild wind takes delight.
Naught but the vacant wilderness is seen,
And grassy mounds, where cities once had been.
    The earth smiles as of yore, the skies are bright,
Wild cattle graze and bellow on the plain,
And savage nations roam o'er native wilds again !

The burden ceased, and now, with head bowed down,
The bison smelt, then grinned into the air.
An awful anguish seized his giant frame,
Cold shudderings and indrawn gaspings deep—
The spasms of illimitable pain.
One stride he took, and sank upon his knees,
Glared stern defiance where I stood revealed,
Then swayed to earth, and, with convulsive groan,
Turned heavily upon his side, and died.

MISSIPOWISTIC.

(Written at the Grand Rapids of the Saskatchewan.)

HERE, in this howling torrent, ends
The rushing river, named
By savage man
Saskatchewan—
In dark tradition famed.

His source, Creation's dread abyss,
Or in the glacier's cell;
His way, the sweep
Of canyons deep,
And clefts and chasms fell.

And forth from many a mountain's side
He leaps with laughter grim;
Their spurs are slit,
Their walls are split,
To make a path for him.

And down into the plains he raves
With dusky torrent cold,
And lines his bed
With treasure shred
From unknown reefs of gold.

And, monster-like, devours his shores,
Or, writhing through the plain,
Casts up the while
Full many an isle,
And swallows them again.

For though, betimes, he seems to sink
Amidst his prairies pale,
He swells with pride
In summer-tide,
When low-born rivers fail.

And knits tradition to his shores
Of savage fights and fame,
When poaching Cree
The Blackfoot free
With magic arms o'ercame.

Of Wapiti and Spanish horse,
And of the bison horde,
A transverse stream,
As in a dream,
Which flowed at every ford.

And of the whites who first espied
His course, their toils and cares;
Of brave Varennes,
The boast of men,
And prince of voyageurs!

Of ancient settlement and farm
Ere France his wantons pressed;
Ere royal mind
For lust resigned
The Empire of the West.

Of him who once his waters churned—
The bluff fur-trader King—
Mackenzie bold,
Renowned of old
For his far wandering.

Of later days, when to his shores
The dauntless Franklin came;

Ere Science lost,
In Arctic frost,
The life, the lofty aim.

Or of the old *Bois-brûlé* town,
Whose huts of log and earth
Rang, winter-long,
With jest and song,
And wild plain-hunters' mirth.

And of the nearer, darker day,
Which saw their offspring leap
To arms, and wake,
With frenzied shake,
Dull Justice from her sleep.

Or, turning to the future, dreams
On Time, and prophesies
The human tide
When, by his side,
Great cities shall arise.

The sordid tide, the weltering sea,
Of lusts and cares and strife;
The dreaded things
The worldling brings—
The rush and roar of life.

And onward tears his torrent still,
A hundred leagues withdrawn,
Beyond the capes
And silvan shapes
And wilds of Chimahaun.

Down through the silent forest land,
Beyond the endless marge
Of swale and brake,
And lingering lake,
Beyond the *Demicharge*.

Till at the Landing-place he lifts
His crest of foam, and, quick
As lightning, leaps
Adown the steeps
Of Missipòwistic!

Whilst o'er him wheels the osprey's wing—
And, in the tamarac glades
Near-by, the bear
And Mooswa share
Their matchless mossy shades.

Whilst echoes of the huskies' yells
From yonder woods are flung
At midnight dim,
A chorus grim,
As if by demons sung!

But, see! Here comes a birch canoe!
Two wiry forms it bears,
In quaintest guise,
With wrinkled eyes—
Two smoke-dried voyageurs!

"We'll take you down! Embarquez donc—
Embarquez donc, monsieur!
We'll steer you through
The channel true,"
Cries each old voyageur.

"Nay, look ye, men—those walls of foam,
Yon swirling 'cellars' fell!"
"Fear not to pass,
Thou Moniyas!
We know this torrent well."

"I've roamed this river from my youth—
I know its every fork."

"And I have made,"
The other said,
"Full many a trip to York!"

Soho! I'll go! The Rapids call!
With hamper at my wing
We sally down
Their foaming crown
Like arrow from the string—

Into the yeast of waters wild,
Where winds and eddies rave!
Into the fume
And raging spume
And tempest of the wave!

Past rocky points, with bays between,
Where pelicans, bright-hued,
Are flushed to flight
With birds like night—
The cormorant's impish brood!

And madly now our frail craft leaps
Adown the billows' strife,
And cleaves their crests
And seething breasts
As 'twere a thing of life.

As dips the pandion for his prey
So dips our bark amain.
We sink and soar,
And sink and soar,
And sink and soar again!

Till, following the foaming fall
Of one long, throbbing wave,
Enrapt we glide,
And seem to slide
Down, down into its grave!

"O break! O break! sweet balm, soft air!"
No, no, we mount! we rise!
Once more the dash
And deafening clash
Of billows flout the skies.

Till, swept o'er many a whirling swell,
The final surge is past,
And, like the strife
Of human life,
We reach calm floods at lāst.

Now, thanks, ye grim old voyageurs!
No man has flinched in fear—
Yet in earth's round
I've seldom found
This life and death so near.

Thanks, thanks to you, good men and true!
Here we shall rest awhile,
And toast the bold
Coureurs of old
Upon the Prisoners' Isle.

THE IROQUOIS AT THE STAKE.

(*Ancien Règime, circa* 1680.)

BROTHERS! all things have end, as hath this feast—
This farewell feast of sweet sagamity
And fine brown flesh of beaver and of bear.
Your own provision I have thus set forth
After the ancient custom. Whilst you ate
I sat aside, and thought how we are one—
In language, race—in all things one save love.
I sat aside, and pondered in my soul
The severing hate which seals my lingering death,
Yet sweetens still the foretaste of its pangs.

The feast now over—bowls well scraped—but first,
Confess I run the gauntlet well! Ah, ha!
No hatchet hit this loftier head than yours,
And, save these mangled hands, all's right with me!
Why not, since you, the quarry of my chase,
Have ne'er o'ertaxed my speed to run you down?

This galls you! Good! Let womanish passion rise—
Your childish rage—and break my leave to speak!
When captives of your nation give us feasts
We let them speak; yet, I remember me,
They but beseech their miserable lives—
Not death, with torture, as we do.

One word!
In lieu of him who perished by this axe
Yon dotard will not take me for a son—
A substitute worth fifty of his tribe!
Belike, that wench rejects my brotherhood,

Though thus she might be sister to a man,
Not to a Yendat dog with soul askew,
Who sneaked and snarled. This is your Chief's desire—
As far from mine as I am from your power
To make me quail at aught that you can do.
What! Lift you up! An Onondaga help
Your recreant breed to rise! Nay, were this urged,
Then would your torture strike!

You bear with this!—
Struck dumb, mayhap, by some ancestral thought.
For, Yendats, I perceive we might be one
But for this flood of hate which, turned to love—
For now my thoughts clear up with coming death—
Might well oppose the flux which threatens all;
Those pale, thin streams which up our inlets pour—
Diverse, yet deadly. Ah! "Yonondio
Is still your friend with whom you trade," you say,
"As we do with Corlaer"; and, true, their tools
Are finer than our flints, their kettles thin,
And better than our clay, their arms—but, what?
"*No more!*" you cry; then lead me to the stake!
(*He is led by the Hurons to the place of torture.*)
Now here, behold me! Atotaroh's son!
For he it is you ambushed yesterday—
A goodly prize—so now exhaust yourselves!
But, hark! no common cords, since you must tie
An Onondaga's very spirit down!
You will not heed! and I am bound, you fools,
After your fashion! for one strain, and see!
Your moosewood strings and linden lashings snap
Like rotten twigs! (*Flings them in their teeth.*) You
must be taught to bind!

Chut! yelping urchins, hence! Ye wizened crones
And screeching hags, stand off! Your wise men know
I am their sacrifice, and not your sport.
Ye warriors, what I would say is this:

Naught holds the Onondaga but his stocks
Of iron-wood, or the hard gray willow withe.
Bring this, then tie me to our people's tree—
The foliaged elm, leaf-wreathen to the root!

Believe me, chiefs, I have no fear of death—
That lies not in the compass of my soul!
Nay, I rejoice in this your sacrifice
To great Areskoui, who, from the sun,
Looks down upon us all. Yet there are thoughts—
Like storm-clouds beating up against the wind,
Or eddies running counter to the stream—
Which fain would stem our currents of revenge.
For did Yonondio but look on this—
Corlaer! those rival raveners, whose maws
Would drink our rivers and devour our lands!
How they would smile to see you round me now,
And whisper, sidelong, from their screening palms—
"One foe the less, one fertile tract the more!"
Ah, they would gloat upon this dance of death;
For they who still beseech will yet demand,
And dance in grinning triumph round you all!
(*Ironical cries*)
Have we not heard—but wherefore should I speak,
Since you but mock me with assent? forked words
Wherewith unwittingly you stab yourselves!
Have you not heard your fathers' tales of yore—
How the destroyers voyaged with the sun
O'er boiling reaches of outlandish foam,
And, anchoring fast by many a torrid isle,
Woke the mild Arrawac from his livelong dream?
You *have* not! care not! Foes are friends, friends foes,
In the dread turmoil which confuses all!
Yet, if your ears have served not, I have seen
Old Wamesits and Wampanoags who know
Their pale-faced pilgrims from across the sea;
The men who came with faded, upturned eyes,
And, supplicating some outlying land,

With subtle leasing, straight enlarged themselves—
Who from the gift made title to the whole,
And thrust the red man back upon the ribs
Of spiny mountains, bleak with summer snow,
Till great Metàcomet arose, and fell!
And, otherwhere, encased in iron they came,
Or in black robes—and won you to their side!
Through you they smote us, tore our castles down,
And sought to lay the mighty "Long-House" low,
Which else had spread—a shelter for us all!
Away all thoughts and feelings save my hate,
Which burns and hisses in my veins like fire—
Hate infinite and fierce, whose sense will dull
The pangs of all your faggots and your flames!
O fools! we were the tempest, you the leaves
Which fled before it! Traitors to our race,
Where *are* ye? Erie or Andasté, speak!
Ye craven remnants of the Yendat—where?
Your emptied forests tell—your ruined towns!
O you poor creatures of Yonondio, blush!
Your women should deride, your children jeer,
And Atahensic, from her silver home,
Look down and curse you! Ah! come back, my soul!
This rage is viler than the fear of death!
O Jouskeha, give calm! that I may feel,
And so endure, and by endurance please
Arèskoui and thee!

The withes at last!
My meaning has been reached, and I am bound!
No flimsy setting this, half-fast, half-free,
But the triced frame, as stubborn as the elm!
Ah, there is something yet unsaid, but, no—
The darkness falls! Now, torches and the Fire!

KANATA.

THE Eastern and the Western gates
  Are open, and we see her face!
Between her piney steeps she waits
  The coming of each alien race.
Dear Genius of a virgin land,
  Kanata! Sylph of northern skies!
Maid of the tender lip and hand,
  And dark, yet hospitable, eyes.

Thou art our Spirit of Romance,
  Our Faerie Queen, our Damsel lorn,
Who, framed by some mysterious chance,
  In undiscovered woods wast born.
In days of love and life gone by,
  Ere waned the light, ere ebbed the tide,
Wild singers sought thy company,
  And supple forms from forests wide.

They sported on the golden shore,
  And far dim headlands of the past;
Untrammelled all, their spirits bore
  No sense of soil by passion cast.
No philosophic doubts were theirs,
  No tideless, stern pursuit of gain,
No weariness of life, no cares,
  No yearnings underlaid with pain.

But, wild and true and innocent,
  They plucked the blossom of the year,
Where savours of the woods were blent
  With music of the waters clear.

Death had no tears; it but revealed
   A spectral world to spectral eyes,
Where spirit-wildings roamed afield,
   And spirit-pinions swept the skies.

Where still the chase they would pursue,
   And o'er the vacant rivers glide
With ghostly paddle and canoe,
   With phantom forests on each side—
Forever, where no frost should fall
   To waste the sweetness of the light,
Nor old age and its funeral,
   Nor bitter storm, nor ancient night.

'Tis past, Kanata! Weightier days
   Strain tight the girdle of the year;
Pale feet are in thy forest-ways,
   Pale faces on thy plains appear;
And eyes, adventurous, behold
   The gathering shadows on thy brow,
Where sacred graves of grassy mould
   Turn black beneath the westering plough.

Thy plains are whispered of afar,
   Thy gleaming prairies rich increase;
And, leaning on their tools of war,
   Men dream of plenitude and peace.
For Europe's Middle Age is o'er,
   And still her ways are undefined,
And darker seem the paths before
   Than the dark paths which lie behind.

Perchance! but still I see them come—
   Her uncouth peasants, seeking rest,
Sighing for sympathy, a home
   And shelter in the peaceful West,

Where ancient foes in race and creed
  May never more the tyrants see,
Who eat the bread of craft and greed,
  And steal the wine of liberty.

Vain promise and delusive dreams
  Which gloze the hidden, narrow heart;
Here man's own vile and selfish schemes
  Will yet enact the tyrant's part.
Alas! for equal life and laws,
  And Freedom 'neath the Western sun;
Here must they stand or fall—her cause
  On these fresh fields be lost or won.

Still must she fight who long hath fought;
  Still must she bleed who long hath bled;
There is no consecrated spot,
  No clime where she alone doth tread.
Devise for her your "simple plan,"
  Or "perfect system," as of old;
They count not where insensate man
  Spurns his own right to be controlled.

VAIN REGRETS.

WHEN I recall the days misspent,
The unabiding hours of youth,
The erring thoughts with pleasure bent,
The poor and shallow search for truth,
Then vain regrets take hold of me
That, sailing on the summer sea,
I dreamt not of a wintry flood
Which I must cross in solitude.

Had I but thought of this—descried
The stormy winds, the tempest strong,
The heaving wave, the darkling tide—
Discretion then had found a tongue.
I should have studied well the art
Of seamanship—the pilot's part—
Re-rigged my craft, without, within,
And laid my soul's provision in.

Repining ! 'Tis the way with man :
Repine not ; rest, O heart, secure !
Affections lie within thy span
Of thoughtlessness which must endure.
There friendship had its steadfast root,
There true love bore its fadeless fruit.
If these condemn, then let me be
Wrecked on the future's stormy sea !

Call back the past, and let us hear
Its tender voices as of yore ;
Let the old welcomes greet the ear,
The old friends meet us as before.

And, ah! let memory fulfil
Her perfect task—bring back the thrill
Of chords long hushed, of loving sighs,
And eyliads from vanished eyes!

They are not dead, they do but sleep;
  They come! I see, I feel them all.
By recollection touched, they leap
  Responsive to the spirit's call.
Depart from me, ye vain regrets,
Ye selfish fears which time begets!
The future, like the past, is mine,
For memory's light is light divine.

Then courage! to the helm, the sail,
  And let the roaring tempest frown!
What though the billows should prevail,
  What though the whelming waters drown?
They cast us on the further shore:
Think not they change what nature bore—
Fond, unreflecting souls, yet true
To friendship, love, and Heaven, too!

OPEN THE BAY!

"The navigation of Hudson's Straits is impracticable."—*Enlightened Hudson's Bay Company Trader from Ungava.*

"The Hudson's Bay route is a chimera."—*Patriotic Toronto Newspaper.*

OPEN the Bay, which o'er the Northland broods,
Dumb, yet in labour with a mighty fate!
Open the Bay! Humanity intrudes,
And gropes, prophetic, round its solitudes,
In eager thought, and will no longer wait.

Open the Bay which Cabot first espied
In days when tiny bark and pinnace bore
Stout pilots and brave captains true and tried—
Those dauntless souls who battled, far and wide,
With wind and wave in the great days of yore.

Open the Bay which Hudson—doubly crowned
By fame—to science and to history gave.
This was his limit, this his utmost bound—
Here, all unwittingly, he sailed and found,
At once, a path of empire and a grave.

Open the Bay! What cared that seaman grim
For towering iceberg or the crashing floe?
He sped at noonday or at midnight dim,
A man! and, hence, there was a way for him,
And where he went a thousand ships can go.

Open the Bay! the myriad prairies call;
Let homesteads rise and comforts multiply;

Give to the world the shortest route of all,
Let justice triumph though the heavens should fall!
This is the voice of reason—manhood's cry.

Open the Bay! Who are they that say "No"?
Who locks the portals? Nature? She resigned
Her icy reign, her stubborn frost and snow,
Her sovereign sway and sceptre, long ago,
To sturdy manhood and the master, Mind!

Not these the foe! Not Nature, who is fain
When earnest hearts an earnest end pursue;
But man's old selfishness and greed of gain:
These ancient breeders of earth's sin and pain—
These are the thieves who steal the Nation's due!

Such are the heirs of traders Gillam led—
Such were they in the past, with souls obtuse
When duty called—who, recreant, and dead
To England's honour, hung the craven head,
And struck the British flag to La Perouse.

And such are they who, in their Eastern place,
Say, "It is folly and the purpose vain!"
The carrier and the shallow huckster's race—
Theirs are the hands, not Nature's, which efface,
And seal the public good for private gain.

Open the Bay! Let Earth's poor people in!
What though the selfish interests lie and flout—
Open the Inlet! Let them growl and grin,
And Power still hobnob with them in their sin—
Humanity, their master, is about!

It looks abroad, and with purged vision sees
Man's wily nature bared, not overcast;
It comes to scatter to the winds his pleas,
His privilege and bland accessories,
And with strong arm right the wronged land at last.

IN MEMORY OF WILLIAM A. FOSTER.

AND he is gone, who led the few
  Forecasters of a nation fair;
That gentle spirit, strong and true
  As ever breathed Canadian air!

Forever fled? the kindly face,
  The eager look, the lambent eye,
Still haunted by a boyish grace—
  Can these from recollection fly?

The counsel sound, the judgment clear,
  The mild thought brooding over all,
The ready smile, the ready tear—
  Can these from recollection fall?

Ah! well do I remember still
  The sultry day, whose sun had set;
The hostel near the tower-crowned hill,*
  The parlour dim where first we met;

The flush of hope, the joy divine
  On that pale eve of loftier times,†
When, with his friendly hand in mine,
  He praised my poor Canadian rhymes;

And sung the old Canadian songs,‡
  And played the old Canadian airs,
Then turned his smile on fancied wrongs,
  And laughed away a youth's despairs;

---

* Parliament Hill.

† Confederation.

‡ Mr. Foster was fond of French-Canadian song; its vivacity and plaintiveness equally touched him.

And said: "Throw sickly thoughts aside—
Let's build on native fields our fame;
Nor seek to blend our patriot pride
With alien worth or alien shame!

"Nor trust the falterers who despond—
The doubting spirits which divine
No stable future save beyond
Their long, imaginary line!

"But mark, by fate's strong finger traced,
Our country's rise; see time unfold,
In our own land, a nation based
On manly deeds, not lust for gold.

"Its bourne the home of generous life,
Of ample freedom, slowly won,
Of modest maid and faithful wife,
Of simple love 'twixt sire and son.

"Nor lessened would the duty be
To rally, then, around the Throne;
A filial nation, strong and free—
Great Britain's child to manhood grown!

"But lift the curtain which deceives,
The veil that intercepts the sight,
The drapery dependence weaves
To screen us from the nobler light.

"First feel throughout the throbbing land
A nation's pulse, a nation's pride—
The independent life—then stand
Erect, unbound, at Britain's side!"

And many a year has fled, and now
The tongue which voiced the thought is stilled;
The veil yet hangs o'er many a brow,
The glorious dream is unfulfilled.

Yet Ocean unto Ocean cries!
  For us their mighty tides go forth.
We front the sun—behind us lies
  The mystery of the unconquered North!

And ardent Aspiration peers
  Beyond the clouds, beyond the night,
Beyond the faltering, paltering years,
  And there beholds the breaking Light!

For, though the thoughtful mind has passed
  From mortal ken, the generous hand—
The seed they sowed has sprung at last,
  And grows, and blossoms through the land.

And time will realize the dream,
  The light yet spread o'er land and wave;
And Honour, in that hour supreme,
  Will hang his wreath o'er Foster's grave.

Written in 1888.

ABSENCE.

MY thoughts are full of gloom to-night, my heart is full of pain ;
And tears, dull as a blind man's, roll adown my cheeks like rain.
And yet the moon is beaming bright, the stars are shining true,
Yet dimly, in their distant skies and fields of palest blue.
Within my home the lamp-light shines a chamber's length along,
And there my children's voices rise in laughter and in song.
Without, assembled here and there, the trees like phantoms stand,
And cast their spectral shadows down upon the spectral land.
And all around are sweetest sounds—the music of the night,
The sidelong whisper of the leaves, the churme of waters bright.
A dream of fragrance fills the air, the moon-flower's cup o'erflows,
And subtle ears, perchance, may hear the breathing of the rose.
The dark green earth, the pale blue heaven with mellow grace are clad,
The night-flower blows, the music flows, and yet my heart is sad.

For my delight is far from me—it comes not at my call,
The perfect womanhood, which gave a meaning to them all.
The burning rose turns to the moon its folded heart, dew-fed,
The gentle lily shrinks and hides its pure and stainless head.

They are but parts of Nature's plan ; my love unites the whole,
As if the rose's glowing form possessed the lily's soul.
Full well I know, behind the veil, a loving purpose reigns
Through all the mystery of earth, its pleasures and its pains.
Tree sighs for tree, flower sighs for flower, love binds them in its thrall ;
But she is far away whose love, with mine, discovered all.

THE RIVER OF PAIN.

THERE is a stream which flows beneath the skies,
  Whose flood is fed by aching hearts and eyes.
Onward it rolls forever down the years,
In seeming peace, yet brimmed with secret tears.

Few seek to trace it to its hidden source;
Few arms are stretched to stay it in its course.
With life it flows, with life's expiring breath
It leaps in anguish to the sea of death.

Yet time's allurements on its surface glow,
And on its banks the flowers of passion blow;
Its charmèd water silvers on the oar,
Its hollow laughter peals from shore to shore.

For there the worldlings sail, affect to rest,
Or, sated, sleep upon its fleeting breast;
Or, fevered, wake to find themselves again
But further borne adown this stream of pain.

Beset with fears, perturbed by human ill,
They dread the fated flood, yet haunt it still,
Like Custom's slaves, who, blinded by desire,
Build and rebuild o'er subterranean fire;

Nor note that counter current's strong employ—
The grief, the tears which thrill with finer joy—
The stream which, set against the world's device,
Flows back to Heaven through self-sacrifice.

Or catch a glimpse of that immortal clue,
Yea, clearly see when sense to soul is true ;
Yet coldly turn aside, nor seek to gain
The simple issue from the maze of pain.

But idly sigh—" Sufficient for the day
The ills thereof, inseparate from Life's clay ; "
Or, " Other men may come when we are gone,
And solve the problem—let the stream roll on ! "

CABOT.

WHAT matters it if on the stormy shore
Of wild Newfoundland or stern Labrador
His foot first fell, or on Cape Breton's strand?
The dauntless sailor somewhere hit the land!

The Land! No pent-up nursling of the seas,
Fanned in the Gulf-stream by the torrid breeze;
For Ocean grim this grim sea dog had cast,
Triumphant, on his furthest shore at last.

With loud huzzas St. George's banner flew,
First o'er the main—a world, an Empire new!
Whilst woke the Continent, and, from his lair,
The wilding rushed, and shook his streaming hair!

Time sped, and saw full many a flag unfurled
In fierce contention for that virgin world;
Saw France's star by Britain's sun effaced,
And Britain's flag by kindred hands abased.

Yet time beheld the trampled banner rise
Victorious beneath Canadian skies,
And races nurtured 'neath its sway go forth,
In welded strength the Nation of the North.

And where is he who gave a realm to these
Large heirs of Freedom, rulers of its seas?
What recompense was his? What high acclaim?—
An unknown grave, a half-forgotten name!

But, no! The hour is ripe; its tumult stills
Whilst Canada her sacred task fulfils.
At last* the triumph sounds, the laurels twine,
And incense burns at Cabot's matchless shrine!

---

* The Cabot celebration at Halifax, N.S., in 1897.

DEMOS TYRANNUS.

AVAUNT, thou monstrous product of the time,
Cruel, remorseless, shallow and untrue!
Vain charlatan that ever lead'st anew
The yearning world along the paths of crime,
Misusing Science—thou that seek'st to climb
To ruinous control with more ado
Than monarch to his Throne! What meed is due
Thy horrid bent, save scorn in prose or rhyme?
Art thou Democracy's incarnate dream?
Is thine the Gospel of its better day?
Wisdom, high mind, compassion, honour spurn
The foul imposture. No, a holier gleam—
The thought humane which leads, but not astray,
Is still the light to which true spirits turn.

The thought of frail Humanity; its tears,
Its plenitude of suffering and sin,
Its tender heart when shame first enters in,
That self-same heart grown callous with the years.
Its visage hardened by the sounds it hears—
The moil of countless miseries, the din
Of wrangling schemes which end where they begin—
Its mind so fit for joy, so worn with fears.
We stumble yet discern, Humanity!
These are the burdens which oppressed Christ's soul,
Wrought up to triumph, midst earth's vanity,
By self-effacement; this the aureole
Which yet shall crown thy brows with light divine—
The emblem of His victory—and thine!

THE RECOMPENSE.

(To a Great Poet.)

THE world still juggles with its pleasure, feigns
Wherein it lacks, and lives pretentious days,
Spurning calm joys, truth, beauty, simple ways—
These old inspirers of the poet's pains.
O Solitary ! still be these thy gains,
The harvest of thy thought, the things of praise,
The solemn chords of thy remembered lays,
The notes which live when worldly mouthing wanes !
Nor these alone thy glory and reward ;
For Inspiration hath a sexless joy
Sweeter than lover's dreams. Thy flights afford
Fairer nativities than Love's employ ;
The offspring of a Spirit set apart,
Yet knit forever to the human heart.

RUINS.

THERE is a forest in the wild north land
  So weird and grim the very lynxes thread,
With quickened pulse, its glades and shadows dread.
  Its jagged stems, black and fire-blasted, stand
  Close-rooted in the dull and barren sand;
And over league-long hills and valleys spread
Those ruined woods—a forest dark and dead—
  A giant wreck in desolation grand:
Like to that other world, the mind of man,
  Wherein are wastes once innocent and dear,
Where beauty throve till fires of passion ran,
  And blighted all. When to such deserts drear
The spirit turns, in retrospection wan,
  The proudest starts, the boldest shrinks in fear.

THE CHAIN.

ONCE from the bitter page of Doubt it hapt
That, wearily, I turned me to the wall,
And, lo ! there, in the hearth's dull embers, all
The self-same thoughts which harrowed me seemed mapt.
But near were coiled a cat and kitten, lapt
In furry dream ; then next, where lay in thrall
Of slumber softer than a feather's fall
Dear wife and babe, I stood in silence rapt.
O endless chain of being and of love,
O paths and pathos of mysterious sleep,
Ye pointed to a world yet undescried !
Strange calm befell me, light as from above,
And thoughts which man can neither yield nor keep :
My heart was filled, my house was glorified !

FULFILMENT.

TWICE has the Winter sallied from his lair,
In seeming triumph, and as quick retired
Into the north again. So things desired,
And loved, still linger in St. Martin's care.
The flowers have vanished, and the woods are bare;
But, all around, stray forms, by Autumn fired,
Still glow like flowers, and many a thought inspired
By Summer, yet is fit for later wear.
Fit and unfit—since naught consists with Time!
For, 'twixt this being and what is to be—
Brief space where even Pleasure holds his breath—
All's incomplete. Life's but a faulty rhyme,
Conned half-contentedly o'er land and sea,
Till comes the infinite Creator—Death!

NOTES TO "TECUMSEH."

TECUMSEH AND THE PROPHET.

Note 1. Page 11.

The tribe from which Tecumseh sprung was a branch of the wide-spread *Lenni Lenapé*, or Delaware race, which had long been settled in the South, and which, for this reason, received the name of the Shawanoes, or "Southerners." Having become involved in disputes with the Creeks, Yamasees, and other powerful tribes in Georgia and the Floridas, the Shawanoes removed to the Valley of the Ohio, in the first half of the last century, or earlier, and spread themselves along the banks of the Scioto River and Great Miami. The immense region west of the Alleghanies was then an unbroken wilderness, with the exception of the villages, or towns as they were called, of the red men; and it was in one of these that Tecumseh was born. The name has given rise to much conjectural interpretation, the most plausible being that of the Indian missionary, Kah-Keway-quonaby (the Reverend Peter Jones), who derives it from Ta-Kuh-mo-sah, "He Who Walks Over the Water." But this is a misnomer, for the chief's proper name was Tecumtha, not Tecumseh, the "a" being sounded as in the word "far." Two seemingly very divergent interpretations have been given by various writers, viz., "The Shooting Star" and "The Panther Crouching, or Lying in Wait," and owing to the recondite origin of the name both are correct. The research of the distinguished philologist, Professor Gatschet (Report for 1892-3 of the Smithsonian Bureau of Ethnology), has at last made the meaning perfectly clear. He says the two renderings of Tecumseh's name, viz., "The Shooting Star" and "The Panther Crouching, or Lying in Wait," have a common origin. "The name of Tecumtha is derived from *nila-ni-tkamthka*, 'I cross the path or way of somebody, or of an animal.' This indicates that the one so named belongs to the class of the round-foot or claw-foot animals, as panther, lion, or even racoon. Tecumtha and his brother belonged to the clan of the *manetuwi msipessi*, or 'miraculous panther'—*msi*, great, big; *pishiwi*, abbreviated *pessi*, cat, both combined meaning the American lion. So the translations, 'panther lying in wait' or 'crouching lion,' give only the *sense* of the name, and no animal is named in it. But the *msi-pessi*, when the epithet 'miraculous' (*manituwi*) is added to it, means a celestial tiger, *i.e.*, a meteor, or shooting star. The *manituwi msi-pessi* lives in water only, and is visible not as an animal, but as a shooting star, and exceeding in size other shooting stars. This monster gave name to a Shawano clan, and this clan, to which Tecumtha belonged, was classed among the claw-foot animals also. The quick motion of the shooting star was correctly likened to that of a tiger or wild-cat rushing upon his prey. Shooting stars are supposed to be souls of great men all over America. The home of the dead is always in the West, where the celestial bodies set, and since meteors travel westward, they were supposed to return to their western home." Tecumseh is thus a corruption of Tecumtha, but the former has so completely displaced the latter in books, place-names and conversation, that the author, in conformity with long-established usage, retains it.

The portrait in this volume is, with the exception of the British uniform, a reproduction of the one given by Lossing in his "Pictorial Field-Book of the War of 1812," the head in which was taken from a sketch made by Pierre le Dru, at Vincennes, Indiana, before Tecumseh espoused the British interest. The uniform was borrowed by Lossing from another sketch which he saw in Montreal in 1858, and which, he says, was made at Fort Malden soon after the surrender of Detroit. Tecumseh may have donned a major-general's uniform upon some special occasion—a review or a banquet—but, if so, it was soon discarded for his simple buckskin tunic, leggins, quilled fillet, and eagle plume. The costume as now restored corresponds with contemporary description, and the portrait is in other respects an authentic likeness.

Tecumseh was born about the year 1768, either at Piqwa, on a tributary of the Great Miami River, or at Chilicothé, another old Indian village on the Scioto, in what is now the State of Ohio. His father was killed at the battle of Kanawha, where, on the 10th October, 1774, Lord Dunmore's forces defeated the celebrated Chief Cornstalk. His mother was a Cherokee woman, and is said to have been delivered of Tecumseh, the Prophet, and a third brother at the same time. Tecumseh became celebrated in early manhood for his exploits against white encroachers on the Ohio, and was engaged in almost every struggle of his people against the Americans down to the day of his death. Engrossed in projects for the defence of his race, he did not marry until long after the usual period, and then only as a matter of policy and in deference to the urgent desire of his friends. His genius was first aroused to its fullest activity by certain transfers known as the Treaties of Fort Wayne, whereby an extensive region on the Ohio, running up one of its tributaries, the Wabash, on both sides, for a great distance, was ceded to the whites. These treaties, made by alleged irresponsible Indians or village chiefs, as they were called, meant, of course, displacement to a number of tribes, whose war chiefs alleged that their people, not having been consulted in the making of them, had been swindled. Tecumseh had foreseen that nothing but combination could prevent the encroachments of the whites upon the Ohio, and had long been successfully endeavouring to bring about a union of the tribes who inhabited its valley. The Fort Wayne treaties gave a wider scope to his design, and he now originated his great scheme of a federation of the entire red race. In pursuance of this object his exertions, hitherto very arduous, became almost superhuman. He made repeated journeys, and visited almost every tribe from the Gulf of Mexico to the Great Lakes, and even north of them, and far to the west of the Mississippi. In order to further his scheme he took advantage of his brother's growing reputation as a prophet, and allowed him to gain a powerful hold upon the superstitious minds of his people by his preaching and predictions. The Prophet professed to have obtained from the Great Spirit a magic bowl, which possessed miraculous qualities; also a mystic torch, presumably from Nanabush, the keeper of the sacred fire. He asserted that a certain belt, said to make those invulnerable who touched it whilst in his hands, was composed of beans which had grown from his flesh; and this belt was circulated far and wide by Indian runners, finding its way even to the Red River of the north. These, coupled with his oratory and mummeries, greatly enhanced an influence which was possibly added to by a saturnine countenance, made more forbidding still by the loss of an eye. Unfortunately for Tecumseh's enterprise, the Prophet was more bent upon personal notoriety than upon the welfare of his people, and, whilst professing the latter, indulged his ambition, in Tecumseh's absence, by a precipitate attack upon Harrison's force on the Tippecanoe. His defeat discredited his assumption of supernatural powers, led to distrust and defection, and wrecked Tecumseh's plan of independent action. But the protection of his people was Tecumseh's sole ambition, and, true statesman that he was, he joined General Brock at Amherstburg (Fort Malden), in Upper Canada, with a large force, and in the summer of 1812 began that series of services to the British interest which has made his name a household word in Canada and endeared him to the Canadian heart. As Colonel Coffin says, in his "Chronicles of the War of 1812," "His death sheds a halo on a much-abused and fast-departing race. May the people of England, and their descendants in Canada, never forget this noble sacrifice, or the sacred obligation it imposes. It should be held as the seal of a great covenant: 'And Jonathan said to David, The Lord be between thee and me, and between my seed and thy seed forever.'" Those who buried Tecumseh never revealed the secret of his burial place, and the Indians resented, for many years, any attempt to explore the region of his last battle for his grave. It is not likely that his bones will ever be recovered; but to Canadians, whose fathers were the friends of his race, there remains the duty of perpetuating his memory. There is not in all history a nobler example of true manhood and patriotism.

Note 2. Page 12

" The Prophet! Olliwayshilla, who probes
The spirit-world."

The Prophet assumed several names. His first was Laulewasikaw, or Lalowe'thika, sometimes written Olliwayshilla. According to Professor Gatschet, it means "a rattle," or similar instrument, hence its common interpretation by the whites, "The Loud Voice." After the burning of Tetaboxti and others for wizardry he changed his name to Tenskwatawa, "The Open Door"—from *Skwat'e*, a door, and *the'nui*, to open. "The Prophet was held to be an incarnation of Manabozho, the great 'first-doer' of the Algonquin system." In the year 1808, in order to facilitate the project of a confederacy, Tecumseh and he established a village at the junction of a stream called by the Indians Tippecanoesipi, or Night-Owl River, with the Wabash (The White River), one of the largest tributaries of the Ohio. The site of the village was well chosen, being far above the white settlement of Vincennes, yet having easy access to it down the river. The village, which was known as the Prophet's Town, soon became the resort of large numbers of Indians, who flocked to it as the headquarters of the revived faith and of Tecumseh's military power. After the battle of Tippecanoe the Prophet fell into disrepute, and is said to have ultimately retired with the remnant of his tribe to the Indian Territory, where he died some sixty years ago.

In the foregoing note the author has followed the hitherto accepted authorities as to the origin of the Prophet's Town. In the Fourteenth Annual Report of the Bureau of Ethnology, Smithsonian Institute, however, a different account is given, as follows: "The new settlement, which was on the western bank of the river, just below the mouth of the Tippecanoe, was known to the Indians as *Kehtipaquononk*, 'the great clearing,' and was an old and favourite location with them. It had been the site of a large Shawano village which had been destroyed by the Americans in 1791, and some years later the Potowatami had rebuilt upon the same place, to which they now invited the disciples of the new religion. The whites had corrupted the name to Tippecanoe, and it now generally became known as the Prophet's Town."

Note 3. Pages 12, 13.

" For I should treat our foes to what they crave—
Our fruitful soil—yea, ram it down their throats,
And choke them with the very dirt they love."

After the defeat of Harmar and St. Clair's forces by the Indians, many of the American dead were found with their mouths crammed with earth—a grim satire upon the land-hunger of the white man.

Note 4. Page 13.

"*The Prophet's robe,*
That I assumed when old Pengasega died."

The Prophet, or Josakeed, is held in reverence by all pagan Indians. He uses an unknown tongue in important ceremonies and in the mysteries of the *Metay-win*—the most sacred festival of the Algonquin race. To the back of his robe, or to some other part of his person, is affixed the skin and outspread wings of a raven or other bird—the invariable badge of the Prophet's office. Though some Josakeeds are impostors, yet generally they are firm believers in their own powers. They appear to exercise more beneficent functions than those of the Medicine-man, and to aim at the moral elevation of their people. The Medicine-man, on the other hand, is a juggler and exorcist, whose mysterious doings are a puzzle to the onlooker. He is feared as a man who has dealings with Evil Spirits. Tecumseh's famous brother assumed to succeed Pengasega (the Change-of-Feathers), a Prophet whose death was much lamented amongst the Shawanoes of his region. The more sinister functions of a magician he superadded, in order to increase his influence and further his selfish ambition.

Note 5. Page 14.

"*Old Shataronra's grave*
Sends up its ghost, and Tetaboxti's hairs—
White with sad years and counsel."

The somewhat sudden rise of the Prophet provoked at first much jealousy amongst certain of his tribe, who felt that he was undermining them. To counteract it, he instituted a persecution for sorcery, which involved both sexes. Numbers were burnt, including those named, before Tecumseh, who was absent, could interfere.

Note 6. Page 16.

"*Of Long-Knife forts, encampments, and their chiefs.*"

. . . .

"*Then he declared he was a Saganash.*"

The American is called by the Indians of the Algonquin race *Chemo-komaun*, or the Long-Knife, from the sabre. The Englishman, or Canadian, they call *Saganashay*, the Ojibway form of the Cree word *Aka-yas-see: Aka-yas-see-wuk*—"People who have sailed across." These were general names, understood or made use of by most Indians; and nations other than the Delaware made use of them, or simply translated them into their own tongue, according to their custom. Other names, however, were sometimes given. The Shawanoes, for example, called the Englishman *Metticosea*. The Algonquin word *Chemo-komaun* became greatly softened in the southern dialects, and is scarcely recognizable in the musical Shawano word *Shemaunthé*.

Note 7. Page 17.

"*In headship with our Saganash allies.*"

Tecumseh, who foresaw a war between England and the United States, dreamed of taking part in it as the leader of an independent power, and of coming in at its successful end as one of the signatories to a treaty of peace, securing the rights of his people.

Note 8. Page 17.

"*And agent sent by General Harrison.*"

General William Henry Harrison was born at Berkley, in Virginia, in 1773, and was the son of Benjamin Harrison, one of the signers of the Declaration of Independence. He was aide-de-camp to General Wayne in his campaign against the Indians in 1794, and in 1801 was appointed Governor of the newly-formed Indiana territory, a vast region which, extending from the Ohio to the Mississippi, contained at that time but three small settlements of white men, including the old French village of Vincennes. This region was inhabited by numerous tribes of Indians, many of whom cultivated maize, possessed orchards, and had on the principal streams considerable villages, consisting of rude log cabins but little inferior to those of the early white settlers. The destruction of these towns, as they were called, and the treatment of the aboriginal inhabitants of this region, now constituting numerous populous States, is one of the dark chapters in history. Year by year the irresistible tide of whites poured into the territory in ever-increasing volume ; and though Harrison, a man of humane and generous nature, meditated nothing but kind and just treatment of the native races, and warmly advocated it both publicly and privately, yet nothing could restrain the rapacious adventurers, who spread themselves everywhere, and looked upon Indian treaties as so much waste paper. To have opposed their grasping spirit too strongly would have brought upon Harrison political extinction, and he was therefore, it may be taken for granted, compelled to wink at aggression and injustice too often veiled under the specious name of progress. Harrison's victory at Tippecanoe won him great repute, and was the precursor of the war of 1812. His subsequent victory, with a greatly superior force, over Tecumseh and Proctor at the Moravian Town, established his fame amongst his countrymen. He shortly afterwards resigned his commission, disgusted with unfair treatment at the hands of the Secretary of War, and retired to his farm at North Bend, on the Ohio, whence in 1839 he was called to the Presidency of the United States. He died deeply regretted by the American people, shortly after his inauguration.

Note 9. Page 17.

"*You are an enemy to the Seventeen Fires.*"

At this time the United States numbered seventeen, and were called by the Indians the Seventeen Fires, in accordance with their own custom of Council Fires, around which all their deliberations took place.

Note 10. Page 23.

"*First comes his pioneer, the bee.*"

It is a curious fact in natural history, that the wild bee has been in America the pioneer of the white man. Its first appearance on the Saskatchewan is within the memory of men still alive.

Note 11. Page 23.

"*His flowers, his very weeds, displace our own.*"

The European flowers and weeds are usurping the place of the indigenous flora of North America. The white clover, for example, which, it is said, forty years ago had only reached the Sauk Valley, in Minnesota, is now found hundreds of miles farther to the north-west.

Note 12. Page 26.

"*So that your cabin flows with mouffles sweet,*
And hips of wapiti, and bedded robes."

The mouffle is the nose of the moose, or American elk. When boiled for a long time it becomes very tender and jelly-like, and is a delicacy. The wapiti is the American red deer, frequently miscalled the elk.

Note 13. Page 28.

"*Who fought, as devils fight, until the lodge*
Shook to its base with struggling."

The performances of the Indian Medicine-men in their medicine lodges are very curious. The lodge is a structure of poles and dressed skins, sometimes large enough to accommodate fifty people. The Medicine-man enters it alone, and presently the sounds of altercation are heard in an unknown tongue; flashes of fire issue from the lodge, which begins to rock, and is, at last, so violently shaken as to threaten its overthrow. These feats are performed simultaneously, and sometimes for prolonged periods. Collusion must be very adroitly employed, for intelligent half-breeds, who have frequently witnessed the performance, assert that there is none. The belief is prevalent amongst them that the genuine Medicine-man possesses extraordinary and occult powers; and, certainly, their performances deserve more investigation than they have yet received.

Note 14. Page 29.

"*Roped round with scars and cicatrized wounds.*"

The initiation of warriors is a solemn ordeal amongst most Indian nations. On reaching manhood the candidate prepares himself for his trial by a severe and sleepless fast, lasting several days. This is followed by elaborate religious ceremonies, after which the aspirant, in presence of the chiefs and warriors of his tribe, is subjected to dreadful tortures. Sharp splinters are thrust between the skin and muscles of his breast and back, and from these he is suspended by cords, and turned round slowly, so as to produce excruciating pain, which must be borne without a murmur to be accounted a satisfactory test of the candidate's endurance. Other trials and ceremonies follow, and the candidate, if he acquits himself heroically throughout, assumes the status of a trusty warrior of his nation. The marks of this ordeal remain in hard, cord-like scars, which are ever after the proud evidence of fortitude and unquailing courage. These ordeals are sometimes repeated in after life, and warriors are to be met with on the western plains to-day who exhibit five or six rows of these great cicatrices on their breast, back and arms. The preliminary initiation of boys was, and probably is still, practised by the southern tribes. It was called the *Huskenaw*, and began with dancing, in which the old and young of both sexes took part. The boys "ran the gauntlet," and were then confined in the woods for several weeks and fed solely upon roots. The object each boy most frequently dreamt of during this period became his guardian spirit for life. Implicit faith is placed by the Indians in dreams, and fasting is often resorted to in order to induce them. If an Indian dreams of things above the earth, as of stars, clouds, etc., the dream is considered favourable; if below, the reverse.

Note 15. Pages 30 and 33.

"*And made their hosts a winter's feast for wolves.*"

. . . .

"*And old Kanaukwa, famed when we were young.*"

General Harmar was defeated in September, 1791, by Michi-Kanaukwa, or Little Turtle, as he was called by the Americans. In the following November General St. Clair was defeated by the same chief, with great loss. Hundreds of the American dead were left unburied on the field, and were devoured by wild animals. After the treaty of Greenville, consequent upon the victory of General Wayne, in 1794, the Little Turtle settled at Eel River, and lived in a house furnished by the American Government. This conduct subjected him to the suspicion of his people; and his equivocal attitude in the negotiation of the Fort Wayne Treaty of 1803 confirmed it.

Note 16. Page 32.

"*And with the peace-pipe sits beside their fire.*"

The calumet—a corruption of the Norman *chalumeau*—was constantly employed by the Indians in treaty-making. The Ojibway pipe was made of green porphyry, and was called the *pwagun*. The pipe of the Plain Indians was made of a red sand-stone taken from the ancient pipe-stone quarry in western Minnesota.

Note 17. Page 35.

" *White wampum, not the dark, till we can strike
With certain aim.*"

Wampum (once greatly valued by the Indians) was made from several kinds of shells, particularly the mussel, the clam and the conch. Pieces of the thickness of a small clay pipe-stem, and about half an inch in length, were with great labour cut from the enamel, perforated, and strung on sinews, so as to form belts. These, according to the adjustment and colour, were tribal records or the symbols of peace or war. The colour of the war-belt was purple or red; of the peace-belt, white. European traders substituted porcelain for the shell wampum, and degraded its value; for, like the *cowry* in India, it was used by the Red Indians as money. It has long been disused.

Note 18. Page 37.

" *You've heerd o' them Delaware Moravians, surely?*"

The horrible incident recorded in this passage is an historical fact. The descendants of the remnant that escaped are still in possession of their lands at the Moravian Towns, Ontario, and are still presided over by a Moravian missionary.

Note 19. Page 41.

" *Gold is the king who overrides the right.*"

The better class, the thoughtful people of the United States, feel deeply the want of honour in the treatment of the Indians. The late Mrs. Helen Hunt Jackson wrote a most powerful appeal in their favour, and entitled it "A Century of Dishonor." Bishop Whipple, of Minnesota, in the preface he contributed to the work, says: "The sad revelation of broken faith, of violated treaties, and of inhuman deeds of violence will bring a flush of shame to the cheeks of those who love their country."

Note 20. Page 41.

" *But look at him! Look at Tecumseh there—
How simple in attire!*"

Tecumseh had hazel eyes, an aquiline nose, and a somewhat oval countenance. "He was," says Colonel Coffin ("Chronicles of the War of 1812"), "about five feet ten inches in height, and of a well-knit, active figure. Contrary to the Indian nature, he had an aversion to external ornament. His invariable costume was the deer-skin coat and fringed pantaloons. Indian moccasins on his feet, and an eagle feather, completed his simple and soldierly accoutrements." The foregoing is the gist of minute accounts left by the late Colonel Glegg, of Thursteston Hall, Cheshire, General Brock's *aide*, and Colonel Hatch, one of General Hull's officers at the surrender of Detroit.

Note 21. Page 48.

"*He'd better put a lump o' bacon in his mouth to keep his bilin' sap o' passion down.*"

In making maple sugar the settler suspends a piece of fat bacon on a string over the cauldron to prevent the sap from boiling over. The Indians use a spray of the balsam spruce for the same purpose.

Note 22. Page 57.

"*My fear sits like the partridge in the tree,*
And cannot fly whilst these dogs bark at me."

Settlers in the backwoods of Canada train their dogs to flush the ruffled grouse, miscalled the "partridge." The birds take refuge in a tree, at whose root the dogs keep up an incessant yelping, which seems to puzzle them, so that they stick to their perches and become an easy prey. In order to secure them all, they must be shot successively from the lowest bird upwards.

Note 23. Page 58.

"*Each coulee and ravine.*"

In western America certain prairie water-courses are called coulees. The melted snow, etc., is carried off by them in spring, but in summer and winter they are generally quite dry.

Note 24. Page 60.

"*Hark! 'Tis the war-song.*"

Ye-awe! hi, ya! whe, ya wha! a-a-a-a-a, whe, ya wha! a-a-a-a-a.

The foregoing chant, which is taken from Peter Dooyentate Clarke's "Origin and Traditional History of the Wyandots," is substantially the same as that now in use by the Indian tribes in the British North-West Territories and elsewhere. The chant, which to the uninstructed on-looker appears to be mere gibberish, is an invocation to the Great Spirit—the changes being rung upon the sacred syllables, *yo* and *wah*. Yo-he-wah is the Indian's sacred name for the Deity. The sacred syllables enter into the construction of many words applicable to the Deity, such as power, light, goodness, etc., and those who think the Indians descendants of the Lost Ten Tribes connect the Indian word with the Jewish Jehovah. The warriors begin the chant in a high key, the voice gradually falling until the sounds are almost indistinct, then swelling up to full pitch again. At intervals the chant is interrupted by war-whoops.

Note 25. Page 64.

"*Go bring the braves to view the Mystic Torch*
And belt of Sacred Beans grown from my flesh."

See Note 1 concerning the above and the Prophet's Magic Bowl.

Note 26. Page 67.

"*Go to the corn-dance, change your name to villain!*"

The corn-dance is held in the middle of August. Children are named at it, and warriors can then change their names if they choose.

Note 27. Page 69.

MAJOR-GENERAL BROCK.

This distinguished soldier was born in Guernsey, in 1769—the year which gave Napoleon and Wellington to the world. At the age of fifteen he entered the British Army as an ensign, and at twenty-eight became lieutenant-colonel of the 49th Regiment. He served in Holland, and was wounded at the battle of Egmont-op-Zee, and subsequently took part in Nelson's attack upon Copenhagen as second in command of the land forces. He was sent to Canada in the spring of 1802, and, after nine years of valuable service, was advanced to the rank of Major-General, and stationed in the upper Province, where, Lieutenant-Governor Gore having gone to England on leave of absence, he succeeded him as Administrator of the Government of Upper Canada in October, 1811. He had been for some time negotiating for a transfer to Wellington's command in the Peninsula; but the breaking out of the war with the United States in 1812 changed all his plans, and his fortunate union of offices gave him control of the civil and military affairs of the Province at the most critical period in its history. Boldness, energy and decision characterized his every movement, infused enthusiasm into the loyal, confirmed the wavering, and overawed the disaffected; and so prompt and speedy were his operations, that in eighteen days from his departure with his force from York (now Toronto), he had conquered Michigan Territory, provided for its government, and returned to Fort George. His intention when he left Detroit was to proceed immediately to Sackett's Harbour on Lake Ontario, and destroy the American naval arsenal there. To his mortification he found that an armistice had been proposed by Sir George Prevost, and consented to by the American General, Dearborn, the intelligence of which only reached him on his way down Lake Erie. In all likelihood he would have succeeded at Sackett's Harbour, and so prevented the Americans from equipping the fleet which gave them the command of Lake Ontario, and enabled them twice to capture the capital of Upper Canada. Strange to say, after Brock's death this unfortunate armistice was capped by another, granted by General Sheaffe at the instance of the American General Smythe, by which the Americans were enabled to equip their fleet at Presqu' Isle, and gain the command of Lake Erie. This preponderance upon the lake was dreaded by Brock, whose movements, however, were paralyzed by the continuous policy of inactivity of the Commander-in-Chief. In one of his letters from Fort George, he says: "The enemy is making every exertion to gain a naval superiority on both lakes, which if they accomplish, I do not see how we can retain the country. . . . I shall refrain as long as possible, under your Excellency's positive injunctions, from every hostile act, although sensible that each day's delay gives him an advantage." On the expiry of the first armistice, and when hostilities began again, Brock exhibited his usual vigilance and promptitude until, on the 13th October, 1812, he met his death gloriously on Queenston Heights. He fell early in the day, but inspired by his example his followers won a complete victory, and signally avenged his death. His monument, erected by the Canadian people on Queenston Heights, is one of the finest in the world, and attests the respect in which his memory is regarded by them, who look upon him as the Americans look upon Washington. His remains, and those of his Canadian aide-de-camp, the gallant Macdonell, who fell in the same battle, rest side by side under the monument.

Note 28. Page 69.

"*Hull's threatened ravage of our western coast.*"

William Hull was born in Connecticut, and upon the outbreak of the Revolution took service in defence of the revolted colonies. He was present in numerous battles, and after the peace became a collector of customs. When well advanced in years he was made Governor of Michigan Territory, and resided in Detroit, then a village. He in Washington in the winter of 1812, and, preparations being then afoot preparatory to a declaration of war, he reluctantly accepted the appointment of brigadier-general in command of the Ohio volunteer militia, embodied to march upon Detroit with a view of a descent upon Canada, to which he was opposed. The fourth regiment of regulars, which had helped to defeat the Prophet at Tippecanoe, and three regiments of militia, were joined to his command. "On the march," says Lossing ("Field-Book of the War of 1812," note to page 260,) "General Hull had been subject to much annoyance from the Ohio volunteers. . . . They were frequently quite insubordinate." . . . This fact was brought out on Hull's trial. "One evening," says Lieutenant Barron, "while at Urbana, I saw a multitude, and heard a noise, and was informed that a company of Ohio volunteers were riding one of their officers on a rail." On arrival at Detroit, Colonel Cass, a young eastern lawyer of fire-eating tendencies, in command of the 3rd Regiment of Volunteers, and others of a kindred spirit, urged a descent upon Canada, which the general opposed, until the arrival of instructions from Washington. These having at last reached him, he issued a boastful and threatening proclamation to the people of Canada (the composition of which has been attributed to Cass), and crossed the Detroit on the 12th July, 1812, but retreated on the 8th of August following. General Brock reached Sandwich, nearly opposite Detroit, on the 15th, and, in conjunction with Tecumseh, quickly matured his scheme of attacking Fort Detroit. The next day Hull capitulated to a force greatly inferior in numbers, and consisting mainly of Canadian volunteers and Indians. He was subsequently tried by court-martial at Albany, N.Y., in January, 1814, and sentenced to be shot. "Mr. Madison pardoned him," says Lossing, "and he returned to his farm to live in comparative obscurity, under a cloud of almost universal reproach." Dispassionate criticism has since to a large extent justified Hull in his conduct.

Note 29. Page 69.

"*Bid Colonel Proctor come.*"

It may be thought that the traits of this officer have been too strongly shaded in the drama. There can be no doubt that his retreat from Amherstburg had its justifiable and prudential side, and what a more daring General, Brock for instance, would have done under the circumstances, one can only conjecture. But General Proctor, by basely casting the blame of the disaster at the Moravian Town upon his troops, weaned from himself all sympathy. He is still held in poor remembrance in Canada. The General Order of the Prince Regent confirming the court-martial held at Montreal in December, 1814, and ordered to be read at the head of every regiment in His Majesty's service, concludes thus: "His Royal Highness has directed the general officer commanding in Canada, to convey to Major-General Proctor His Royal Highness's high disapprobation of his conduct; together with the expression of His Royal Highness's regret that any officer of the length of service and the exalted rank he has attained, should be so extremely wanting in that professional knowledge, and deficient in those active, energetic qualities which must be required of every officer, but especially of one in the responsible situation in which the Major-General was placed."

Note 30. Page 74.

"*Enter two U. E. Loyalists, separately.*"

On the revolt of the American colonies, in 1776, a large number of the colonists remained loyal to the Crown, and fought under the British colours for the maintenance of a United Empire. They were known as the United Empire Loyalists. At the close of the war these loyalists, driven from their homes, came to the wilderness of Canada, where, under severe hardships and trials, they carved new homes in the forest, under the same flag they had fought so hard to uphold. When the war of 1812 broke out, the old loyalists and their hardy sons, burning under the recollection of their wrongs, and valuing deeply the privileges they had sacrificed so much to retain, rallied around Brock to defend once more the unity of the Empire. It was this element that gave tone to public feeling in Upper Canada in 1812. The whole population turned out to fight for Canada. Few but the old men, the women, and the children were left at home in the lonely clearings; and many instances are recorded of tenderly-nurtured ladies, whose husbands were at the front, being left with the little children to protect themselves as best they could against the wolves, which at that time often howled around the log cabins of the early settlers.

Note 31. Page 75.

Colonel Nichol.

Very little is known as to the early career in Canada of this remarkably able man. His grandson, the Rev. R. T. Nichol, an Anglican clergyman, wrote to the author in 1891 for information, and, in a subsequent letter, stated that his grandfather's papers had been entrusted by his uncle, Robert Nichol, to a Major Lundie, an English officer who was in this country many years ago, and who had in hand a history of the war of 1812. The Major died in England, and the papers, so far as the author knows, have not yet been recovered. If lost, it is a grave misfortune to Canadian history. Colonel Nichol was General Brock's right hand. His experience was great; his knowledge of the inner side of affairs during the war thorough; his discernment of character seldom at fault. General Brock, who before the war had recognized his singular ability, took him from civil life and gave him perhaps the most important command after his own. He received a pension from the Imperial Government when the war ended, and became a member of the Upper Canada Legislature, where his career was characterized by scrupulous integrity and an almost ultra-independence of character. He lost his life by driving on a dark and tempestuous night over the cliffs near Niagara Falls. A memorial should certainly be erected to this able loyalist's memory, for his services to Canada were vital.

Note 32. Page 77.

"Not mine, but thine, thou dull and fatuous House!"

In 1812 the House of Assembly of Upper Canada refused to suspend the Habeas Corpus Act, though urgently desired to do so by General Brock. The Lower House roughly reflected the crude, isolated and unprotected condition of Upper Canada. Loyal at heart, it yet contained numbers of disaffected members, and others timid and hesitating, who allowed themselves to be swayed by the boasting and threats of aliens, domiciled in the Province for that very purpose. The invasion of General Hull engendered additional fears and despondency for a time ; and the general procedure of the House was provoking to loyalists of bold and decisive temper.

Note 33. Pages 89, 90.

" *How those giant pears*
Loom with uplifted and high-ancient heads,
Like forest trees ! A hundred years ago
They, like their owner, had their roots in France."

The remarkable old French pear trees, once plentiful along the Detroit River, are now rapidly decaying. The annual rings of one blown down two years ago were found to number one hundred and seventy, so that it must have been planted by the French colonists who founded the settlement of Detroit under de la Mothe Cadillac, in 1701. They are of immense size, and are prodigious bearers ; but, strange to say, cannot be propagated, and before many years will become extinct.

Note 34. Page 90.

" *That hospitable roof*
Of thine, thou good old Loyalist, Baby."

The interesting old Baby mansion, at Sandwich, is still standing. The Baby family (pronounced Baw-bee), which ever since the conquest has been distinguished for its loyalty to the British crown, is one of the most ancient in Canada. The owner of the Sandwich mansion, in 1812, was Colonel the Hon. James Baby, a son of the Baby who rendered such valuable assistance to Major Gladwyn during Pontiac's investment of Detroit in 1763. Colonel Baby was born at Detroit in 1762. He was in the Battle of the Thames, and was taken prisoner there by Harrison, who sent him to Chilicothé, in Ohio, where he was detained for many months. His hospitality and kindness of heart were as proverbial as his loyalty, and after many years of active public service, he died at York (now Toronto), in 1833. In early life Colonel Baby was largely engaged in the fur trade—the engrossing occupation of that day—and in the hall of the mansion is still to be seen the hook from which the balance was suspended upon which the beaver-packs were weighed. The first room to the right of the hall was occupied by General Brock as his headquarters, and there he wrote his demand for the surrender of Detroit. General Harrison subsequently made a similar use of the house, and in it have been successively entertained nearly all the Governors of Canada from an early date down to Confederation.

Note 35. Page 90.

" *Oh, have I eaten of the Spirit-plant !*"

The wild carrot is called by the Indians *Manitou-o-ska-task*, or the Spirit-plant. It has intoxicating or deadly qualities.

Note 36. Page 92.

"*The dancing grouse, at their insensate sport.*"

There is not in animate nature a more amusing sight than the dancing of the prairie grouse during the love-making season. The birds have in their various localities a customary meeting-place, where they assemble and enjoy a veritable "ball," bowing and scraping, crossing and re-crossing, pirouetting and setting to each other in the most grotesquely ceremonious fashion. They often become so rapt in their singular exercise that they can be approached quite closely without taking alarm.

Note 37. Page 101.

"*Here are my pistols—take them from a friend.*"

Brock's presentation of his sash to Tecumseh is said by most writers to have taken place in Detroit. The late Honourable François Baby was present when the pistols were presented, and he is the authority for the latter incident, which is less generally known.

Note 38. Page 103.

"*We heard the crash of battle yesterday.*"

The Battle of Lake Erie was fought near Put-in-Bay, on 10th September, 1813, and resulted in a victory for the Americans. The sounds of the engagement were distinctly heard at Amherstburg, sixty miles away.

Note 39. Pages 104, 105.

"*A fool who beats Sheaffe's folly at the game.*"
"*Force him,*
Who would not face yourself, to face five thousand!"

Squire Reynolds, commissary to H. M. forces at Amherstburg during the War of 1812, in his narrative (see Colonel Coffin's "Chronicle of the War"), describes an altercation between Elliott and Proctor which resulted in a challenge. Proctor's responsible position as commander justified him in refusing to go out. The challenge arose out of his half-hearted attack upon Fort Meigs, in April, 1813, and his disposition to retreat, which was strongly resented by Tecumseh. "Our father," said the latter, "has brought us here to take the fort; why don't we take it? If his children can't do it, give us spades, and we will work like beavers; we'll eat a way in for him." Proctor's vacillation and want of tact reacted in all directions. "He was on bad terms," says Col. Coffin, "with his own regiment, the 41st, of which he was Lieut.-Colonel. There was discord amongst the officers, and the men had lost confidence, and suffered besides from malarial fever induced by long-continued outpost duty and exposure." "He treated the Canadian volunteer militia badly," says Reynolds. "When they saw his guns on skids (at Fort Meigs), and knew the siege was over, they sent respectfully to ask leave to go home, only to put in a crop for his men and their own children. He sent them home and disarmed them. He tried to disgrace them, but they would not be disgraced, because they knew they did not deserve it. Brock was another sort of man. He thought, and felt, and spoke for the men, and other men loved him, and fought for him, and died for him."

A reference to the massacre of prisoners by the Indians at the Raisin River and at old Fort Miami, which so greatly incensed the Americans against General Proctor, may be made here. After the surrender of General Winchester to Proctor in the affair at the former place, a rumour arose that Harrison was advancing rapidly with a large force. Proctor, alarmed at this, beat a needlessly precipitate retreat, leaving not only a number of wounded prisoners but his own wounded and dead. Some of the prisoners were murdered by loose and disorderly Indians who had got at liquor and were drunk, and are said not to have been in the action at all. At the Miami, or Fort Meigs affair, a similar scene was enacted after the capture of an escort, in which Proctor has been much blamed by Americans for non-interference, whilst Tecumseh has been as highly praised for putting an end to the massacre by braining one of the participants with his own axe. Cold-blooded deeds were common to both sides, however, at this period, though too many American historians attribute them solely to the Indians.

Note 40. Page 111.

"*He comes! Yohewa! The Great Spirit comes!*"

Ellen Russell Emerson, in her delightful collection entitled "Indian Myths," extracts from "Archæologia Americana" a description of the Indian ceremonial worship of the sun which suggested this scene. The book referred to is radiant with just thought and the tender sympathies of a true woman.

Note 41. Page 113.

"*The night-sun set in cloud, and curling mists*
Hid the plumed star from sight."

In the Algonquin dialects the moon is called *tipik-ghezis*, or "the night-sun." The Evening Star is called the "plumed star." It is also called "the woman's star." (See "Schoolcraft's Legend of Osseo.")

Note 42. Page 114.

"*Oh, cherish her! for she is dear to me*
As is the Intercessor to your race."

The Indian's Intercessor is Nanabush—the Guardian of the Sacred Fire. Nanabush is supposed to be a dialectic name for the Manabozho of the Ojibways, who is regarded, says Mr. Schoolcraft, "as the messenger of the Great Spirit sent down to them in the character of a wise man, and a prophet. But he comes clothed with all the attributes of humanity, as well as the power of performing miracles."

Note 43. Page 114.

"*Yes for his huskenaw—you call it that.*"

"'*Tis from the self-piece cut, and quilled all o'er—*
Your gathered edges show not half so well."

Among the numerous nations who contributed support to Tecumseh's force were the Dahcotas or Sioux, of the Wisconsin and Upper Mississippi, numbers of whom were with him at the capture of Detroit and at the Battle of the Thames. The Winona of this scene is a Dahcota girl, and her name is that invariably given by a Dahcota mother to her first-born daughter, viz., "the only one." The Dahcota moccasin is cut out of one piece; whereas the Delaware, or Algonquin race, always make theirs with a piece let into the instep, the edges of the sole being turned up and drawn in around it. Some writers say the word Ojibway, frequently written Chippeway, is derived from the peculiar fashion of the moccasin, meaning "gathered"; but this is a mistake. The name Ojibway—*O-cheepo-way*—is given to the Indians of Lake Superior and the Red Lake region from their peculiar manner of dropping the voice toward the end of a sentence; *cheepo* meaning "tapering," and *way*, "sound, or voice."

Note 44. Page 116.

"*All gone! all gone! naught here but smoking ruins!*"

General Proctor burnt Fort Malden, the ship-yard, and the public stores before retreating from Amherstburg.

Note 45. Page 123.

"*Ah! this is our own tree.*"

One of the Indian names for the sugar maple is *nen-au-tick*, "our own tree."

Note 46.

An additional note re *General Proctor.*

Several years after the publication of the first edition of "Tecumseh," a controversy was raised by "Historicus," a Toronto man of letters, in the columns of the Toronto *Daily Mail*, over the character of General Proctor as depicted in the Drama. A number of civil and military correspondents took part in the controversy, which had lasted for some time before the author knew of it, he being then in the remote wilds of

the Saskatchewan. The point raised by "Historicus" was whether it could be proved that General Proctor was a coward. It is impossible to quote authorities *in extenso* here. But history, and emphatically the tradition as to General Proctor's conduct, still extant upon the Detroit frontier, are, to the author's mind, very clear. As a recent Edinburgh reviewer says, "To set up the incomplete records of the past against the incontrovertible testimony of authentic tradition is often the shallowest pedantry." Perhaps the author is astray in his notion of what constitutes cowardice; for if a soldier's running away at the beginning of a battle is not it, then truly it is a hard matter to determine. A report of Colonel Nichol, evidently intended for the information of the Prince Regent, and which has never seen the light, but which the author has permission to use, contains the following passage:

"On the 8th September, 1812, I left Amherstburg for the headquarters of the army under General Brock, but, owing to contrary winds, did not reach Niagara until the 15th. Immediately on my arrival I was ordered to make a confidential report on the state of that part of the country to the General (Brock), which I did, and among other things felt it my duty to state several strong reasons which, in my opinion, totally disqualified General Proctor for so important a command. The General, on perusing my report, was pleased to express his satisfaction at what he chose to call the full and comprehensive view I had taken of the subject, and added, respecting General Proctor, that he was fully aware of all I had stated, concluding in these words: 'I think him a brave man, and believe he will fight, but I fear he will disgust everybody with whom he has anything to do; but I have no other officer to send.' His fears were, alas! prophetic; and the ruin of our affairs to the westward was the consequence."

Brock's opinion of Proctor was formed in a time of peace, and therefore he could not foretell, with certainty, what his conduct would be in a great emergency. Down to the Commander's death Proctor's experience on the Detroit frontier had been comprised within a few months, and his unhappy reputation was largely added to by his subsequent transactions there.

In a letter of "Historicus," replying to Mrs. Curzon—one of the author's defenders—and referring to an extract from "Tecumseh," he says:

"She will find even here quite enough to challenge inquiry. Proctor is made to give timid counsels at Detroit (Sandwich); Brock is made to leave him in command only because he is 'straitened for good officers'; there is a sneer at his prudence; and Tecumseh is made to express his misgiving at the appointment on the ground that while Brock says 'come,' Proctor says 'go'—in other words, that Proctor is wanting in gallantry as a leader."

As regards the first point in the foregoing passage, it is enough to quote the following extract from General Brock's letter to his brother after the surrender of Detroit:

"I crossed the river contrary to the opinion of Proctor, etc. It is, therefore, no wonder that envy should attribute to good fortune what, in justice to my own discernment, I must say proceeded from a cool calculation of the *pours* and *contres*."

That Brock, at the beginning of hostilities, was greatly hampered for want of efficient officers is made plain by the following passage from his letter to his brother Savery, written from Fort George on September 18th, 1812. Proctor was Colonel of the 41st regiment, and this is what Brock says about it:

"I have now officers in whom I can confide. When the war began I was really obliged to seek assistance among the militia. The 41st is an uncommonly fine regiment, but wretchedly officered."

The foregoing, compared with the extract from Colonel Nichol's report, makes it a certainty that Proctor was one of the "wretched officers."

Tecumseh's description of Brock as the soldier who said 'come,' whilst Proctor said 'go,' is authentic. The reader will find it referred to in Tupper's "Life of Brock." It was for many a day a jocular saying on the Detroit frontier, and elsewhere in Upper Canada.

Note 47.

With the exception of Tecumseh's protest to Proctor against his retreat from Amherstburg, but a few fragments of his speeches are extant. The author has thought it advisable to include a versified portion of the former in the 1st scene of Act V. The reader will recognize it in the passage beginning: "*Brother, my people are before you now!*" The author has made use of a few other equally well-known utterances of his historical characters, and has kept as close to history as dramatic exigencies would permit. Iena and Lefroy, he need scarcely say, are imaginary characters, though not without example in the history of this continent.